NEW YORK UNIVERSITY

STUDIES IN

ROMANCE LANGUAGES AND LITERATURE

2

At the HOTEL de BOURGOGNE, PARIS

May 2nd, 1928

THE CORRESPONDENCE OF

André Gide

and

Edmund Gosse

1904–1928

Edited, with Translations, Introduction, and Notes, by

LINETTE F. BRUGMANS

NEW YORK UNIVERSITY PRESS · 1959

Editor's Dedication
To N.F., J.F., and H.B.

ACKNOWLEDGMENTS

I WANT TO THANK ALL whose help or advice has made it possible to complete this book. Especially am I grateful to Dr. Philip Gosse, son of Sir Edmund, who gave not only permission to publish his father's letters but also some very useful information; to M. Jean Lambert, André Gide's son-in-law, who granted access to unpublished documents; to Madame Anne Heurgon, who gave permission to publish some letters of her father, Paul Desjardins; to Madame Marie-Hélène Dasté for the letters of her father, Jacques Copeau, and Madame Vernier-Dola for those of her brother, Henry-D. Davray; and to Mrs. Dorothy Bussy, M. Jean Schlumberger, and the late Roger Martin du Gard for kindly supplying useful information.

To the library of Rutgers University I am greatly indebted for permission to publish the Gide letters, and to the library of the University of Leeds for allowing me to see many interesting letters belonging to the Brotherton Collection.

Gide's letter of October 25, 1925, is reproduced with the kind permission of The Rutgers University Library; Gosse's letter of December 12, 1926, is reproduced by kind permission of the *Comité Gide*.

To Professor Leslie Marchand of Rutgers University, who first told me about the Gide letters, to Professor Justin O'Brien of Columbia University, to Professors Frédéric Ernst and Richard Parker of New

York University for their good advice, and to Professor Germaine Brée of New York University, whose enlightened guidance has been extremely helpful, I feel deep gratitude.

This work was first prepared for publication in French; the translation is mine except for the quotations from Gide's *Journal,* for which I use the excellent translation by Professor Justin O'Brien. I am indebted to four persons for revising the translation: Professor Leroy Breunig of Barnard College, and Wilson Follett, who both made many valuable suggestions about the English version of Gide's letters; Miss Mary Hagedorn, who revised notes and introduction; and my husband, Henri Brugmans of Hofstra College, who gave both unfailing encouragement and able assistance in preparation of the manuscript. I also wish to thank Professor George Parks for his helpful advice on the preparation of the manuscript, and Mrs. France Anders for kindly reading the proofs.

L.F.B., *Queens College, 1956*

CONTENTS

THE CORRESPONDENCE OF

ANDRÉ GIDE AND EDMUND GOSSE

1904-1928

Introduction

I. THE CORRESPONDENCE

EDMUND GOSSE AND ANDRÉ GIDE exchanged, over nearly a quarter of a century, about a hundred letters, most of them when Gide was writing his most important books. It seems, at first glance, strange that two writers so separated by age and by language should have established relations so friendly and so durable. The relations were based mainly on Gosse's unceasing interest in Gide's art and admiration for it and on Gide's affectionate gratitude for the stimulating comprehension of his English friend at a time when he had achieved, even in his own country, so little comprehension. The relationship ended only with Gosse's death.

The correspondence here printed consists of eighty-eight letters, thirty-four of them by Gosse and fifty-four by Gide. It begins in June, 1904, and ends in May, 1928. Some letters mentioned in the correspondence have not been found; they may turn up someday. The Gide letters are in the possession of Rutgers University Library, New Brunswick, New Jersey. To them have been added three letters fortunately discovered in England among the treasures of the Brotherton Collection of Leeds University: Letters 58, 77, and 88, of September 20, 1916, January 15, 1925, and April 28, 1928, respectively; the third of these closes the correspondence. Gosse's letters, of which Gide himself sent me copies in January, 1951, are now part of the Jacques Doucet Library collections in Paris.

To the eighty-eight letters an appendix adds five from Gide to Philip Gosse, son of Sir Edmund, written between February 8, 1929, and May 2, 1930, about a year after Gosse's death; these contain useful information about the importance Gide attached to his friend's letters. All five belong to the Brotherton Collection. Gide had lent Gosse's letters to Philip Gosse for the use of Evan Charteris when he was preparing *The Life and Letters of Sir Edmund Gosse,* published in 1931. Of the letters in this volume, Charteris printed seven: Letters 2, 40, 47, 57, 73, 80, and 85, of July 5, 1909, January 2, 1914, May 30, 1915, September 16, 1916, August 25, 1924, August 22, 1926, and January 7, 1927, respectively.

The correspondence is of uneven interest. Some of the letters are no more than short notes; but others contain biographical, historical, or literary information that throws light on the background of the period or helps us reconstruct the development of a friendship between important writers. The correspondence falls naturally into three periods. The first is 1904–1914; in it the incipient friendship develops rapidly, with increasingly frequent meetings. In the second, 1914–1918, kept physically apart by the difficulty of crossing the Channel but brought mentally closer by the common danger and by the intensification of Gosse's long-standing devotion to France, the two keep on writing. The third period, that of the postwar years, has but a scattering of letters, but some of them are the most important and the most moving messages that Edmund Gosse and André Gide ever exchanged. The letters here reproduced may lack the special and deep interest of the Claudel–Gide exchange and the Charles Du Bos–André Gide correspondence, the variety and intimacy of the Francis Jammes–André Gide letters and, of course, the Paul Valéry–André Gide letters published in 1955. On the other hand, they seem to me to be of greater value than the letters that Gide exchanged with another foreign writer, Rainer Maria Rilke, during almost the same years.

The first or prewar phase has forty-three letters, nineteen by Gosse and twenty-four by Gide. The correspondence begins with a short but admiring note from Gosse dated June 16, 1904. It is not until 1909 that the interchange takes on real importance, with two letters by Gide and three by Gosse, who by this time is seriously interested in Gide's writing, to Gide's pleasure and gratitude. For 1910 there are only three letters of Gide and one of Gosse; but each sends some of his books to the other, and Gide, who had hitherto known Gosse only as critic, now discovers him as writer. In 1911 the relationship becomes still closer: there are three letters from Gosse and six from Gide, and their more personal tone reflects the fact that the two have talked face to face. There is the beginning of a true friendship. Between early 1912 and the outbreak of World War I there are twenty-four letters, thirteen of them by Gide. The nine letters of 1912 record several meetings; the eleven of 1913 show a continuation of contacts both social and literary and, on Gide's part, a growing warmth and gratitude. War intervenes after only four letters of early 1914, the last of them by Gosse on April 6; but these four show a deepening of the relationship and a decidedly more intensive interest in Gide's books on the part of his English friend.

The second period, that of the war years, includes twenty-six letters. Nineteen of them are Gide's, the first belonging to November, 1914; but some of both men's letters of 1916–1918 have disappeared. The letters missing from the 1916–1917 correspondence may have fallen victims to German submarines; in 1918 Gide, himself in England, may have found it inconvenient to preserve all his mail, or he may have destroyed Gosse's letters as consisting of information and practical advice of no more than transient interest. Gosse, whose mind was pre-empted by the war, wrote only once in 1914 after hostilities began and, apparently, but once in 1915; all seven of the surviving letters of these two years are dominated by the war. But in 1916 Gide has left the Foyer Franco-Belge, the organization for war refugees that had been taking most of his time, and the correspondence mounts to a total of seven letters by him and five by Gosse. Also, Gosse spends some days in France, and Gide goes to Paris expressly to meet him. From 1917 only one long and interesting letter of Gide's survives, and all six of 1918 are also Gide's, the last, of September 7, in the interest of a young Frenchman who was then trying to enlist in England for military service.

The third, or postwar, period begins in 1920 with a resumption after a two years' hiatus. The hiatus is unexplained; but it is to be noted that Gide's diary for this period is extremely short—two pages for 1919—and that his *Journal intime* and *Et nunc manet in te* show him in acute depression and confusion of mind. His gift to Gosse of his *Symphonie pastorale* leads to an exchange of cordial messages in 1920; but the correspondence lapses to a single letter in 1921—this one by Gide, about a project of translating an early novel of Thomas Hardy's for the Nouvelle Revue Française—and from January, 1921, to August, 1924, there are no letters at all. Then Gosse makes a delayed acknowledgment of *Incidences,* which Gide had sent him at a date undetermined, and there follows a renewal of affectionate intimacy. Gosse, now seventy-five, shows no resentment of Gide's apparent remissness, and he follows intently the younger man's books as they appear. Gide's African journey is an impediment to the exchange of letters in 1925; but 1926, with three letters by each man, leads into the most important phase of the entire correspondence—a phase continued into early 1927 in a long and searching letter by Gosse and in Gide's reply. In 1924 Gosse had bought *Corydon,* with a mild reproach because Gide had not sent it to him; and in 1926 he receives *Si le Grain ne meurt* and the *Journal des faux-monnayeurs.* The challenge of these books, the most candid and untrammeled that Gide published, drove Gosse to the utmost frankness of which he was capable on the score of what in Gide's work most troubled and distressed him. His probing questions and Gide's answers constitute the most memorable passages of the entire quarter century's interchange.

This last phase of the correspondence, closed by a single letter in the year of Gosse's death, consists of nineteen letters, eleven of them Gide's. His letter of 1928 is in answer to one of Gosse's that remains untraced. The last letter that we have from Gosse is a brief one explaining his refusal to contribute to a projected volume of tributes to Gide. The whole correspondence comes to a quiet end on the note of the friendship warmly renewed in 1924, with affection on both sides and grateful recognition on Gide's. Clearly he did not undervalue the friendship of the critic, long famous, who for over twenty years past had given him unfailing admiration and support. The death of Gosse on May 16, 1928, meant to Gide the loss of the one influential English friend who from as early as 1909 had cordially recognized and proclaimed the originality of his writings and their lasting value.

II. RESEMBLANCES AND CONTRASTS

A LITTLE OVER FOUR MONTHS BEFORE the correspondence began, the two men had seen each other at an important reception arranged in Paris in honor of Gosse. Early in that year of the Entente Cordiale, 1904, a group of Frenchmen of letters undertook this gesture of grateful esteem for a distinguished critic who was also a conspicuous Francophile. The initiative was taken by Henry-D. Davray, who in 1896 had started in the *Mercure de France* a column, "Lettres Anglaises," in which he missed no opportunity to comment on Gosse's writings. As fellow participants he recruited writers so important as Heredia, Maurice Barrès, Henri de Régnier, Maeterlinck, Verhaeren, Stuart Merrill, Paul Fort, Marcel Schwob, and Gide. The original intention was a comprehensive banquet to be attended by most personages of the Parisian literary and artistic world, but a less pretentious, more selective gathering was eventually decided on. About fifty guests attended a dinner given February 9 in the Restaurant Durand, then famous, and the next day Gosse lectured at the Société des Conférences about French influences on English poetry. The press reported the lecture as a shining success, but it was given in English, and it is permissible to wonder how many of the hearers could follow it.

The reasons why so distinguished a group wanted to honor Gosse are not far to seek. His preoccupation with French culture had been well known for many years; it had dated, indeed, from virtually the beginning of his literary career, in which one important formative influence had been Matthew Arnold and another the early intimacy with Swinburne. The young critic had been cordially welcomed by the Pre-Raphaelites, who, like most of the English literary elite, were firmly Francophile to a man after 1870. Gosse was a devotee of Théodore de Banville in poetry and considered himself a Parnassian; in critical prose he had an unfailing admiration for the fluency and vividness of Sainte-Beuve, whom he regarded as his master. The whole range of French literature interested him, and he was tireless in studying it and in writing about it for English consumption. And of course his general attachment to France lost nothing by his awareness of his own Huguenot ancestry.

Gosse set a high value on the free international exchange of ideas. He was equally ready to discountenance the isolationist tendencies of sundry British writers and the French chauvinism of a Jules Lemaître. A primary role that he took upon himself was the important one of keeping the English informed about European, and particularly French, currents of thought; and he soon acquired the prestige to make himself effective in that role. He may have lacked the loftiness of imagination and the profundity of thought that are measures of the very great critic, but he had made himself a decidedly influential one. He had a real and fervent love of letters, a lively style, energetic curiosity, and taste—the very qualities needed to discover works of merit as yet unknown in Britain and to persuade the British of their merit.

As far back as 1871 Gosse published the first English article about the plays of Ibsen, and several French-language writers before Gide had him to thank for their earliest recognition across the Channel— among them Mallarmé (in the *Academy,* January, 1893) and Verhaeren (in *Cosmopolis,* December, 1896). Well before 1904, then, he was producing articles about French literature, and not in English reviews alone: he contributed five long pieces to *Cosmopolis,* which printed work of well-known English, French, and German writers in the original languages. All five were on contemporary French literature; and the subjects were by no means restricted to novelists, play-

wrights, poets, and critics already famous in France, for Gosse was
concerned to do justice to the most gifted among the younger writers—
a valiant undertaking for a foreigner no longer young whose range
of personal acquaintance was negligible outside literary folk of his
own generation.

Nor were Gosse's Anglo-French undertakings confined to critical
articles. He had for years wanted to see the English reading public
enjoying more of the major European novels, and in 1902 he launched
the substantial enterprise called "A Century of French Romance."
It involved him in the general editorship of twenty novels in translation, each with an introduction by some well-known writer and a
brief monograph. The century of his general title was the nineteenth;
to his thinking the French novels of that period achieved the most
nearly perfect equilibrium of content and form. The authors represented were Stendhal, George Sand, Jules Sandeau, Octave Feuillet,
Dumas père, Dumas fils, Hugo, Gautier, Victor Cherbuliez, Balzac,
the Goncourts, Maupassant, Flaubert, Loti, Mérimée, Edmond About,
Daudet, Zola, and Erckmann-Chatrian. (The prospectus did not
name the translators.) The introductions to *Madame Bovary* and *Memoirs of Two Young Married Women* were written by Henry James;
Gosse himself introduced *The Lady of the Camelias*. Some of the choices
seem, from our perspective, less than happy, but, as the *Bookman*
pointed out at the time, Gosse was deferring to known British prepossessions not easily gainsaid, and he reconciled himself to excluding
works that he doubtless knew to be first-rate—some as impracticably
long, others as affronts to Anglo-Saxon squeamishness. In sum, the
undertaking was a signal service to literature and to international
understanding.

Cross-Channel understanding was becoming, in the mid-1890's,
reciprocally easier. In 1896, the year in which *Cosmopolis* was
founded and Davray's "Lettres Anglaises" began in the *Mercure de
France,* there was in both countries a noticeably expanding interest in
foreign writing.

It was probably through Davray that André Gide learned of the
dinner at which Gosse was to be guest of honor. Gide and Davray
were well acquainted; they met off and on at the *Mercure de France,*

and they were presently to be occasional collaborators. Davray was aware of his friend's lively interest in English literature. Gide was able to read it only in translation, but, even so, in 1900 an article of his about novels by Kipling and H. G. Wells had appeared in the *Revue Blanche*.

Gide attended the dinner, but without getting himself introduced to Gosse. He was as inclined to be constrained in a public gathering as Gosse was to be relaxed and expansive. Did he perhaps know that in the *Contemporary Review* of December, 1898 ("Some Recent Literature in France"), Gosse had named Pierre Louÿs as "the most interesting of the young French writers of to-day"? Whether he did or not, and whatever thoughts he may have harbored in that connection, he certainly knew that he himself had never had so much as a mention in any one of Gosse's numerous articles about French writers and writing.

At this period Gide was somewhat sunk in depression. He would have liked to know that his work was read in England, as for some years past it had been in another predominantly Protestant country, Germany; but the truth was that even in France it had not achieved the broad general recognition that would have gratified him. He had been admired in little reviews that hailed him as one of the "naturists"—for example, by M. Beaubourg in the *Revue Blanche* for the first quarter of 1896. Léon Blum, in particular, had foreseen for him an influential world reputation. In the *Mercure de France* he had been having respectful attention ever since 1891—in June, 1891, from Rémy de Gourmont; in August, 1893, from Camille Mauclair, who paired Gide with Maeterlinck; in February, 1894, and in July, 1895, from Mauclair; in May, 1897, from Henri Ghéon in a long article about all the books to date. But Gide was still being treated, or felt that he was, as a young avant-garde writer and rather a promise than a fulfillment.

Edmund Gosse, who read the *Mercure de France* punctiliously and had moreover a special predilection for writings that dealt with the inner life, could hardly have missed all these eulogies of the early books of Gide. But he was a busy man and much in request. (On this very expedition to Paris he learned that to his other literary and social duties had been added an appointment as librarian of the House of Lords.) It is also not improbable that he was repelled by such books of Gide as he then knew; *Les Nourritures terrestres* (1897) and *L'Immoraliste* (1903) are known to be among the works that he least liked. He did not recommend to English readers the works of young French writers that he found coarse in subject matter or aberrant in point of view, and his criticism of them was often fairly harsh. Whatever the explanation, he had come to February, 1904, without giving a sign of awareness that André Gide existed.

The immediate upshot was that Gide, not long after the February occasion, sent Gosse his latest volume, that containing *Säul* and *Le Roi Candaule*. (Submitting one of his books to a critic was a departure from his habit, very likely conceded at the prompting of Davray.) Gosse, habitually punctilious, wrote (June 16) the acknowledgment that opens the correspondence—a letter too brief to prove its writer very deeply stirred, yet too cordial to be thought entirely perfunctory. ("Your works have no more warm admirer than . . . Edmund Gosse.") And there the matter rested until July, 1909—five years—with no intimation of a relationship that was to involve a prolonged interchange of some moment.

The real beginning of that relationship came with Gosse's reading of *La Porte étroite* in 1909. His response to this newly published work was prompt and unreserved. Not only was he excited by the perfection of its form, but he also found in it a comprehension of the Puritan mind that he would never have anticipated in a French writer. What confronted him was, in fact, an artistically superior counterpart of a major document of his own, published two years before: the chapter of early autobiography called *Father and Son,* in which he had paid his respects to Calvinistic education and had described the grim upbringing of which he had been the victim.

From the age of seven, when his mother died, Gosse had been brought up by his father, who strangely combined great distinction as a zoologist with great fanaticism as a leader of the Plymouth Brethren in his little Devonshire town. Philip Gosse had provided for a soul's salvation by getting young Edmund accepted at ten as one of the sect and saddled with all the religious responsibilities of an adult member. The father was a naturally kind man, besides having an "acute mind," and the son was a naturally obedient boy; but the one had let his theological system narrow his outlook and freeze his heart, and the other could not help applying to everything the inquiring spirit that his father reserved for zoological facts. Philip Gosse unhesitatingly rejected Darwin's books for their incompatibility with the Scriptures as he interpreted them; Edmund Gosse deliberately prayed to a chair as an empirical test of his father's assurance that an angry God would smite whoever bowed down to wood or stone. Thus the pattern of conflict; and young Edmund maintained for years a secret revolt against the sort of life that a nightmare religion imposed on him and against a theology that pitilessly excluded from all hope of salvation the greater part of the ostensibly Christian world. The son's revolt was the more intense because he apparently never had any very deep religious experience of his own.

Young Gosse left Devonshire at seventeen to be a clerk in the catalogue department of the British Museum, but he was still hounded by adjurations to avoid "the pitfalls . . . which surround on every hand the thoughtless giddy youth" and by premillennialist worries lest his soul be ill prepared for the imminent Second Coming. It cost the youth a long and painful struggle to win his mental freedom, and well he knew what he was talking about when, toward the end of *Father and Son,* he denounced the noxious system that "invents virtues which are sterile and cruel; . . . invents sins which are no sins at all, but which darken the heaven of innocent joy . . . the fanaticism that can do nothing with this pathetic and fugitive existence of ours but treat it as if it were the uncomfortable ante-chamber to a palace . . . of which we know absolutely nothing."

Philip Gosse had many times told his son "with a solemn complacency" about an aged nun who discovered on her deathbed the utter uselessness of a long life of devotion and sacrifice lived under the wrong theological auspices. If the son had been able to look into Gide's diary of 1894, he might have read: "Possibility of distress: the soul that thinks it has not adored properly"—words that embody the central thought and impulsion of *La Porte étroite,* which Gide was then meditating. (He meant to call it *La Mort de Mademoiselle Claire.*)

Gide too had been brought up by one deeply Calvinist parent, his widowed mother, though not so fanatically. He had known a counterpart of Philip Gosse in his grandfather Tancrède, an "austere, selfwilled Huguenot . . . overscrupulous, unyielding, and carrying his trust in the Lord to the point of sublimity." Both men had experienced the Puritan spirit and suffered from it—Gide perhaps more than Gosse, who had long got over being preoccupied with religious problems. Gide was, in fact, to be haunted by religious anxieties for years after the publication of *La Porte étroite*. Congenitally inclined toward the mystical, he had experienced more than Gosse would ever know of the insidious perfidy of puritanism, for he had a deep sense of its appeal to the pure and the mystically given.

The two men had in common, then, underlying any differences of circumstance, temper, and capacity, a remarkably solid nucleus of crucial experience and knowledge. It was this that they discovered and shared when Gosse read *La Porte étroite* and Gide read *Father and Son*. Gosse could not fail to penetrate the meaning of Gide's novel, the inwardness of Alissa's strange behavior and desperate death. The book was the revelation of a spiritual tie, and Gosse lost no time in sending its author a letter charged with admiring recognition, sympathy, and eagerness for closer contacts. Some effect remained from this first of their really important exchanges and palpably overhung the rest of their relationship to the end, as the effect of striking coincidence will often do.

The analogies of their childhood and youth were, of course, far from being all that Gosse and Gide had in common. For a major example, one of the rare pleasures of Gosse's arid childhood was accompanying his father on zoological expeditions along the English seaboard, where he developed a great fondness for botany and zoology; marine animals and plants became his equivalent of the fairy tales and books of adventure that he never knew. Gide, at about the same early age, was initiated into the natural sciences by Anna Shackleton, his mother's friend and former governess and, incidentally, the woman of whose solitary death he was thinking when he conceived *La Porte étroite*. His interest in animals and plants was lifelong; his diaries, like his books, are sown with evidences of it. When he read

Father and Son, he was particularly struck by the accurate and beautiful descriptions of the aquatic fauna and flora at which Gosse had marveled as a child on the coast of Devonshire; for Gide himself had had a closely parallel experience on the Mediterranean shore line about Cannes.

But of course the principal bond, the strongest link in the friendship, was the equal absorption in literature. To literature each owed his liberation from the incubus of puritanism, or at least whatever degree of liberation was temperamentally possible to him. Gosse freed himself much earlier in life than Gide, who carried the burden of an obsessive moral preoccupation through virtually all his working years and emancipated himself only piecemeal and with pain by means of his successive works.

The two had approached the conquest of literature by different routes and against different kinds of impediment. Gide's father had left a library of sorts; his mother, after a close watch on the reading of his early youth, conceded him the freedom of this library. She never resisted, and in fact approved, his resolve to be a writer; and, unlike most men of his craft, he never had to face the problem of self-support. Edmund Gosse, on the other hand, had little access as a boy to any reading but religious and scientific books. He had been made to read the Bible so much in his childhood that in manhood he could find in it no interest, no beauty; it had become to him a synonym of ennui—the very word that he coupled with it in *Father and Son.* (He was much addicted to French words and to the citation of French idioms and whole sentences.) On Gide's mind and taste the influence of the Bible was formative; he was constantly drawing on it for ideas, for allusions. For literature as literature, Philip Gosse had had only contempt; he plumed himself on never having read Shakespeare, and when he introduced his son to the Georgics of Vergil, it was not to teach him poetry but Latin. When in later years the son attempted verse of his own, it was in defiance of a father who feared that "the sickly, hollow, fashionable tone of mere human sentiment" would be only the pathway to "deserved hell." It is one of the fairly startling phenomena of literary history that Edmund, arrived in London at seventeen with his spotty education, no money, no influential friends, and a living to drudge out, contrived in so short a time to make himself felt among the younger English poets and critics. The tempo of this achievement is in striking contrast to the long-drawn process of Gide's success.

The explanation is, of course, a congenital gift for letters. Through the Latin of the Georgics Gosse penetrated to their poetry and was deeply moved by it. In some fragments of a novel found in the attic he discovered a world utterly unlike that in which he lived. These scraps fed his inward resistance to his father and led him to odds and ends of surreptitious reading. When he got to London his thirst for knowledge was insatiable; it pre-empted every minute he could spare. His feeling for literature was sheer worship. And it was lifelong. The ingrained puritanism of his make-up took the form of resenting whatever impaired or vitiated the dignity of letters; whence his refusal to admit the existence of some kinds of books and the frequently excessive conservatism of his judgments. As Charteris records in the *Life and Letters,* Edmund in his twenty-fourth year wrote his father (March 4, 1873): "I am a poet, critic and littérateur." It was the simple assertion of a fact. Virginia Woolf, whose father had been a friend of Gosse, summed up Gosse the critic in *The Moment and Other Essays* in the sentence: "Literature to him was an incomparable mistress and it was his delight to dress her charms and make her more beloved."

Gosse had, too, the temperamental advantage of being almost as much interested in writers as in writing. He revered great men; friendship was one of his innate needs; and he enjoyed close and confidential relationships with the greatest English writers of his time— among them Swinburne, Stevenson, Henry James, George Moore, and Thomas Hardy.

Among his literary predilections, French classicism ranked as high as any. To the Racinian harmony and balance he responded in a way not common among the English, and he was correspondingly cool toward symbolist poetry and generally chill about French blank verse. Of one of his lifelong admirations, the Parnassians, he said (*Cosmopolis,* June, 1896): "The Parnassians had their faults, of course, but they will probably stand the ravages of time better than the Decadents. Enamel may get to look old-fashioned, but it makes, in the long run, a better show than gelatine"—a pronouncement interestingly paralleled by Gide in a much later remark that he puts into the mouth of the young apprentice poet in *Interviews Imaginaires:* "It is too easy for us to knead a substance still soft, yielding, incohesive . . . we are modeling in lard"—"*on travaille dans le saindoux.*" Gide, then, eclectic as he was in poetical taste, often exhibited a preference for regular verse akin to Gosse's.

He also shared Gosse's sense of the importance of knowing the literatures of other countries. To the great European books no modern French writer has shown more hospitality. Knowing his own identity to be determinate enough to defy subversion by other men's ideas, he shrank from no influence, and he got sustenance and communion with his kind out of whatever foreign novels, poems, or philosophical essays extended comprehension of the labyrinthine human spirit. His easiest access was to German. For the language he cared little, but he had learned it in childhood and had further studied it in school. (From English, which was coming to be a vogue and contributing to the French vocabulary, particularly in sports, he had been cut off, to his regret, by his parents' fancy for communicating freely in it over his head; see his letter of April 10, 1910, to Gosse.) In a *Mercure* article of 1902, "Enquête sur l'influence allemande," he had said, to be sure, that the best teaching he had got out of Goethe, Heine, Schopenhauer, and Nietzsche was possibly their admiration for France; but such a remark has to be taken as little more than a light pleasantry, for Gide had a towering admiration for Goethe, and Nietzsche's philosophy was of major importance to him, however firmly he believed these great writers to have found in France the initial inspiration of their thinking. Moreover, Schopenhauer and Wagner were two fashions that raged during Gide's student days, and even Maurice Barrès was then still sympathetic to some aspects of German civilization and thought. There was, then, enough in the general atmosphere to encourage and supplement a natural eclecticism, and Gide became instrumental in the dissemination of foreign works in France, if not so systematically or on such a scale as Gosse in England.

There were, of course, radical contrasts between the French novelist and the English critic. The twenty years between them constituted a barrier of a sort. Gosse, whose success was rapid, had become a household word in English letters at a time when Gide, making haste slowly, was still short of general recognition; their contrasting tempos of attainment had the effect of widening the gap to at least a full generation; and the disparity naturally imposed on the younger man a posture of obligatory deference, whether or not it altogether corresponded with his inward feeling. Gosse had the civil servant's inevitable bent toward conformity and a degree of snobbery; Gide, with an income that meant independence, was a congenital solitary and a conspicuously asocial being. In capacity for religious feeling the two were, as has been shown, poles apart. If we couple these divergences with the lack of oral command of each other's language and with their national differences in manners and mores, we see easily enough why the friendship could never attain absolute frankness, entire freedom from self-consciousness, or the ease that goes with real intimacy. What they gave each other, as we find it vested in the letters they wrote, was solid and important. But there were important interests of each about which they never undertook to communicate, areas of privacy that they could not imaginably have shared. In all their exchanges there can be sensed, if not always exactly located or defined, an element of constraint.

III. THE MEN AND THE LETTERS

THE FIRST IMPORTANT STAGE of the Gide-Gosse correspondence began, then, not with the brief unanswered letter of 1904, but with Gosse's understanding tribute to *La Porte étroite* in July, 1909. This letter exceeded the utmost that Gide had yet received by way of admiring recognition from any equally impressive source, and he was much affected by its obvious sincerity and by the writer's cordial wish to meet him. Gide's expression, in his reply, of some genuine emotion did not preclude his thriftily seizing the occasion to suggest that Gosse share his approbation with the British reading public. As it happened, Gosse himself had had an impulse to write something about *La Porte étroite;* he said so to Gide, at the same time asking him for information about *Amyntas;* and on September 2 he wrote Gide that the article in question had just come out in the *Contemporary Review,* "the most influential monthly organ of the Liberal party." Gide's acknowledgment, besides glowing with both surprise and gratification, declares a modest doubt whether he can make his future work live up to the expectations that Gosse's tribute must have aroused.

One practical consequence of this exchange was that Gide began to send Gosse his books as they were published. (The only one of which he made an exception during this period was *Corydon,* which he presented to none but the most intimate of his friends.) In the English critic the books sent found an unfailingly absorbed and generally admiring reader.

Gosse too aspired to be read, particularly as the author of *Father and Son*. Over and above the writing man's normal pride in his work he had, as we have seen, the special excitement of discovering his deep affinities with Gide, and he wanted the discovery to be mutual. For some reason Gide did not receive *Father and Son* until April, 1910, and he let more time elapse before he could confess what he described as the great humiliation of his life: an ignorance of English that made his comprehension of the book a very slow process, impossible without the help of his wife. Gosse was frankly startled. ("But why do you not read English? You shut yourself out . . . from such a wide field of pleasures!") Gide, however, needed no admonishing: the interest in English literature that he had long felt was in a phase of spontaneous growth at this very time, and he would soon be making a vigorous and systematic effort to master the language.

Nor did his interest stop at the language and its literature: it extended to England and the English. In July, 1911, Gide made the first of his adult visits across the Channel. His attempt to call on Gosse the day of his arrival was thwarted by a small mischance, but the critic's slightly delayed welcome was cordial. (It included a luncheon at the House of Lords.) Of course this first personal encounter put the relationship on a permanently different footing.

What it immediately led to was Gide's invitation to the series of literary *entretiens* to be held at Pontigny the next month. Gosse, with Mrs. Gosse, was in Pontigny for the whole *décade,* August 19–28, and he took the liveliest interest in the daily afternoon sessions. He was introduced into the whole circle of Gide's friends, including the group identified with the *Nouvelle Revue Française.* The entire experience made him feel rejuvenated, and he left Pontigny with regret, well aware that his association with Gide had graduated into a durable friendship.

Gide himself found that his daily encounters with Gosse had signally contributed to his interest in the English language and its literature. (There were other influences to the same end: for example, Arnold Bennet, lately met in Paris, prompted Gide to read Fielding's *Tom Jones,* which captured his admiration.) After the Pontigny interlude he applied himself so assiduously to the study of English that he temporarily slighted his own writing. When presently Gosse sent him his *Sir Thomas Browne,* he was able to read it with a good deal less difficulty than he had experienced with *Father and Son.* In his letter of thanks he quoted sentences that had particularly pleased him; and two months later, when he received Gosse's *Collected Poems*—in which, incidentally, he found a piece dedicated to himself—his acknowledgment even ventured upon a few original sentences in English.

Possibly under the stimulus of this early progress, he shortly found himself wanting to see Gosse again. ("I *need* to tell you: à bientôt," he wrote on October 8.) Early in 1912, then, he revisited London, where, after all, he fell a victim to influenza and had to go home without a sight of his friend. (A few days later, according to his journal for January 19, he had dinner with Jacques Copeau "in the little English tavern of rue d'Amsterdam," possibly by way of compensation for what he had missed.) He and Gosse met briefly in Rouen in June, and in August they were together again for a longer time at Pontigny. Gosse had at first not seen how he was to get away from London that summer. But Paul Desjardins sent him repeated invitations; they were seconded by Jacques Copeau, who was preparing an article about *Father and Son;* the program of that year's *décade* was especially interesting to Gosse, its nuclear topic being the English novel; and he finally yielded. He and Gide took daily morning walks together, and Gide talked about his future books—especially and at length about *Les Caves du Vatican,* the "absurd and baroque" novel on which he was then engaged. It was written, he said, more or less in the vein of *Paludes*—with which, unluckily, Gosse was as yet unacquainted, though this aspect of Gide's talent was presently to be a particular delight to him.

That the friendship made appreciable progress during this visit to Pontigny is shown by the perceptibly changed tone of the letters that followed. Gosse had enjoyed his second stay as much as the first, possibly even more, for this time his own work had come in for some attention flattering to his pride of authorship. *Father and Son,* recently translated, was being read at Pontigny and seemingly admired.

In the autumn of 1912 Gosse published his *Portraits and Sketches.* The volume included in amplified form the article of three years

earlier about Gide, who naturally drew encouragement and self-confidence from this renewed evidence that he was understood and appre-
ciated. Indeed, he had an impulse to go to London to deliver his
thanks in person. What deterred him was his absorption in *Les Caves
du Vatican*. For the same reason he intermitted his English studies,
though with reluctance; his grasp of English had become much
firmer, and his *Journal* of this period records that he was pursuing the
language with a "teacher," "madly" studying an English etymological
dictionary, and reading many English books. Also he had acquired a
feeling for the rhythm of English verse, which tends to sound baffling
to the Gallic ear. For this he owed something to Gosse, who had been
reading aloud to him from the poems of Shelley, bringing out the
precise scansion after the manner of his late great friends Swinburne
and William Morris.

On Christmas Eve, 1912, Gide, who was given to acting on impulse, arrived unheralded in London. Gosse, delighted, invited him
to the Christmas family dinner, which was to include, as usual, his old
friend Henry James. On December 30 Gide, again Gosse's guest, met
another Francophile intimate of the critic, George Moore, who, like
James, had spent years in France. George Moore had been an active
participant in the artistic and literary life of Paris in the years 1872–1882;
he, Verlaine, Henri de Régnier, and Mallarmé had been fellow contributors to the *Revue Indépendante;* and he was an English disciple of
Zola. The encounter between Gide and Moore must have been evo-
cative of uncounted reminiscences.

It happened that Moore knew of five important letters of Swinburne
to Mallarmé. Gosse, whose inveterate devotion to Swinburne and to his
memory had lately been incorporated in his life of the poet, and who
was then busy editing Swinburne's complete works, asked Gide to
trace these five letters written in French. Early in the May following
Gide was able to provide copies of them; and he found them so
interesting that he wanted to print them in the *Nouvelle Revue Française*. Gosse tried to get him the necessary English authorization, but
probably without success, for the letters never appeared in the magazine.

Later in May Gide found Mr. and Mrs. Gosse in Paris at the time of
his own return from Rome, to which he had made a quick visit to

verify some final details for *Les Caves du Vatican*. Here was his awaited chance to have the Gosses meet Madame Gide. Gide, however preoccupied with completing his novel, was not too busy to express his insistent hospitality in two letters, one of them containing meticulous directions to his Auteuil villa.

In the months preceding this visit the relationship had been assiduously cultivated on both sides, with frequent visits back and forth, more frequent invitations, and exchanges of books and even of photographs. The latter part of 1913 seems to betray a slackening of interest on the part of Gide; for whatever reason, his letters become less frequent, and Gosse, a thin-skinned and touchy man, feels the difference and shows that he feels it. This oversensitiveness, an ingrained trait of his otherwise enthusiastic and outgoing temperament, is recurrently in evidence in the correspondence. Gosse is nettled when Gide, already silent for some months, fails to congratulate him on his Légion d'honneur. ("You did not write, perhaps you disapproved?") He finds reason to suspect that Gide has not read, or has read but carelessly and partially, a volume of Gosse's essays sent him a good while before. When *Si le Grain ne meurt* comes out he is hurt because he is not among the earliest of Gide's friends to receive a promised copy. When a publisher somewhat tactlessly presses Gosse three times over to write an *éloge* of Gide's works, Gosse reports brusquely to Gide: "I never join in these combinations."

In the summer of 1913 Gide did not participate in the *entretiens* at Pontigny. Neither did Gosse attend, though again besought by Paul Desjardins after the way had been paved by winter visits of Jean Schlumberger and Jacques Copeau. (The Gosses, not in the best of health, went to Wiesbaden for the cure.) And a tentative plan of Gide's to repeat his Christmas holiday visit to London failed to materialize. What correspondence there is has to do chiefly with *Les Caves du Vatican,* which Gosse received with an enthusiasm equal to the impatience of his anticipation.

The dire events that began in August, 1914, kept the friends from seeing each other for two years. They resumed their correspondence, however, in the first war autumn. A patriotic poem of Gosse's in the

Times drew a letter from Gide, and from then to the end of the war the two kept in touch, writing with the warmth engendered by the common peril, temporarily subordinating literary considerations to the overwhelming events of current history, and faithfully sending each other the news of their families and friends.

In neither country was there any shortage of heroic dedication. Jean Schlumberger, one of the Pontigny group, had enlisted in the artillery. Copeau, another, found unfit for active service, nevertheless gave all his time and strength to France, producing plays in Geneva and in the United States, to which he was sent by the Ministère des Beaux Arts. Henri Ghéon, a third, was an army physician and while in the army wrote the *Poèmes de guerre* that Gide praised for their genuineness. And Jacques Rivière, taken prisoner at the very outset of the war, admonished his friends not to try to get him released or exchanged, for he wanted to "bear his ordeal to the end." A young nephew of Gide's, Dominique Drouin, had enlisted in the cavalry. Gosse's letters are sown with examples of an equal ardor on the British side. His only son, Philip, was on the Béthune front with an army ambulance, and many sons of close friends had already fallen on the battlefields of Flanders. In some of the fatalities reported in the correspondence the two friends felt a common interest: the death in early 1915 of Rupert Brooke, perhaps the most gifted of the younger English poets; the death by tragic accident of Emile Verhaeren, long a friend of both; and that of Michel, only son of Paul Desjardins, who fell in the summer of 1918 while leading his company in attack.

Gide himself was immersed in his work for the Foyer des Réfugiés (Charles Du Bos was one of his colleagues there), and he hardly thought of anything else up to the beginning of 1916. He published during the war nothing at all except one small piece written on behalf of the Réfugiés—a piece that Gosse rendered into English for him. Gosse, on the other hand, turned out article after article, chiefly about the war and especially about the part played in it by the country of his undying admiration. Gide, much more analytical in his patriotism, was nevertheless deeply moved by Gosse's enthusiasm for France, which he experienced recurrently in *War Essays,* received in July, 1916; in *Reims Revisited,* Gosse's account of his inspection of devastated regions with Maurice Barrès; and again in a volume of 1918 that included the recent essays "Three French Moralists" and "The Gallantry of France."

Gide derived an exceptional pleasure of a different kind from Swinburne's *Posthumous Poems,* of which Gosse, coeditor of the volume and author of the introduction, sent him a fine copy in 1917. Gide, though he did no publishing in the war years, did a good deal of anguished thinking. As early as 1914 he was finding himself exasperated and dismayed by the general "militarization of the mind." What he got out of English books provided a solace that he really needed. As he said in his journal (December 7, 1915): "Nothing could express the amusement and curiosity with which I hasten to a new English book by a good author whom I don't know yet; an amusement that, for some time now, French literature cannot provide for me since it does not hold in store any real surprises." He followed *Sesame and Lilies* with works by Walter Pater, Charlotte Brontë, Rupert Brooke, Thomas Hardy, Henry James, George Meredith, Joseph Conrad, and the comparatively unknown William Hale White. He also discovered Browning, who came to be his favorite English poet; he reread Milton, and he rested, as he put it, with Keats. Some of these authors he had impulses to translate; and to him translation is well known to have been a means of personal creation. After Rupert Brooke's death Gide wanted to render Brooke's poems, and he asked Gosse to arrange the necessary permission. A few months later he was thinking seriously about two volumes of Mark Rutherford (William Hale White), about whom Gosse supplied him with the relevant information. Gide eventually relinquished both projects.

Soon after leaving the Foyer des Réfugiés, in which for some X months past he had been feeling useless, Gide resumed writing, and to Gosse he sent accounts of what he was doing. He wrote glowingly of his progress with the translation of Shakespeare's *Antony and Cleopatra;* also he confided details about what he thought of as his "posthumous works"—those in which he would disclose, somewhat in the manner of *Father and Son,* his thoughts on fundamental religious and ethical problems, as he was presently to do in *Si le Grain ne meurt.*

In the autumn of 1916 the two friends had not met for three years, two of them war years. Then, in September, Gosse went to France to survey, at the invitation of the French government, the devastation caused by the invader. Gide, notified, hurried to Paris from Cuverville, and Gosse, between the day of his return from his tour of inspection with Barrès about Reims and that of his private interview with Briand, managed to be Gide's host at a luncheon. The occasion, which Gide's *Journal* rehearses in detail, produced one of those awkward mischances that can expose a sensitive man to a suffering out of all proportion to importance. It seems that Gosse, by way of grooming himself for the next day's meeting with the Premier, spoke in French, and Gide, construing too literally a phrase meant as rhetorically graceful formula, kissed him on both cheeks. The immediate result was a visible English wince, and Gide, already prey to one of his characteristic interludes of depression and perturbation, felt a wretched constraint for the rest of their time together. (Two days earlier he had written in his journal: "A disgust, a frightful hatred of myself sours all my thoughts the moment I wake up.") His entry of September 22 records: "This morning lunch with Gosse at the Crillon. More wearing than pleasurable. The conversation exhausts me. Gosse is exquisitely cordial. Nevertheless, I felt two or three times that perhaps I was approaching a bit too closely. Ah! how I should like to plunge into a deep bath of silence." Even so, that conversation over luncheon must have been of interest, for Gide recorded that he had told his wife all about it in a letter of that evening. (Unfortunately we shall never know what was said, for in 1918 Madeleine Gide made the despairing gesture of destroying all her husband's letters to her.) Gide, perhaps thinking to offset the impression of *gaucherie* that he was afraid he had created, had an impulse to see Gosse once more by returning to Cuverville on the train that took his English friend to Le Havre, but fatigue or some other cause unspecified prevented his carrying out the intention. And, anyway, the contretemps seems to have done no appreciable damage to the relationship, which continued to grow in cordiality.

Gide spent the entire summer of 1918 in England, most of it in Cambridge. Inasmuch as Gosse's letters to him are missing for this interval, we have but a partial and one-sided version of the relation-

ship. We do know that the two men met several times in London; and
Gosse seems to have gone out of his way to be serviceable in matters
both important and trifling. He used his influence to enable Gide to
get a prompt visa; he supplied the novelist with an introduction to the
head of a zoo that Gide wanted to visit; he helped Gide get a young
nephew and protégé entered at Cambridge University and, later,
enlisted in the British armed forces.

After the end of the war the letters become noticeably less frequent. Gosse, seventy in 1919 and depressed and saddened by postwar developments, was still writing energetically. (Though the *Daily
Chronicle* had dispensed with his contributions and replaced them with
Arnold Bennett's, the Francophile *Sunday Times* welcomed them, and
to it he was to contribute as long as he lived.) But Gide was absorbed
in the production of his most important books, besides being somewhat harassed by complications in his private life. He was as interested as ever in English literature, but Edmund Gosse no longer
represented his sole or even his principal contact with it. His stay in
Cambridge had made him friends nearer to his own age and interests: for example, Lytton Strachey, whose sister, Dorothy Bussy,
was to be the translator of several of Gide's major works. And his
acquaintance with Arnold Bennett had developed into a friendship,
of which Bennett's sympathetic introduction to Gide's *Dostoievsky*
was one token. Gide did not cease to be gratefully aware of Gosse's
affection for him and interest in his work, but he had less and less to
say to the aging dean of English critics.

Gosse obviously quite realized that he was the object of a dimin-
ishing interest. He said nothing at all to Gide about some signal
distinctions of which he was the recipient—an honorary doctorate
from Cambridge University in June, 1920 (Bergson was similarly
honored at the same time); in the following September a party given
for him in connection with the presentation of a bronze bust and
attended by some two hundred personages including Hardy, Conrad,
Kipling, Arnold Bennett, George Moore, and Chesterton. In January,
1921, Gide asks Gosse by letter to intercede with Thomas Hardy for
permission to translate *The Mayor of Casterbridge* and does not go
beyond this literary errand for the Nouvelle Revue Française. There

follows a three-year silence, the first of any such length since 1909. Nor did the two see each other during it. An honorary degree from the University of Strasbourg took Gosse to Paris in November, 1921, but there is no record of a meeting. There is none for 1922, though Gosse spent a vacation between Dieppe and Caudebec, near Cuverville, where Gide was at home after the annual forgathering at Pontigny; Arnold Bennett, Ivan Bunin, and Lytton Strachey, invited, had been unable to attend, but Mrs. Bussy had been among those present. It is evident that for the time being a once close association had been let lapse by tacit mutual consent.

The renewal of contact came about, almost of course, through a book. Gide sent Gosse a copy of *Incidences,* and in August, 1924, Gosse, after some delay, wrote ostensibly to acknowledge and to praise it, but actually to reproach Gide for having failed to send him *Corydon,* which he had bought and read. Without pretending to understand why it had been necessary for Gide to write such a book, he considered the publication of it an act of admirable courage, and he assured the author that he was shock-proof and could be counted on to read "with sympathy and respect" whatever Gide might write on any subject. Gide's reply was that he had not sent *Corydon* to anyone; but he added with candor that, even if he had distributed the book among his friends, he would not have ventured to send it to Gosse. At the same time he paid tribute to Gosse's profession of open-mindedness by undertaking to send him *Si le Grain ne meurt*—another book, then nearing completion, that he had meant to give to no one of his acquaintances.

Within a few weeks Gosse, now president of the Royal Society of Literature, got Gide elected as an honorary fellow of the Society—an English recognition that gave the novelist the more pleasure because he was being violently castigated in his own country. Henceforward he makes a point of prompt acknowledgment, obviously in the realization that Gosse values expressions of esteem and gratitude and is especially sensitive to omission of them. Gide does not fail to congratulate him when, at the beginning of 1925, he is knighted; and during his African tour he takes pains to write to Gosse, as he does to few others. His New Year's message from Bangui, brief but charged with cordiality, shows that its writer has never forgotten the hospitality that he himself had received in London during a holiday season of years before. And, back in Cuverville, Gide writes again, for no reason but to maintain contact with the critic whom he had addressed from the Congo as *mon cher grand ami.*

Gosse, meanwhile, had read and reviewed *Les Faux-Monnayeurs,* of which he liked nothing much but the style; it was in tacit reference to this book that in his reply he adjured its author to rid himself of the pernicious influence of the Russians and especially of Dostoevski, whom Gosse refers to as "this epileptic monster" and "the cocaine and morphine of modern literature."

When, after long hesitation, Gide published *Si le Grain ne meurt,* he did not carry out his undertaking to send this autobiographical work to Gosse, though he did present him with a fine copy of the limited edition of *Journal des faux-monnayeurs.* Gosse, however, demanded the promised book in a note that veiled a real insistence under a light manner, and Gide, with no choice, forewarned his friend that *Si le Grain* was being received with a mixture of applause and outrage. He hoped that, whatever Gosse might think of it, it was not going to deprive its author of a friendship that he had valued so highly. Gosse reassured him on that score and also declared his admiration of the art with which the book was written and of its originality. As to the central disclosure, Gosse was by no means startled: he had been aware of it for twenty years. What he could not comprehend was why such a disclosure had to be shared with all and sundry, and this question he put in terms that precluded anything short of a full and candid answer.

Gide's explanation, which was prompt, ought perhaps to be called the high point of his side of the long correspondence. Written with simple directness and devoid of either cynicism or self-deprecation, it makes the point that his definition of truth to himself had compelled him to write as he did. Any other course would have been cowardice. The time had come when he could neither live nor die in peace of mind with a major part of himself disguised. He had rather be hated for what he was than loved for what he was not; and he cited Montaigne's declaration that he would come back from beyond the grave to give the lie to anyone who falsified him, even if the intention were to do him honor.

Gosse, two years earlier, had written to his young friend J. C. Squire, editor of the London *Mercury,* that hypocrisy, "conscious moral falsity," seemed to him a much graver failing than an "instinctive abnormality" and that an abnormality could not affect his recognition of a writer's general merits. Unfortunately, Gosse's reply to Gide is missing; his last extant letter to Gide is a mere note in a somewhat testy vein about a literary favor solicited by a stranger. But it is clear enough from Gide's acknowledgment of the missing letter (April 8, 1928) that Gosse stood by his own doctrine and declared an unswerving respect for the novelist's moral position.

Gide's April, 1928, letter, undoubtedly his last to Gosse and written about a month before the older man's death, is such as to leave no doubt of either the critic's sympathetic comprehension or the novelist's gratitude for the unfailing deference that he and his work had received. Gosse, facing a major surgical operation at seventy-seven, found that he had to see his beloved France once more, though in 1926 he had written: "I shall certainly never come to France again." In late April, then, accompanied by his young friend William Bellows, he went to visit for a few last days the scenes he had loved and to see historic stones and the waters of the Seine touched by the clear Parisian light. His was first of all a pilgrimage to places, not to persons. He did not call on anyone; he did not even let anyone know that he was there—with a single exception. The one man he wanted to see was the friend whose books had seemed to him for nearly thirty years both beguiling and important. André Gide, on invitation, went to the Hotel de Bourgogne, ostensibly to have tea with Gosse. The two old friends spent an hour together, talking about their inveterate subjects, politics and literature. Two days later, on May 4, Gosse returned to London; he entered the hospital the next day. On the sixteenth he was dead.

IV. GOSSE AS CRITIC OF GIDE

How IMPORTANT the purely literary judgments of Edmund Gosse were to André Gide is a question difficult enough to answer at all and impossible to answer exactly. It is a foregone conclusion that in the course of twenty-five years Gide's estimate of the critic underwent modifications and was subject to ups and downs; in any such long association men discover each other's capacities, but they also discover each other's limitations. And there is no way to distinguish between Gide's appreciation of the Englishman's intellectual and critical gifts and his gratitude for a potent public influence exerted in his interest.

Gosse was a man disinterestedly devoted to literature, given to searching thought about it, and concerned to arrive at true and lasting judgments of its qualities; but he was also a man who had accumulated no little power to make and unmake reputations, to affect the standing and the circulation of particular books. It is clear that Gide first turned to him in the hope of tangible support—of wider recognition and an enlarged audience. It is as clear that he was presently warmed by Gosse's personal understanding and approbation. Of the expressions of deferential regard that abound in Gide's side of the correspondence, no one could say what part belongs to Gosse the perceptive critic and what part to Gosse the vigorous public advocate; because either without the other would account for the terms in which Gide writes.

There is the further difficulty that the novelist, knowing his critic for a thin-skinned, somewhat oversensitive man, undoubtedly treated him at times with a calculated tact that he would have found unnecessary in dealing with a less petulant friend, especially one of his own age and country. There was enough of the *faux-monnayeur* in Gide—as in whom mightn't there be?—to make him convey the impression that he was going to Paris or London expressly to see Gosse, when actually he had substantial other reasons for going. He avoided all reference to other friends who succeeded or supplemented Gosse as the mentors of his English studies. There is, for example, never a mention of Arnold Bennett, who presently supplanted Gosse as Gide's principal English confidant; Bennett was in much closer touch with *Les Faux-Monnayeurs* than Gosse had been with *Isabelle* and *Les Caves du Vatican,* and his correspondence with Gide discloses an easy camaraderie never suggested by the Gide-Gosse letters. Gide carefully refrained from sending *Corydon* to Gosse and sent *Si le Grain ne meurt* only belatedly and under protest, in both instances because he was afraid of alienating the critic's sympathy—a loss that he said would have been one of the great regrets of his life. On that point he must have been sincere; there is every indication that he was well aware of owing something substantial to Gosse. The English critic, besides writing tirelessly and with solicitude about Gide's work in the correspondence itself, paid his public respects to it in the *Contemporary Review* as early as 1910 and in the *Sunday Times* as late as 1927, in pieces reprinted in *Portraits and Sketches* and *Books on the Table*. That Gide's work was felt and respected in England as early as it was is clearly ascribable to Gosse's efforts in its behalf.

These efforts, as we have seen, were not prompted by his earliest exposures to Gide's writing. He did, to be sure, profess warm admiration for the force of design and the purity of style that he found in the two very original plays *Saül* and *Le Roi Candaule;* but, significantly, he left Gide unmentioned in *French Profiles,* published the following year at a time when, intent on the discovery of merit in the latter-day French writers, he was excited about Vigny, Barbey d'Aurevilly, A. Daudet, Zola, Fabre (first urged upon him by Walter Pater) Loti, Paul Bourget, Anatole France, René Bazin, Henri de Régnier, and the poets Verlaine, Mallarmé, Verhaeren, Albert Samain, and Paul Fort. It is evident that as yet Gosse contemplated Gide with more reservations than enthusiasm. *Les Nourritures terrestres* struck him as having more audacity than unity; *L'Immoraliste* he found "extremely painful" as the portrait of a young man with "too definite a divergence from the comfortable type"; it was hardly to be expected that the rhythmic prose of *Le Roi Candaule*—which seemed to him to be free verse—could appeal to a critic captivated by the orotund Alexandrines of *Cyrano de Bergerac;* and he was offish to the subject matter of both of Gide's plays. In the author of all these works he detected a sort of arrogance "tending a little to lawless eccentricity." But when Gosse encountered *La Porte étroite* all was suddenly different. Here was "one of the most beautiful books . . . printed in Europe for a long time," and under its compulsion he wrote the *Contemporary Review* article that left the novelist permanently grateful.

Gosse was impressed by the originality of *La Porte étroite* and by what he called its "sober fullness"; but what was really important was his penetration into the real inwardness of the book as a searching exposition of "the moral psychology of Protestantism," a statement of the suffering caused by a morbid conviction of sin. (Paul Claudel, too, saw in the book "an invaluable document about Protestantism," while questioning whether it were Christian.) In Alissa, Francis Jammes had identified only a saint, Rainer Maria Rilke only an "incarnation of immaterial love"; but in the same character Gosse had no difficulty in recognizing the desperate soul. Was he not himself well acquainted with the rigors of Calvinism? He would never forget how his hand had been wrung by the mother who died when he was seven years old—the mother who, after years of self-denial dedicated almost entirely to what she believed was the Lord's service, would express no joy in entering upon eternal life—"It would not do to go into eternity with a lie in my mouth"—and could profess no more than that her soul was at peace. Gosse perceived, underlying the profound comprehension and the sympathy with which Alissa was portrayed, her creator's abhorrence of "the futile and wretched sacrifice . . . against nature, against happiness, against common sense"—the tragic result of a Puritanism that Gide himself had utterly renounced. " . . . here . . .

a man of modern training, clear–eyed and cool, ... entirely appre-
ciates the nature of the error he so clearly describes and regards it
with deep disapprobation." In this rebellion against the suffering
and the waste entailed by certain kinds of moralistic and religious
preoccupation, Gosse identified the ruling impulse of Gide's fiction
and the mainspring of the "strictly symbolic" works.

In this eight-page article of September, 1909, Gosse went on to pay
his respects to other works of Gide and to trace his development. He
made a point of Gide's particular interest in the exceptional or the
aberrant individual, the "elected spirit," and of his indifference to
types and classes—an implicit consequence of his protest against the
curtailments imposed by the modern collective discipline. He had
emancipated himself, Gosse observed, from symbolism; his growth,
though not rapid, had been continuous; and "the delicate firmness of
his touch as an analyst" was at its best in the very beautiful pages of
La Porte étroite, where the novelist had also attained a deeper human
sympathy and serenity. He had "completely outgrown" the "willful
oddity of aim" that Gosse had found in such comparatively youthful
achievements as *L'Immoraliste, Le Roi Candaule,* and *Philoctète.* Yet
even in these books, unlikely ever to be popular, he perceived distinguished qualities, among them a noteworthy purity of style. Gide's
work, he thought, was less akin to the French spirit than to the
English as manifested in sundry "tender individualists" of the immediate past—Pater, Shorthouse. In fine, it was the privilege of English
readers to become aware of a promising and original career and to
follow it attentively.

Three years later Gosse included the *Contemporary* article, revised
and expanded, in *Portraits and Sketches,* where it stood out as a tribute
to "one living friend, ... a fascinating writer, still young," among
essays on figures whose careers were ended. So Gosse observed in a
preface that went on to predict for Gide a place among the greatest
European writers. The matter added to the essay was chiefly about
Paludes—which, as appears in the correspondence, Gosse read at the
suggestion of Gide himself—and *Isabelle. Paludes,* in which Gide is
satiric about both the humdrum bourgeois mind and his own literary
pretensions, was the more beguiling to Gosse because he had not

foreseen this comparatively frivolous side of Gide's talent; he found *Paludes* to be one of the most delightful of modern books.

Isabelle seemed to him to be an experiment and, as that, possibly somewhat short of "positive perfection" despite its great charm. Gosse was bothered by the circumstance that, in a novel aimed at a "more purely objective effect" than Gide had ever attempted before, the narrating of dubious behavior is done in the first person. ("The young guest listens at key-holes, he spies out the movement of his hostesses, he opens and reads and acts upon a letter intended for no eyes as little as his own.") Curiously illuminating about Gosse's processes is the fact that what disconcerted him in *Isabelle* was not so much the pattern of Isabelle de St. Auréol's life as Gérard's want of punctilio; and that despite the critic's declaration in a letter of two years earlier to his friend E. Marsh: "I should like to know what you think of the new craze for introducing into fiction the high-bred maiden who has a baby? It is the craze of the moment; it is beginning to attract the wonder of the Continent. I have read three English novels this autumn of which this is the motif. The French, who allow themselves every other aberration, have at least preserved their horror of this one, which never occurs in their novels. . . . I do not know how an Englishman can calmly write of such a disgusting thing, with such sang froid." The apparent inconsistency is partly chargeable, no doubt, to Gosse's realization that Isabelle's story was not the true subject of the book. But, after all, what disturbed him in an English novel did not, when it came to the actual test, disturb him so much in a French one.

He was enthusiastic about the style of *Isabelle:* he quoted a whole page by way of illustrating the author's prose rhythm. It seemed to him that Gide's manner here was a departure from that of the preceding books, though still unmistakably Gide's. Indeed, one of his central points was that Gide's career thus far had been an affair of incessant experimentation. Gide wanted to give a new direction to the form of the novel—exactly *what* direction, he seemed as yet hardly to know himself, for every new novel meant a change of direction. Gide occupied an independent "midway position" between literary extremes; he was happily no friend of the "rash and undisciplined improvisation" to which many of the new writers were prone, but there was also a "something northern" in his gift that saved him from oversubservience to the rigorous formalism of the French tradition.

Gide was highly gratified by the rewritten essay. It was much better supported by chapter and verse than the 1909 article; at the same time it was even more laudatory, and it carried the implication that an i telligent and sensitive audience was already intently following development of a writer of exceptional originality and power. score of his style in *Isabelle,* however, Gide was not so easily satisfied as Gosse had been. He thought the verbal manner too given to subtleties and nuances, and he meant his next and forthcoming invention, *Les Caves du Vatican,* to achieve a quite different effect; as he said in his journal (October 20, 1910), " . . . beside a flat tone I shall boldly place another flat tone."

When, in January, 1914, the opening chapters of *Les Caves du Vatican* appeared in the *Nouvelle Revue Française,* Gosse's reception of them was enthusiastic. For some months he had been keeping track of the progress of the novel, which its author had discussed with him in some detail; and he had awaited it with impatience. Now he wrote to congratulate Gide on "perhaps *by far* the greatest thing you have written." He saw in the new novel a development of some tendencies experimentally hinted in *Paludes* and *Isabelle.* (In fact, Gérard seems to have an authentic if limited kinship with Lafcadio, and are not the St. Auréols and the Floches prefigurements of the fantastic couples to be encountered in the later book?) Gosse was nothing short of delighted by the satirical exploitation of a bourgeois Roman Catholic milieu, with every character's behavior pushed to the logical extreme of downright caricature. He rejoiced in the violent contrasts of personality, the "air of mystery and of mystification," the "sparkling irony" in the account of Anthime Armand-Dubois' ludicrously abrupt conversion—in short, every intimation of the *saugrenu* in this curious modern *sotie.* His disappointment came later, when he saw the rest of the book: he wished that Gide had not "dropped so completely the spiritual and religious element"—a pretty clear disclosure that he did not, after all, quite grasp the rules of the queer game that Gide had elected to play.

In all likelihood Gosse found it impossible to read far in *Les Caves du Vatican* without being reminded of Fielding. The genesis of the modern novel—which Paul Desjardins, like most orthodox commentators, credited to Richardson and Fielding—had been rather thoroughly discussed at Pontigny in 1912, and Gosse himself had addressed the gathering about these two English progenitors. Gide's extravaganza uses Fielding's structural device of books divided into chapters; his Lafcadio, like Tom Jones, is a bastard; and, as Gosse noticed, the whole procedure of the story is nothing if not picaresque. Moreover, Gide's manner is more than a little reminiscent of Fielding's in *The History of Tom Jones, a Foundling,* particularly in the matter of confidential asides to the reader about the thoughts and behavior of the characters. ("I don't know what to think of Carola V . . . "; "Did Protos intend to deliver Lafcadio to the police? . . . I don't know.") Gide had not resorted to this expedient before: his nearest approach to it had been narration in the first person, especially in the form of the journal. Gosse, as we have seen, had reservations about the use of the first person in *Isabelle* (though on moralistic rather than aesthetic grounds); but Gide found it a comfortable technique and a way to circumvent the novelist's objectionable pretense of omniscience about the inner life of his characters. He was in chronic quest of narrative methods that would enlarge his canvas and frame it in something better than the mere *récit*—something that could be called, by his exacting definition, an organic novel. It was natural enough that he should draw inspiration from the naturalness, freedom, and robust directness of Fielding.

Gosse, however much or perceptively he may have admired *Les Caves du Vatican,* seems not to have said anything about it to the public. After reading the last installment, he wrote Gide that he needed more time to formulate what he thought of the story and that he meant to reread it carefully when it was published as a book, but he did not say that he was going to review it. He may have been too preoccupied with the tumultuous events of 1914 to go back to Gide's curious *sotie;* or his inveterate caution and conservatism may have made him shrink from recommending to a miscellaneous public a book that, as he correctly foresaw, was going to be widely attacked and debated. It is perhaps odd, whether or not seriously regrettable, that he should have been publicly so reticent about a book that in private he described as destined to be "finally immortal."

The spring of 1914 also brought forth Gide's *Souvenirs de la Cour d'Assises,* about which Gosse made polite enough remarks while somewhat deploring ("You must not indulge this hunger") the expenditure on "juries and judges and prisoners at the bar" of some time and tissue that might have gone into imaginative creation. "You have other and larger fish to fry" was the gentle form his admonition took.

For the larger fish he had to wait six solid years: Gide was publishing no fiction while the war lasted. But 1920 brought Gosse *La Symphonie pastorale,* which drew from him a prompt word of "emotion and admiration" and an undertaking to review the book; he promptly did so for the *Sunday Times,* in an article collected the following year in *Books on the Table,* under the title "Psychology of the Blind." Curiously, two of the most eminent of French writers, Gide and Paul Claudel, had come out almost simultaneously with books on the same subject, a blind girl and her effect on the lives that touched hers. Gosse's piece paid tribute to Gide's talent, which Gosse considered at that time "the most exquisite in Europe," and he cited passages from other works by the same "protean moralist" to exhibit the variety of a writer by turns "paradoxical in *Paludes,* whimsical in *L'Enfant prodigue,* farcical in *Les Caves du Vatican* and sinister in *L'Immoraliste.*" At the same time Gosse made no secret of his own preference for the works in which Gide "shone beyond all the rest" by being a "delicate and translucent mirror of humility"; specifically, *La Porte étroite* and *Isabelle. La Symphonie pastorale,* Gosse thought, belonged in this choice company, and he was gratified to find Gide being once more "calm, austere and evangelical," though he foresaw that the mood would be but fleeting.

Gosse had, however, his reservations about the way the theme was worked out. He found much that was beautiful and touching in the opening scenes, much understanding and humor in the minister's and his wife's feeling for the blind child; but he was left unsatisfied by the explanation that the child did not know how to talk or how to listen because she had been so little spoken to. And the close of the novel, in which the blindness is cured by surgery, struck him as melo-dramatic, "worthy of an *ambigu comique*." Also he found the ending hurried and scamped, as if the author had tired of his subject. Fifteen hurried pages to retrace Gertrude's operation, her discovery of the visual world and of sin, her conversion on the heels of Jacques's, and her death! Gosse wished that Gide would rewrite the ending to show, without benefit of any miraculous cure, what happened to the minister and his wife and their son when Gertrude in her blindness comes to understand their predicament. In this preference he was doubtless judicious and right, and Gide himself was not far at variance. It is disclosed in *Hommage à André Gide,* "A propos de la *Symphonie pasto-rale*" (*Nouvelle Revue Française,* November, 1951), that he gave this book a very low rating among his works, and his journal, in a passage that records his reading of the first forty-five pages to his wife, betrays his despair of completing the story to his satisfaction.

Gide may never have seen what Gosse wrote about *La Symphonie pastorale:* the two exchanged no letters in the three years after publi-cation of *Books on the Table.* Gide knew, however, that Gosse had detected his weakness for losing his grasp of a present work because he was letting his mind become surcharged with a future one. Wil-liam Bellows, in *Edmund Gosse: Some Memories,* records that Gosse said to Gide during his last Paris visit in May, 1928: "You often tire of your characters before you have quite disposed of them; and you even get tired of yourself."

Gide's next announcement to Gosse of a forthcoming novel was in late 1924; and he knew enough about the English critic's prepossessions to anticipate his reception of *Les Faux-Monnayeurs.* What Gosse wrote about this book—"The Coiners," in the *Sunday Times* of March 21, 1926, when Gide was on his journey to the Congo—was the expression of a distaste far exceeding anything that he had de-clared before. He thought this novel one of the most disheartening he had ever read; it had given him a "saddening, disagreeable shock." What disturbed him was not so much the treatment of a subject theretofore most commonly relegated to "medical jurisprudence"— after all, Marcel Proust had dealt with homosexuality much more outspokenly—as an "atmosphere of sordid depravation" uncompensated by any sufficiently pervasive countereffect. Gosse cited episodes in the behavior of the corrupt youths in the book, the least reprehensible of whom steals a valise and rifles its contents. A less unpleasant character—the oddly "incompetent school-teacher" M. de La Pérouse, little but an old fool—struck Gosse as hopelessly unreal, a fantastic puppet of a Dostoevskian kind; and he frankly hated to see Gide crouch in the shadow of the barbarian giants of Russian fiction. (Gide himself thought La Pérouse a failure, but for the radically different reason that the portrait was too close to its real-life model, Marc de La Nux, his excellent former piano teacher, to whom Gide showed great kindness in his lonely old age. "It is difficult to imagine when memory holds you back," he pointed out in *Journal des faux-monnayeurs*. It is, however, undeniable that his mind was much under the influence of Dostoevski while he was writing *Les Faux-Monnayeurs*.) On more counts than one, then, Gosse was considerably upset by this novel.

A part of his disturbance was the borrowed trouble of construing an imaginative work as a factual, a sociological document. Identifying the point of view of Edouard, the novelist in the book, with that of Gide himself, Gosse proceeded from the assumption that Gide was offering *Les Faux-Monnayeurs* as a whole and balanced representation of Parisian life—as, in fact, his first attainment of the "authentic novel" toward which he had been groping his way through a variety of fictional experiments. On this basis Gosse was at pains to argue that the depiction of society was one-sided and wrong; that Gide could never have assembled such a cast of deplorably unrepresentative characters unless he had egregiously deceived himself; that to accept this book as a veritable slice of life would be to despair of France. In fine, the critic who had for twenty years been watching Gide's efforts to reconstitute the French novel now quite failed to realize that any sort of logical consummation had been attained. He perceived neither the striking originality of what he had read nor the inordinate complexity of the task that the novelist had deliberately imposed upon his reader. When, the next year, *Les Faux-Monnayeurs* appeared in translation as *The Counterfeiters,* it was widely received as Gide's masterpiece, especially by the younger and more alert American critics; but of all Gide's works it was the one that Edmund Gosse least understood, and it seems not to have occurred to him that it might be of them all the most important to understand. Perhaps it should be noted in Gosse's defense that he was not the only distinguished critic to find the book difficult. In *Je dois à André Gide,* Lucien Combelle quotes Gide as saying, "*The Counterfeiters,* my most important book, was more or less understood only by Strowski and (I think) Lalou. All the others said inanities, especially Arland and Jaloux." Whether Gosse's condemnation was ultimately right or wrong is, of course, a matter of opinion, but it was critically wrong because based on a radical oversimplification that falsified what the novelist had undertaken to do.

Gosse would gladly have persuaded himself that *Les Faux-Monnayeurs* was some obscure species of satire; but he could find in it neither censure nor underlying irony, and he had to fall back, hopefully and vaguely, on an ascription of "a certain temper of pity" that saved the book from being too formidably inhuman. Gide was, after all, a major writer, a conscious artist who wrote a distinguished style; whatever he did was done with care and for meditated effects; no one must judge him precipitately or dismiss him peremptorily—thus Gosse, with his inveterate discretion. He had a far from tough-minded gift for explaining away what disturbed him. This he had shown even in a short *Sunday Times* article of May, 1925, about Gide's sale of his library just before his African journey. The novelist had written the preface to his catalogue in an ironic vein all his own, and Gosse was aware that many tongues were busy over Gide's reasons for "selling Peter and keeping Paul," for "blandly and defiantly" ridding himself of the books of former friends; nevertheless he insisted on detecting in the sale a Protestant impulse toward renunciation of worldly possessions and commitments on the eve of a momentous departure. No one need be greatly astonished, and perhaps no one was, that such a man should fall something short in comprehension of *Les Faux-Monnayeurs.* Gosse was a critic firmly entrenched in his limitations, some of them congenital and some systematically built up; he believed in most of them devoutly; he had never had overmuch of the patience that he would have needed to untie, even in his own language, the kind of knot that Gide had patiently designed; and he was seventy-seven.

On Gide's return from Africa Gosse wrote him at some length without overt mention of either *Les Faux-Monnayeurs* or his own piece about it, though he must have had the novel in mind when he adjured Gide to release himself from his bondage to the Russians. The *Journal des faux-monnayeurs* might perhaps have set him to reconsidering some of his impressions if he had made a point of studying it very intently, but he seems to have given it only a rather perfunctory interest. The reason was, at least in part, that his mind was now stretching forward to still another work: the piece of autobiography that was to produce the nearest approach to an absolute showdown ever reached by these two men, probably the nearest possible to them.

Gosse's first letter about *Si le Grain ne meurt,* a letter of late December, 1926, is missing; the answer to it shows that it dwelt on the early pages about Gide's Puritan upbringing, some aspects of which brought back memories of Gosse's own childhood as chronicled in *Father and Son*—ground covered years earlier in connection with *La Porte étroite.* But some days later the critic, having reread *Si le Grain ne meurt* with care, declared his qualms about its deliberately confessional Part II. The facts there disclosed, he said, did not startle him: he had divined the central one more than twenty years earlier, on reading *L'Immoraliste,* and had since found repeated corroborations. But why carry confession to this unprecedented length? Need it be done so overtly, made so explicit? "Was it wise? Was it necessary? Is it useful?" He marveled at the courage shown; he disclaimed any impulse to pass moralistic judgments or to let his friends' peculiarities blind him to their qualities; he was sure that much of the book would bear comparison with the best modern writing; he admitted that Gide's kind of genius might be entitled to enact its own laws. But he could not see what benefit to anyone could accrue from such selfexposure, and he besought Gide to tell him, if he could, why it had to be.

Gosse's position, it may be said in passing, was essentially that of Gide's closest friends in France. Charles Du Bos, to whom Gide had shown *Si le Grain ne meurt* at Pontigny in the summer of 1923, had at first been aware of nothing but the artistry of the book, its inner harmony; but then Jean Schlumberger, who was both his friend and Gide's, had made him realize the practical consequences of publishing such a self-revelation. Du Bos did not intervene: he felt sure that Gide's mind was made up and that he no longer had an ear for any considerations but artistic ones. But Roger Martin du Gard made an energetic attempt to head off immediate publication, which, among other considerations, would be gravely prejudicial to the full further development of Gide's capacities; the book, he maintained, should be a posthumous one. (Gide's answer was that he could wait no longer; he was obeying an imperious inner necessity stronger than anything else. "I feel a need of finally dissipating that cloud of lies in which I have been sheltering myself all through my youth and my childhood. It suffocates me!") And Jacques Copeau arrived at the same conclusion by a somewhat psychoanalytic route. In the public avowal he detected a "nostalgic aspect of martyrdom"—such a prompting as might originate in contemplation of Oscar Wilde's disaster. Roger Martin du Gard, who could be psychoanalytic too, thought he recognized in Gide's resolve "a Slavonic intoxication"; he referred to the mania for public confession as a "contagion"; Gide was "burning, like the hero of a Russian novel, to brave society, to expose himself to its buffets; he longs to undergo insult, shame, the pillory"—words that might have come from Gosse himself.

Gosse printed nothing expressly about *Si le Grain ne meurt,* but he did take account of it in reviewing (for the *Sunday Times* in November, 1927) Paul Souday's book about Proust, Gide, and Valéry. Souday, whom Gosse described as the most influential of living French critics, had begun by dealing rather cordially with Gide, but he had become comparatively censorious after 1914. He had never cared for the sort of humor that he found in *Paludes; Les Caves du Vatican* irked him by excess of irony; on the whole he deplored the publication of *Corydon, Les Faux-Monnayeurs,* and *Si le Grain ne meurt;* and he had taken to declaring himself baffled by Gide's "protean and elusive" talent—the talent of "a wizard and perhaps a demoniac," as Gosse put it—in contexts in which the word *clandestin* kept turning up. Gosse, in partial agreement, admits the sinuosities of the novelist's mind and the difficulty of defining his fundamental purposes; resurveying his earlier works, Gosse detects in him a satirist whose sense of the moral order has been warped, especially in *L'Immoraliste,* by the leverage of Nietzsche; Gide "concealed, under an exterior of the gentlest sophistry, an iron obstinacy . . . he has formed a conviction that the time has come to replace our old conventional morality by a new system." Nevertheless, Gosse continues to maintain that Gide is "one of the most interesting writers now at work in Europe." It is an error to charge him with "complacency to crime": he seems to be indulgent to the criminal because he lets impulsive pity take precedence over "all recognized moral discipline"—a turn of temperament that Gosse ascribes to the influence of Dostoevski, whose poison, "if poison it be," has infected Gide to the marrow. In fine, Gosse tends to make the most of what he takes to be Gide's merits and to explain away what he construes as faults; and he is confident that Gide will keep on growing, experimenting, conquering new domains.

Gosse is, of late years, obviously pretty much in eclipse. It has become the fashion to minimize the value of his criticism, to think of it as prevailingly conventional and hidebound. He had, to be sure, like anyone else, the defects of his qualities, and the defects as well as the qualities are certainly traceable through the decades of his association with Gide. But a depreciatory over-all estimate of his capacities will not stand up against the facts of this association—the facts incorporated in the Gide-Gosse correspondence and in Gosse's published writings about Gide. He discovered the French novelist for himself, and discovered him early, with no pressure or prompting except from the novelist's work and his own taste and conscience. He was urging Gide upon English readers well before Gide had captured any great body of French readers or any impressive volume of plaudits from French criticism. He saw in Gide, at the outset as at the end, a writer of the first originality and of international stature, and he unfailingly gave Gide's works, both those published and those at any stage of incubation, the most solicitous attention. Edmund Gosse (1849–1928), a critic of the generation of Anatole France (1844–1924), maintained an open-minded hospitality to a succession of works produced when he was between fifty-five and seventy-eight; works of a generation not his, foreign to him in language and even more foreign in ethos—works that freely trampled on his most important preconceptions about the moral responsibility of authorship, and by their untrammeled individualism affronted his lifelong code. About one of the most crucial of these works he arrives independently in his seventy-eighth year at almost exactly the position taken by one of the most gifted of the younger critics, Charles Du Bos, and by two of Gide's literary intimates, Jacques Copeau and Roger Martin du Gard—an exhibition of disinterested and disciplined acumen hardly to be contemplated without deep respect. That André Gide himself could have contemplated it with anything short of that respect is unimaginable; and there is every reason to suppose that he was speaking with sincerity and well within his convictions when, in a letter to Gosse's son two years after the critic's death, he paid tribute to the man who had spoken of his work "with such broad, enlightened and generous understanding."

The Letters

I. GOSSE TO GIDE, *June 16, 1904, from London*[1]

MY DEAR SIR, Allow me to thank you for your kindness in sending me "*Saül*" "Le Roi Candaule."[2] The latter I had read before, the former was new to me. Both are admirable for force of design and freshness of execution. Your works have no more warm admirer than

Yours very faithfully, EDMUND GOSSE

[1] Gosse's letters from London were all written from his home, 17 Hanover Terrace, Regent's Park, N. W.

[2] What Gide sent to Gosse was the first edition of *Saül* and *Le Roi Candaule* together, published by the Mercure de France early in 1904. It included the preface to the second edition of *Le Roi Candaule,* in which Gide cited the opinions of critics after the performance. This play, a three-act drama in verse, had been printed by the *Revue Blanche* in 1901 and produced in May, 1901, by Lugné-Poë. *Saül,* written in 1896, had been privately printed in 1903 by the Mercure de France in a limited edition of twelve copies. Parts of it—fragments III, IV, V—had been published in the *Revue Blanche* June 15, 1898. This play was naturally less known than the other, and it is not surprising that Edmund Gosse was not aware of it. Antoine had wanted to produce *Saül,* but had been prevented by lack of money. It was performed for the first time in June, 1922, at the Vieux-Colombier; Jacques Copeau and Louis Jouvet were among the actors.

The 1904 edition was not very successful. On October 14 Gide wrote Francis Jammes: "Save for the excessively kind and charming article by F. de Miomandre, the critics have not been interested in Saül. Since I am hard to classify, I embarrass them.... so much the worse for me!" (Francis Jammes–André Gide, *Correspondance*, p. 215.)

2. GOSSE TO GIDE, *July 5, 1909, from London*

DEAR MONSIEUR ANDRÉ GIDE, Your beautiful story of "La Porte Etroite"[1] has caused me a real emotion. I do not know how long it is since I have read a book which has so profoundly moved me. I can witness to the penetration, the truth, the bitter sweetness of your searching analysis of Calvinistic pietism,[2] so far more tragic, so far more hopeless and desolating than any of the ecstasies of the Catholic Church. What are the sufferings of S. Catherine of Sienna, of S. Fina of San Gimigniano, by the side of the slow and cruel suicide of Alissa? Pages 191 to 203 are among the most poignant in litterature, and the most true: I did not read them without the sense of an almost personal agitation and despair.

For many years past, dear Monsieur Gide,—I have felt that between you and me there exist some very close spiritual and intellectual ties. Am I presumptuous in saying so? I wish that we might meet. Do you ever come to England? There is no one whom I should more eagerly welcome, or from whose conversation I should anticipate a keener pleasure.

I wonder if you ever saw a book of mine, called "Father and Son?"[3] If not, will you let me have the pleasure of sending it to you? When you read it, you will see why I particularly desire that you should read it.

Pray believe me to be, with deep gratitude for the pain and pleasure which "La Porte Etroite" has given me

Yours very sincerely, EDMUND GOSSE

¹ *La Porte étroite* (Mercure de France, 1909) had been printed in installments in the *Nouvelle Revue Française,* February–April, 1909. Gide had finished writing it October 8, 1908; he had been thinking about it ever since 1894.

² In July, 1910, Gide was to write in the *Nouvelle Revue Française,* in answer to an attack by Eugène Montfort in *Les Marges,* May 15: "As far as I am aware it is impossible to imagine any school of thought more alien to a work of art ... or even more hostile to it ... than Calvinism. This is the reason why I broke with it as soon as I began writing." Gide often declared that a work of art should not demonstrate anything; all he wanted was to disturb—to incite to thought. About *La Porte étroite* he wrote to Jules Renard: "What did I want to offer except a portrait? My heroine made me suffer a good deal. I depicted her with love. Some persons thought I sympathized with her; others thought my book a satire on Protestantism, and that was neither less false nor less true."

³ *Father and Son* had been published October 25, 1907. It combined autobiography with a biography of Gosse's father. In the first edition Gosse had changed names and published anonymously. Philip Gosse, respected as a specialist in natural history, exposed himself to ridicule by undertaking to refute Darwin out of Holy Writ, or rather out of his own interpretation of it.

La Porte étroite was Gide's first success. In thanking Francis Jammes for his tribute in the *Occident* (October 26, 1909) Gide wrote: "*La Porte étroite* is selling well ... a success that surprises the Mercure." (Jammes–Gide, *Correspondance.*) *Father and Son,* even more successful, was reprinted in December, 1907 and in January and April, 1908.

3. GIDE TO GOSSE, *July 14, 1909, from Cuverville*¹

CHER MONSIEUR EDMUND GOSSE   Quelle joie me cause votre excellente lettre! La chaleureuse expression de votre sympathie me touche profondément; elle m'est précieuse entre toutes, non seulement à cause du grand cas que je fais de votre jugement — mais aussi parce

que vous êtes, aujourd'hui, mon seul "correspondant," (et j'allais
dire: mon seul lecteur) en Angleterre. Oui, je n'ai envoyé en Angleterre d'autre exemplaire de ma "Porte Etroite" que le vôtre, et si
votre jugement m'importe à ce point, c'est aussi parce que c'est le
jugement d'un Anglais. Depuis si longtemps mes goûts, mes sympathies, mes passions tournent mes regards vers l'Angleterre — et
je ne m'y connais pas un ami! Quoi! tandis qu'en Allemagne, où
j'ai peut-être plus de lecteurs qu'en France, mais à l'égard de qui
je garde plus d'attente que de réelle curiosité, mes livres sont traduits
aussitôt que parus, ou même avant de paraître, comme il advient de
ce dernier — l'Angleterre resterait à mon égard sans oreille et sans
voix! . . . Mais voici votre lettre réconfortante. Cher Monsieur Gosse,
je sais de quel poids est votre parole et de quel crédit jouit votre
opinion: est-ce à vous que je devrai de n'être bientôt plus un inconnu
pour la littérature Anglaise où ma pensée habite si souvent?

Oui certes j'aimerais vous connaître. Mais quand pourrai-je aller
en Angleterre? je ne sais. Vous avouerais-je qu'elle m'effraie autant
qu'elle m'attire et que, précisément parce que je n'y connaissais personne, je craignais de m'y sentir perdu.

Oui, certes il faut m'envoyer "Father and Son"; je suis extrêmement impatient de vous connaître sous un nouvel aspect, n'ayant lu
de vous jusqu'à présent que des études de critique. Croyez à mon
attention très vive et à ma reconnaissante sympathie.

ANDRÉ GIDE.

[How much delight your fine letter gives me! The warm expression of your understanding stirs me deeply; it has a unique
value to me, not only because of the great store I set by your
judgment, but also because you are at present my one corre-
spondent—I had all but said my one reader—in England.
Actually, I have sent to England but one copy of my Porte
Etroite, yours, and another reason why your verdict matters so
much to me is that it is the verdict of an Englishman. For a good
while now my tastes, sympathies, and enthusiasms have been
drawing me toward England—and without my being acquainted
with one friend there![2] It is curious that in Germany, where I

have possibly more readers than in France[3]—though toward it I feel rather open-mindedness than true interest—my books are translated on publication or even before, as this latest one was, whereas England continues, so far as I am concerned, both deaf and dumb! But now here is your consoling letter. Dear Mr. Gosse, I know what weight your word carries and how your opinion is looked up to:[4] am I presently to owe to you my ceasing to be an utter stranger in English letters, on which my mind so often dwells?

To be sure, I should love to make your acquaintance. But when can I get to England? I don't know. Shall I confide to you that England frightens as much as it draws me, and that, just because I knew no one there, I have dreaded the feeling of being lost there?

By all means you must send me *Father and Son;* I am most eager to know you in a guise new to me, having hitherto read nothing of yours but pieces of criticism.[5]]

[1] Cuverville-en-Caux, canton of Criquetot-L'Esneval, district of Le Havre, is the village of Mme André Gide's country house, in which Gide was accustomed to spend several months of each year.

[2] Actually, Gide knew and corresponded with the young French anglicist Valery Larbaud. (J. G. Aubry, *La Jeunesse de Valery Larbaud,* Monaco, 1949.)

[3] Books already translated were *Philoctète,* 1904; *Paludes, L'Immoraliste, Le Roi Candaule,* 1905; *La Tentative amoureuse,* 1907; *Saül, Le Prométhée mal enchaîné, La Porte étroite,* 1909. (The first English translation of *La Porte étroite,* by Dorothy Bussy, was not published until 1924.) Gide knew German rather well; he had studied it in school, and he sometimes read it with his wife. He had made a number of visits to Germany; in 1903 he gave a lecture in Weimar. He had friends among the liberal-minded German writers—R. Kassner, F. Blei, R. Curtius, Rainer Maria Rilke, Thomas Mann, Rathenau; some of them were his translators. But the German press had been severely critical of *Le Roi Candaule,* produced in Berlin January 9, 1908, and Gide resented the critics' treatment of it. (Cf. R. Lang, *A. Gide et la pensée allemande,* Paris: Egloff, 1949.)

⁴ Gosse was then a very influential combination of critic and pub-licist—a redoubtable specimen of the independent scholar who cir-culates and explicates ideas and introduces to the readers of his own country all the writers whom he finds worthy of interest. (Cf. H. Davray, "Lettres Anglaises," *Mercure de France,* August, 1904.) Gide had almost never sent books of his to critics or journalists, but he now seriously aspired to becoming known in England. He also sent *La Porte étroite* to Georg Brandes, probably at Jacques Copeau's instance; Brandes never mentioned it in print. (Rilke–Gide, *Corres-pondance,* p. 39.)

⁵ Gide probably knew the articles published in *Cosmopolis,* 1896–98, and perhaps those in *French Profiles,* 1905, which dealt with Vigny, d'Aurevilly, Alphonse Daudet, Zola, Fabre, Verlaine, Anatole France, Loti, Bourget, Bazin, Régnier, Mallarmé, Verhaeren, Sa-main, and Paul Fort.

4. GOSSE TO GIDE, *July 28, 1909, from London*

DEAR MONSIEUR GIDE, I have wholly withdrawn from periodical writing, which I think belongs to a generation younger than mine. But I am so strongly tempted to make your writings better known in this country, that I intend to make an exception to the rule I have laid down for myself, and, when I can find time to do so, to say something about "La Porte Etroite." [1]

Yours truly, EDMUND GOSSE

What is "Amyntas?" [2]

¹ Gosse's article was "The Writings of M. A. Gide" in the *Con-temporary Review* of September, 1909. The critic, then sixty, had all but ceased to write for literary magazines, but in 1909 he did print, besides the piece about Gide, an article on the centenary of Edgar Allan Poe and another of reminiscences about Swinburne.

² *Amyntas* (Mercure de France, 1906) was a volume of Gide's African reminiscences containing, besides the title piece, "Mopsus," "Feuilles de Route," "De Biskra à Touggourt," and "Le Renoncement au voyage"; "Feuilles de Route" had been previously published (Brussels, 1899). The title *Amyntas* is from Vergil: "*Quid tunc si fuscus Amyntas?*" (What matter if Amyntas be dark?) Gide's imagination construed Amyntas as no human being, but "an imaginary idol"—the "Saharan Apollo." (*Journal,* April 9, 1930.) Criticism received the book with a concerted silence, thanks partly to Gide himself, and it is not astonishing that Gosse was unaware of its existence. Gide's *Journal* for January 9, 1907, records: "I am the one who created this silence around me... not the *Ermitage,* nor *Vers et Prose,* nor *L'Occident,* all friendly reviews, has said a word about my *Amyntas*... I did not want any articles where praise was almost obligatory." Gide was, however, anticipating with some dread an article by Jean de Gourmont in *Vers et Prose:* "I did not send *Amyntas* to Jean de G———I wish he would not write that article; he cannot but do it badly. He does not like me." (Jammes–Gide, *Correspondance,* p. 234.)

5. GOSSE TO GIDE, *September 2, 1909, from London*

DEAR MONSIEUR GIDE,   You will see that I have fulfilled my promise.¹ The "Contemporary Review" is the most influential monthly organ of the Liberal party, and has a very large circulation.

Yours truly, EDMUND GOSSE

¹ Gosse's article sketched Gide's French Huguenot background, quoted his first books, his plays, and his first real novel, *L'Immoraliste,* and made mention of his essays, of "Feuilles de Route," and of *Prétextes,* a volume of criticism. Gide's bent for incessant experimentation, which was later to fascinate and to disconcert Gosse by turns, here drew the compliment that Gide was "never satisfied to be a cliché of himself."

6. GIDE TO GOSSE, *September 9, 1909, from Cuverville*

CHER MONSIEUR GOSSE   Malgré que votre avant dernière lettre me l'annonçât, j'osais à peine croire à cet article — et le voici pourtant! Je le trouve en rentrant d'une courte absence, ce qui vous explique que je ne vous en aie pas remercié plus immédiatement. Vous me demandiez si je ne viendrais pas en Angleterre; grâce à vous j'en ai désormais le plus vif désir, car je ne pourrai bien vous exprimer que de vive voix ma gratitude.

Vous parlez de mon œuvre avec une rare compréhension et compétence — auxquelles mes compatriotes ne m'ont guère habitué. Quelle joie — où n'entre pas rien que de l'orgueil — de pouvoir se pencher sur un miroir aussi clair, aussi plan, aussi flatteur pourtant que celui que vous me tendez; et combien délicieux à lire ce que vous me dites de mes qualités d'écrivain. (Je ne connais rien de Shorthouse, mais depuis longtemps me sens en effet en étroite parenté d'art avec W. Pater.)

Et maintenant je tremble... Désormais les lecteurs de la Contemporary R. vont *attendre de moi;* vous leur aurez appris à compter sur moi. Le livre auquel je travaille à présent ne va-t-il pas les décevoir? les indigner peut-être? Du moins ce n'est déjà plus d'un cœur aussi léger que j'oserai le publier.

Mais votre étude avertit sagement le public; le happy few auquel ma littérature s'adresse saura n'exiger que la *qualité* de mes écrits; votre article aidera cette confiance en soi, qui n'a rien à voir avec l'infatuation, mais qui seule permet les belles et fortes œuvres de "l'âge mûr."

Croyez cher Monsieur que je vous en suis profondément reconnaissant   ANDRÉ GIDE.

[Even though your last letter but one promised this article, I hardly dared believe in its existence: yet here it is! I find it waiting for me on my return after a short absence,[1] which will explain to you why I have not thanked you more promptly. You ask whether I shall not be coming to England: thanks to you, from now on I shall be keen to do so, for only face to face can I thank you adequately.

You speak of my work with rare understanding and authority—qualities that my fellow countrymen have hardly taught me to count on. What a delight—to say nothing of mere pride —to be able to look into so clear, so smooth, and so flattering a mirror as the one you hold up to me! and how luxurious to read what you say about my gifts as a writer. (I know nothing of Shorthouse,[2] but I have long felt a close artistic kinship with Walter Pater.[3])

And now I tremble. From now on the readers of the *Contemporary Review* are going to expect things of me; you will have taught them to rely upon me. Is this book I am now writing[4] going to disillusion them, perhaps anger them? Anyway, now I shall not dare to publish it so lightheartedly.

But your article gives the public a wise forewarning: the *happy few*[5] to whom my books are addressed will manage to extract only the *merits* of what I write. Your article will bolster the self-confidence, devoid of vanity, that alone makes possible the beautiful and powerful works of the riper years.]

[1] Gide was as yet being read by only a limited public, but his friends Henri Ghéon, F. de Miomandre, and F. Jammes had recently written comprehensive articles about him. On August 11, 1909, Gide wrote from Banyuls to thank Jammes for his fine article in the July *Occident*. It contained a thoroughgoing analysis of *La porte étroite*; Jammes spoke of having met Alissa in "grass-grown Normandy"—a reference to Mme Gide, who did indeed tragically resemble the heroine. "Nothing, except life itself, is more filled with blood and tears than this story." (Jammes–Gide, *Correspondance,* p. 261.) It was on Gide's return from the Pyrenees that he found Gosse's article.

[2] Henry Shorthouse, 1834–1903, was the author of *John Inglesant* (1880), the story, in its day widely read, of a mystic at the court of

Charles I, involved in the clash of Anglican and Roman Catholic dogmas and forces.

³ Gide seems to have read very little of Pater's work at this time. Later he was to be "enraptured" by Pater's Greek studies (*Journal*, August 4, 1922).

⁴ Gide was working on *Isabelle*, which he was to finish November 14, 1910, but the reference may be to *Les Caves du Vatican*, which had been long and persistently on his mind.

⁵ Gide borrows the English phrase from Stendhal, who was given to using it in his letters or as a dedication at the end of a novel. Gide was a confirmed admirer of Stendhal's spontaneity of style and incidentally a sharer of Stendhal's hope of being read by future generations.

7. GOSSE TO GIDE, *March 7, 1910, from London*

MY DEAR MONSIEUR GIDE, Two little books of yours, "Le Retour de l'Enfant Prodigue"¹ and "Oscar Wilde"² have reached me through your kindness, and have given me immense pleasure. They have—different as they are—the same kind of beauty, the beauty of pure thought, strong and clear expression, and that moral elevation which is so characteristic of your genius. There is no one now writing in France whose works give me more pleasure than yours,—perhaps no one at this moment who gives me so much.

Of course, I had already read most of the "Oscar Wilde" in your admirable "Pretextes."³

There has been a great deal of folly written about Wilde. I like the complete sanity of your picture. Of course he was not "a great writer." A languid romancier, a bad poet, a good (but not superlatively good) dramatist,—his works, taken without his life, present, to a sane criticism, a mediocre figure. But the man was consistent, extraordinary, vital even to excess, and his strange tragedy will always attract the consideration of the wise.

Some time ago I sent you my book "Father and Son." I never heard that you read it. I should be disappointed to think that you could never find time to do so, for I put the whole passion of my mind into it, and I should like to think that you, for whom I have so great a sympathy, had some sympathy for me.

Believe me always, with the greatest esteem,

Yours sincerely, EDMUND GOSSE

---

[1] *Le Retour de l'enfant prodigue* was published by *Vers et Prose* in 1907; in 1909 an edition de luxe was printed for the Bibliothèque de l'Occident.

[2] *Oscar Wilde: In Memoriam, Souvenirs: Le "De Profundis"* was published by the Mercure de France in 1910. "In Memoriam" had been included in *Prétextes,* 1903. Gide had known Oscar Wilde fairly well: he had met him in Paris, in Florence, and again in Africa.

[3] *Prétextes: Réflexions sur quelques points de littérature et de morale* (Mercure de France, 1903) includes "Lettres à Angèle," "De l'Influence en Littérature" (a lecture at La Libre Esthétique, Brussels, and published separately in 1900), and "Les Limites de l'art," a Paris lecture printed in 1901. In *Oscar Wilde* Gide maintained that Wilde, without being a great writer, "spoke and lived his wisdom," and he quoted Wilde's *mot,* "I have put my genius into my life and I have put only my talent into my works."

Gosse, on March 13, 1908, had written to Wilde's faithful friend Robert Ross about a new edition of *De Profundis* that Ross had just sent him. The critic said that he had always felt an aversion to Wilde's personality, but added: "...the older I get the more individualistic I get. I detest nothing so much as the cliché in mankind. And more and more personal liberty becomes a passion, almost a fanaticism, with me. Less and less can I endure the idea of punishing a man— who is not cruel—because he is unlike other men. Perhaps poor Wilde (who alas! was in life so distasteful to me) may come to be known as a protomartyr to freedom, now he is in his grave." Gosse further added that he detested not so much Wilde's vices as his lack of reality. (Charteris, *The Life and Letters of Sir Edmund Gosse,* p. 310.)

8. GIDE TO GOSSE, *March 10, 1910, from Villa Montmorency, Auteuil*[1]

CHER MONSIEUR GOSSE Votre exquise lettre me touche profondément. Je suis tout à la fois très reconnaissant de savoir que vous m'avez envoyé votre livre — et désolé de ne l'avoir *pas* reçu. (Croyez bien que sinon je vous en aurais déjà remercié.)

J'écris tout aussitôt au Mercure de France, priant qu'on regarde si ce livre ne s'est pas égaré dans quelque armoire. Jacques Blanche qui m'en parlait longuement il y a quelques jours augmentait encore le désir que j'ai de le lire.

Croyez que vous n'aurez pas plus attentif lecteur que votre affectueux et respectueux

ANDRÉ GIDE.

[Your fine letter moves me deeply. I am at once very grateful for knowing that you sent me your book and unhappy at having failed to receive it. (Do believe that otherwise I should have thanked you before now.)

I am writing at once to the Mercure de France asking them to make sure whether the book has not been sidetracked in some closet. Jacques Blanche,[2] who was talking to me at length about it the other day, made me even more anxious to read it.

Believe me, you will have no more attentive reader.]

[1] Villa Montmorency was the house that Gide had built in Auteuil and moved into in 1905.

[2] Jacques Emile Blanche, 1861-1942, painter and critic, was a friend of Gide.

9. GIDE TO GOSSE (post card), *April 4, 1910, from Barcelona*[1]

CHER MONSIEUR GOSSE,   Une lettre de Paris m'annonce l'arrivée de votre livre très désiré. Merci déjà! Je me réjouis de le trouver dans quelques jours à mon retour.

Croyez à mon très attentif dévouement.   ANDRÉ GIDE.

[A letter from Paris reports the very welcome arrival of your book. I thank you right now, and I am happy that I shall find it there in a few days, when I get back.]

[1] This post card was sent during a visit to Spain that Gide made with Jacques Copeau.

10. GIDE TO GOSSE, *April 10, 1910, from Cuverville*

CHER MONSIEUR   C'est avec l'émotion la plus vive que je lis votre beau livre. J'y pénètre avec une grande lenteur et vous écris bien avant d'en avoir achevé la lecture — car, il me faut bien vous avouer la grande honte de ma vie: je sais fort mal l'anglais.

Du temps que j'aurais facilement pu l'apprendre c'était la langue que se réservaient mes parents pour dire devant moi tout ce qu'un enfant ne devait pas entendre; en fils respectueux, je me gardais de faire effort pour découvrir ce qui devait rester secret. Depuis, sans doute parce que la langue anglaise m'attirait autant que me rebutait la langue allemande, c'est vers cette dernière qu'ont porté tous mes efforts.

Mais, autour de moi, tous parlent anglais, à commencer par ma femme. C'est avec elle que je lis votre livre, et soyez assuré que vous n'aurez pas rencontré lecteurs plus attentifs ni plus émus.

Comment, pourquoi un pareil livre n'a-t-il pas encore été traduit...?

Votre dévoué et reconnaissant ANDRÉ GIDE.

[It is with keen excitement that I am reading your fine book. I am getting into it very slowly, and I write you well before I have finished it—for I must confess to you the worst of my disgraces: I know next to no English.

All the time when I could easily have learned it, it was the language my parents saved for saying in front of me all the things that a child is not to hear; like a dutiful son I avoided trying to penetrate what was supposed to stay secret. Since then, no doubt because English attracted me as much as German repelled me, it is on the latter that I have bent all my efforts.[1]

But everyone around me speaks English, beginning with my wife. It is with her that I am reading your book, and you may be sure that you will have reached no readers more attentive or more affected.

How is it, why is it, that such a book is still untranslated?[2]]

---

[1] Gide, though he took up English belatedly, took it up very seriously; he wanted to read it fluently, for he thought English literature "the richest in the whole world." (*Ainsi-soit-il ou les jeux sont faits,* pp. 75–76.) Years later he recorded his youthful visit to London —a very brief one made in the company of a Protestant clergyman, Elie Allégret—and his first opportunity to make use of his one English sentence, "I can't speak English." The pastor took him to hear a famous preacher. When they were leaving the church, a young woman addressed him in English, and he answered politely, "No, thank you"; whereupon his mentor told him that the young woman had asked if he wanted to be saved. Gide, for the rest of the trip, did not open his mouth. (*Ainsi-soit-il,* p. 75.)

[2] *Father and Son* was to be translated by Henry Davray and Auguste Monod and published in June, 1912, by the Mercure de France as *Père et fils, étude de deux tempéraments.* (Cf. Letters 19, 22, 24.) What

particularly interested Gide in *Father and Son,* aside from its general theme, was the amount about natural history in it. "I was a naturalist before being a writer, and natural adventures have always taught me more than those related in novels." (*Journal,* June 19, 1910; see also Letter 84.)

11. GOSSE TO GIDE, *March 22, 1911, from London*

DEAR MONSIEUR GIDE,   Thank you for the kind gift of your Nouveaux Pretextes,[1] which I had read before, but which give me a new pretext for expressing to you my admiration.

But why do not you read English?[2] You shut yourself out, thus obstinately, from such a wide field of pleasure!

Yours sincerely, EDMUND GOSSE

Your correspondence with Renard—admirable![3]

[1] *Nouveaux Prétextes*: *Réflexions sur quelques points de littérature et de morale,* Mercure de France, 1911. (One of Jules Renard's letters is printed in the appendix.) On June 19, 1911, Gide stated: "I am not writing criticism at all any more—I have written only what was needed to fill out a second volume of *Prétextes*—and I have almost promised myself to abstain from it.... It was taking too much of my time." (Jammes–Gide, *Correspondance,* p. 277.) In 1918, however, Gide was planning a third *Prétextes,* though he never wrote it. (*Journal,* June 8, 1918.) In the same year, when Lady Rothermere wanted to translate some parts of *Prétextes,* Gide wrote her: "The chief difficulty comes from the fact that my sentence constantly suggests rather than affirms, and proceeds by insinuations—for which the English language, more direct than the French, feels rather a repugnance." (*Journal,* January 7, 1918.)

[2] When Gosse asked this question, Gide was rather intensively pursuing the study of English, taking up the language with an informal teacher and, every night for an hour before going to bed,

reading from the works of Milton, Defoe, Thomson, Lamb, Stevenson, Wells, or Conrad. English literature remained one of his permanent interests.

³ The letters are printed in the *Journal sans dates (Œuvres complètes,* tome 6, p. 32). Gide says that he went to see a play by Jules Renard, *La Bigote,* at the Odéon. "Until recently I thought my admiration for Jules Renard was boundless, but this evening made me realize its limits in a rather painful way. The audience responded fervently to every anticlerical stroke. One almost felt like plunging into holy water." Renard answered that he deeply regretted losing something of Gide's admiration, but he wondered if the play was, as Jacques Copeau said, a failure. Of Gide's surprise at the intensity of his anticlericalism, he averred that his anticlericalism was basic, that to him "a priest never made any sense," and that he was an anticlerical in the same way that he was trying to be a poet, or rather "a fairly good prose writer... for important reasons." His admiration for *La Porte étroite* is unbounded, and he cannot relinquish it for the mere reason that the book is involved with religion. Gide retorts: "If you are impelled to express your anticlericalism, write a tract. A work of art must not prove anything—cannot prove anything without cheating. You are cheating, and that is what I reproach you for; also for confusing literary genres." In *La Porte étroite,* Gide added, he had wanted no more than to paint a portrait. (Cf. note 2, Letter 2.)

12. GOSSE TO GIDE, *July 9, 1911, from London*

MY DEAR MONSIEUR GIDE, I am indeed unfortunate! I was merely walking in the garden, when the maid so foolishly told you I was out.¹

Now, is it possible for you to lunch with me *to-morrow* (Monday) at the House of Lords, at 1:30? I do hope you can do so. Will you kindly send me the enclosed telegram?²

I am longing to see you. You are no stranger! May I not say that we are old friends? Very sincerely yours, EDMUND GOSSE

¹ On this visit to England Gide, besides seeing Gosse, joined Valery Larbaud and Miss Agnes Tobin, and with them visited Arthur Symons and Joseph Conrad, both in Kent. On July 21 Gide sailed from Southampton for Le Havre. (Jammes–Gide, *Correspondance*, p. 361.)

² The telegram mentioned by Gosse is missing, and Gide's name does not appear that summer in the "Book of Gosse." (Cf. note 1, Letter 28.)

13. GIDE TO GOSSE, *July 21, 1911, from Hotel Curzon, London*

CHER MONSIEUR GOSSE: Combien je suis heureux de voir Madame Gosse approuver elle aussi ce projet, et quelle joie me cause votre lettre!

J'écris à Paul Desjardins tout aussitôt. Vous aurez reçu n'est-ce pas la petite brochure, que je n'ai mise à la poste qu'avec un peu de retard — excusez-moi.

J'ai trouvé votre lettre en rentrant d'une courte expédition à Harwich; je quitte Londres ce soir par Southampton — heureux de pouvoir vous dire: à bientôt.

Votre reconnaissant et dévoué ANDRÉ GIDE.

[How delighted I am that Mrs. Gosse too approves this plan,¹ and what pleasure your letter gives me!

I am writing to Paul Desjardins at once. You will probably have received the little pamphlet, which I got off rather tardily; I'm sorry.

I found your letter on my return from a short trip to Harwich.² I leave London this evening by way of Southampton, happy to be able to say to you *à bientôt*.]

[1] Gide wrote Jammes in October, 1911: "I have stayed quietly in Cuverville the whole summer and the whole autumn, except for twelve days in London... and ten in Pontigny."

The reference to the "plan" is to the ten-day gathering scheduled for August 19–28 at Pontigny, to which Gide invited Gosse on this visit to England. The founder and leader of this annual institution was Paul Desjardins, 1859–1940. Desjardins, son of a historian, taught Greek and French literature at the Lycée Condorcet in Paris, also literature at the Ecole Normale de Jeunes Filles in Sèvres, and he was a contributor to the *Journal des Débats,* of which Edmund Gosse was a reader. Desjardins had established the Union pour l'Action Morale, the name of which he changed in 1905 to L'Union pour la Vérité. Beginning in November, 1904, this organization arranged annual "free discussions" on important religious, political, and social subjects, and Desjardins invited writers and thinkers of note. He bought near Auxerre (Yonne) the old Cistercian abbey of Pontigny (visited in its time by Thomas à Becket and Louis IX) and there arranged an annual series of *entretiens* to which he invited foreign as well as French guests. They convened for ten days to discuss a program decided on in advance, with an *entretien* each afternoon. The August, 1911, program:

1. The struggle for autonomy of politically oppressed nationalities; modes of oppression and of resistance.
2. Methodological, historical, and psychological problems related to religion.
3. The psychology of work; modern technology.
4. Round table on the Tragic.
5. General culture: the necessity, the definition, and the attainment of it.

Some writers of the *Nouvelle Revue Française* group came under the influence of the Pontigny atmosphere—Alain (Emile Chartier), Roger Martin du Gard, Jean Prévost, Jean Schlumberger, and Pierre Hamp. (J. Dietz, "Paul Desjardins," *Cahiers de la Quinzaine,* 17ème-19ème série, June 20, 1930.) The sessions were brought to an end by World War II; Gide attended the last of them in August, 1939. The Gestapo eventually looted the place, and Desjardin's papers disappeared.

[2] The short trip to Harwich was made July 19. (J. G. Aubry, *op. cit.,* p. 180.)

14. GIDE TO GOSSE, *July 26, 1911, from Cuverville*

CHER MONSIEUR   Tout est arrangé pour Pontigny.

Desjardins m'écrit aujourd'hui pour me dire la grande joie que lui cause votre venue.

                                    Bien cordialement, votre dévoué   ANDRÉ GIDE.

[Everything is settled about Pontigny.

Desjardins[1] writes me today expressing his great pleasure that you are coming.]

---

[1] Paul Desjardins wrote Gosse the following letter, opening a correspondence that was to last to November, 1914, when Pontigny became an asylum for wounded soldiers:

                                    Abbaye de Pontigny (Yonne), France
                                    Saturday, August 12, 1911

SIR: Had I known your address I should certainly have written you before this. The news of your coming to Pontigny, which A. Gide passed along to me two weeks ago, gave me so much pleasure that I had an impulse to write and thank you. I have known you so long through your books! Once more the ancient vaults that welcomed Thomas Becket, Stephen de Langton, and St. Edmund, your patron saint, are to be honored by the presence of an illustrious Englishman. Will you please convey my wife's kindest regards to Mrs. Gosse. We will have the room you wish ready for you. If you had rather have two rooms instead of one with double bed, please kindly just let us know. The easiest arrangement for you when you come is to stay overnight in Paris Friday, August 18. The next morning you take the 8:20 train at the Gare de Lyon, with through tickets to Pontigny via Laroche. At the station you would meet M. André Gide, M. and Mme. Jean Schlumberger, M. F. Vielé-Griffin, and others. Anyway, when you leave the train at Laroche (the first stop) at

10:25 you inquire for the little train for Chablis that leaves at 10:45; you will get to Pontigny (the fourth station) at 11:28, and I shall be waiting for you on the platform.

Please give my regards to Mrs. Gosse. . . .

15. GOSSE TO GIDE, *July 31, 1911, from London*

MY DEAR MONSIEUR GIDE, "Isabelle"[1] is a masterpiece of ingenuity, grace and subtlety. I must (at Pontigny!) talk much with you about it. I intend to reprint my little study of your work in a book, and to enlarge it considerably.[2] I shall, on that occasion, add a page or two on "Isabelle."

We look forward incessantly to meeting you on the 18th of August. Please make the arrangements for us: we are leaving it to you. You will let us know in time all we have to do. To whom, and when, do we pay the 300 francs?

Yours very sincerely, EDMUND GOSSE

J'ai déjà visité Pontigny — en 1906.[3]

[1] First printed in the *Nouvelle Revue Française,* 1911. Jacques Rivière, in a striking 1911 analysis of Gide's works, deplores the neglect by his fellow countrymen of an author regarded in other countries as one of the more eminent French writers. In *Isabelle* Rivière sees a transitional work in which Gide has ceased to transfer his personal problems to his fiction. (J. Rivière, *Etudes,* p. 244, note 1.)

[2] Gosse refers to *Portraits and Sketches* (1912) and to his *Contemporary Review* piece of 1909.

[3] What took Gosse to Pontigny in 1906 may have been either the twelfth-century Cistercian architecture or the pious memory of Thomas à Becket. Gosse was often in France, and he was given to leisurely exploration of the different provinces.

16. GIDE TO GOSSE, *August 11, 1911, from Cuverville*

CHER MONSIEUR GOSSE   Combien je me réjouis en songeant à ce prochain revoir! Ainsi, le 19 au matin, nous nous retrouverons à Paris — à la *gare de Lyon* vers 8 ʰ pour le train de *8 ʰ 20.*

J'ai fait le nécessaire pour vos chambres et vous n'aurez à vous inquiéter de rien que de venir.

Votre amicale lettre me touche profondément, et ce que vous me dites au sujet du remaniement de votre étude sur la Porte Etroite... Mais je garde le meilleur de mes remerciments pour Pontigny. Quelques uns de mes amis qui doivent se retrouver là-bas, se font une fête de vous voir. A bientôt. Déjà veuillez présenter mes hommages à Madame Edmund Gosse et croire à mon amicale reconnaissance. Votre   ANDRÉ GIDE.

[How delighted I am to be looking forward to seeing you again soon! On the morning of the 19th, then, we meet in Paris —at the Gare de Lyon about eight, to take the 8:20.

I have arranged about your rooms, and you won't have to give a thought to anything but coming.

Your friendly letter moves me deeply; also what you say as to reworking your essay about *La Porte étroite.* But I am saving my best thanks for Pontigny.[1] Several friends of mine who are to get together there are congratulating themselves on meeting you. *A bientôt.* Meanwhile please give my regards to Mrs. Gosse.]

[1] The Gosses were at Pontigny August, 19–28. Gosse wrote Evan Charteris on August 27: "It has been an experience charming and delicate beyond almost anything in the rest of my experience.... [Pontigny] now belongs to that unsurpassed Hellenist, Paul Desjardins, who gathers a group of some thirty people round him. Here are André Gide, the poet F. Vielé-Griffin, Jean [*sic*] Bédier who is

the first authority in the world on the Chansons de Geste, several professors of the Collège de France, several ladies... one of them... runs down the meadow in front of my window in the morning, in a thin white robe that scarcely conceals a contour. She is like a Botticelli.

"Well! we sit in a circle, under the elm trees, and we discuss in libres conversations the Tragic—Le Tragique, vous savez, non pas la Tragédie. Paul Desjardins takes the lead, firmly, modestly, slowly, with beneficence and gaiety. It is not at all pedantic or scholastic.... Bursts of laughter intervene, calembours, je ne sais quoi!... Alas! we are to part to-morrow.... The new ideas that I have got here, the new impressions! I could sob with chagrin to think that I am sixty-two, not twenty-two.... Enjoy life while you can." (Charteris, *op. cit.,* pp. 325–27.)

Paul Desjardins to Edmund Gosse

Abbaye de Pontigny (Yonne)
Monday morning, October 2, 1911

DEAR MR. GOSSE, MY DEAR FRIEND: I leave Pontigny two hours from now, but I do want the expression of thanks that I owe you to be dated from here. Here I was able to become better acquainted with you in ten days than I could have in Paris or London in ten years. The old vault of the "library," where I am writing you, seems still vibrant with your moving rendition of the *Dutchess of Malfy* [sic]; when, on these first chilly autumn days, I walk by myself on the road to Venouse and Vouvray, I think of the searching ideas you expressed to me there about the co-operation of our two peoples. It makes me happy to hear that you too remember our talks. Thank you for the kind things you say of our hospitality. Truth to tell, I accept them, not for the little family group that we are, but for my country, which, at Pontigny, at Auxerre, at Vézelay, opened its ancient inmost heart to Mrs. Gosse and you. The tourist eye sees but land, trees, stones; whereas you, with your preparation and your sensitiveness, experience the very spirit and inner harmony of these places. Dear guest of ours, no French person has a subtler understanding of France than you have. Moreover, nobody left pleasanter impressions with us this year than your compatriots did—Mrs. Gosse and you, Miss Petrie and Miss Taylor and Vernon Lee, who arrived last week like a gust in the midst of equinoctial gales.

Pray do what in you lies to see that next year, if there is to be a next year for us, the British pilgrims shall be numerous at the shrine of Saint Edmund. If only William Archer could come! or little Tom Archer, aged three in 1888, to whom Stevenson used to write from Tahiti.

I received the day before yesterday the priceless letters of your friend. I might well add that they are as much classics as the letters of our own Flaubert, though in a different way. I am deeply impressed by their vividness, vigor, mental abundance, and petulant good nature. But what affects me the most—and this I want to lose no time about saying to you—is that your nearness to the author, which shows through the letters he wrote you, makes your gift worth even more to me. It is a token of esteem that you give me, as well as a mark of trust. Let me say that I am as touched by the second as honored by the first. The Pontigny library, without ceasing to hope to make itself the richer by your own books, thanks you for having bestowed on it, with more modesty but no less warmth, the writings of a friend, the great and beloved Tusitala.

If there is no war and I have to go to London in late October to represent our International Association for the Defense of Right, I shall not fail to go and present my regards to Mrs. Gosse and remind you of my affection.

I have been thinking some more about your big book on Denmark. The very conception of it, its point of view, and, of course, its organization, excite my interest, and I am sure I shall enjoy it. . . .

You wouldn't have a good picture of yourself?

17. GIDE TO GOSSE, *September 4, 1911, from Cuverville*

CHER MONSIEUR GOSSE, ET AMI   Cette lettre vous trouvera-t-elle encore à Aix? Y aurez-vous reçu les deux livres que je vous y ai fait envoyer il y a trois jours? — (les poésies de Signoret et le *Crépuscule* d'Elémir Bourges) (il me souvient vaguement d'un troisième que je m'étais également promis de vous envoyer — mais, lequel?...)

Que vous dire des regrets que m'a laissés notre séparation, sinon que constamment je songe à un prochain revoir — à Londres, au printemps... En attendant je lis beaucoup d'anglais. —

Veuillez présenter mes respectueux hommages à Madame Gosse; je suis votre reconnaissant et bien affectueusement attentif

ANDRÉ GIDE.

[Will this letter find you still at Aix?[1] Will the two books that I sent you there three days ago have reached you? (Signoret's poems[2] and Elémir Bourges' *Crépuscule;*[3] I vaguely remember that I likewise undertook to send you a third one, but—what was it?)

How am I to express how sorry I was at your going, except by saying that I am continually looking forward to seeing you again—in London, next spring? Meanwhile I am reading a lot of English.[4]

Please give my kind regards to Mrs. Gosse.]

[1] The spa in Savoy.

[2] E. Signoret, 1872–1900, was the object of considerable admiration on the part of Gide, who included some of Signoret's poems in his *Anthologie de la poésie française* (1949) and thought them "among the most beautiful in our language." Among Signoret's works were *Daphné* (1894), *Vers dorés* (1895), and *La Souffrance des eaux* (1898). The Mercure de France published his *Poésies complètes* (1908) for the relief of his young widow, the poet having died in Cannes in extreme poverty.

[3] Elémir Bourges, 1852–1925, who wrote *Le Crépuscule des dieux* (1884), three less known novels, and *La Nef* (1904), a long epic and philosophic poem in prose, became a member of the Goncourt Academy in 1900. Paul Claudel, who considered Bourges one of his dearest friends, nevertheless thought his literary gifts inferior to his mind and his moral qualities. *Le Crépuscule des dieux* was much admired by F. de Miomandre and Guillaume Apollinaire; English

authors, e.g., Arnold Bennett, tended to reservations about the form
and subject of the book and even its title, which seemed to echo that
of *Götterdämmerung.* (*Journal of A. Bennett,* 1904, p. 160.) Joseph Conrad found in it only a few admirable pages.

⁴ Gide recorded (*Journal,* July 3, 1911): "After Robinson Crusoe I
read Tom Jones, and in the intervals Olalla and The Bottle Imp by
Stevenson, numerous essays by Lamb, then aloud with Miss Siller
The Mayor of Casterbridge, and The End of the Tether by Conrad;
some Milton (Samson Agonistes), Thomson (Evolution of Sex —
the first four or five chapters); Stevenson, Weir of Hermiston."

18. GIDE TO GOSSE, *October 8, 1911, from Villa Montmorency, Paris*¹

CHER MONSIEUR GOSSE, CHER AMI, Je ne puis attendre d'avoir
achevé votre *Sir Thomas Browne* pour vous remercier de l'envoi de
ces volumes et vous dire combien votre affectueux souvenir m'a
touché. Je pensais travailler beaucoup, sitôt au retour de Pontigny,
mais je n'ai pu parvenir à écrire une ligne; ma presque unique oc-
cupation a été de lire de l'anglais: j'ai lu le *Mayor of Casterbridge,*
puis le *End of the Tether* de Conrad. Votre envoi est arrivé comme
j'achevais cette lecture et répondait à la précise curiosité que j'avais
du *Religio Medici* (dont j'entendais parler et ne connaissais encore
rien), aussi exactement que les textes de Webster et de Fielding, à
Pontigny, sont venus répondre à l'appel.

Peu de lectures emportent mon attention aussi facilement que ces
monographies; je comprends avec quel amour vous avez pu écrire
celle-ci — et si vous me l'envoyez, c'est que vous avez bien pressenti
la sympathie que je ressentirais à la lire. "His peaceable spirit desired
to learn rather than to dogmatise" (tout le passage est *excellent*) Et
quel admirable paragraphe, celui que vous citez: "I have been shipwrecked, yet I am not enemy to sea or winds" et "In brief, I am
averse to nothing..." Enfin la manière dont vous indiquez la position des problèmes à cette époque est remarquable — (Je n'ai lu

encore que les deux premiers chapitres, car, de retour à Paris, je me suis trouvé un peu submergé par de menues occupations) — et ce livre augmente encore le grand désir que j'ai de causer avec vous. Je ne puis admettre que nous restions jusqu'au prochain Pontigny sans nous revoir — et maintenant que j'ai découvert que Londres est si près de Paris...! — j'ai *besoin* de vous dire: à bientôt. Veuillez présenter mes hommages à Madame Gosse et croire à ma respectueuse affection.   ANDRÉ GIDE.

J'ai lu dans la correspondance de Stevenson (avec quelle émotion!) l'admirable dernière lettre dont vous me parliez à Pontigny. Les conseils qu'il donnait à Schwob, le 7 juillet 94, sont exactement ceux que je me donne à moi-même aujourd'hui, "more nourished, more commonplace — and not so pretty, perhaps not even so beautiful." J'ai commencé *Weir of Hermiston.*

[I can't wait to finish your *Sir Thomas Browne*[2] before I thank you for sending me these volumes and tell you how this mark of your regard has affected me. I was expecting to get through a lot of work as soon as I got back from Pontigny, but I have not managed to write a line; I have done practically nothing but read English. I read *The Mayor of Casterbridge* and Conrad's *End of the Tether.* Your gift arrived just as I was finishing this reading, and it was the specific answer to my interest in the *Religio Medici* (which I had been hearing about but as yet did not know at all), precisely as at Pontigny the works of Webster and Fielding came as the answer to a need.

Little reading matter absorbs me as these biographical studies do. I understand how much devotion you were able to put into the writing of this one, and your sending it to me proves your intuition of the response that I would make in the reading of it. "His peaceable spirit desired to learn rather than to dogmatise" —this whole passage is very fine. "I have been shipwrecked, yet I am not enemy to sea or winds," and "In brief, I am averse to nothing...." In short, the way you point out the bearings of that period's dilemmas is wonderful.—I have read only the first two chapters, because when I got back to Paris I found myself rather drowned in trivialities. And the book makes me want even more to talk with you. I can't conceive our waiting until the next session at Pontigny to get together again; and now that I have discovered how near London is to Paris—! I *must* say to you *à bientôt*. Please give my regards to Mrs. Gosse.]

I did read in Stevenson's letters—and with what excitement! the fine last letter[3] that you told me about at Pontigny. His advice to Schwob[4] of July 7, 1894, is just what I give myself now: "more nourished, more commonplace—and not so pretty, perhaps not even so beautiful." I have begun *The Weir of Hermiston*.]

[1] The year, omitted from the date line of this letter, is easily supplied by means of the references to Pontigny and to Gide's reading. (*Journal,* July 3, 1911.)

[2] Sir Thomas Browne was the subject of a biography by Gosse (Macmillan, 1905) in the "English Men of Letters" series, edited by John Morley. The tremendous lines that Gide quotes are part of a beautiful letter quoted in Gosse's first chapter; the paragraph from which Gide quotes begins: "I have no antipathy, or rather idiosyncrasy in diet, humour, air, anything." Gosse does justice to Browne's remarkable open-mindedness in youth, shows what the teaching of medicine was like in Oxford, Montpellier, Padua, and Leyden, and describes the intellectual climate of each university. Browne, when he got back to England, had assimilated the variegated aspects of European culture as a scholar and physician, not at all as a judge — a mental posture sufficient in itself to make him a sympathetic figure to André Gide. The *Religio Medici* (1642), translated into several languages and widely discussed, found a place on the Church's Index Expurgatorius.

[3] Stevenson's letter of December 1, 1894, two days before its author's sudden death, was to Gosse, to thank him for the dedication of *In Russet and Silver,* poems of meditation and contemplation. R. L. S. congratulated his friend on his "changing with the years to the proper tune.... Here I am with nothing in my foolish elderly head but love stories." He added: "I have lost the path... to descend the hill. I

am going at it straight, and where I have to go down it is a precipice."
At the end Stevenson wishes Gosse a long and happy life and signs
himself "the vanished Tusitala." (Sydney Colvin, ed., *Letters of
Robert Louis Stevenson,* IV, 376–79.)

⁴ The letter to Marcel Schwob (p. 322) was a criticism of *Les
Mimes,* just published. Stevenson had read it twice with admiration, but
he expected an even better book from its author. "As we go on in
life, we must part from prettiness and the graces... life is a series
of farewells, even in art."

The month of this letter from Gide and of the one from Paul
Desjardins, October, 1911, also brought Gosse a letter from Jacques
Copeau, 1879–1949, close friend of both Gide and Desjardins, a
founder and the director of the *Nouvelle Revue Française,* lifelong
worker for the revival of poetry and truth in the theater, and founder
of the Vieux-Colombier. Copeau wrote on October 14 from the
offices of the *Nouvelle Revue Française:*

> ...I shall be telling you face to face in a few days how faith-
> fully we have been thinking of you since you went away and
> how much it meant to me to receive your beautiful books by
> way of memento.
>
> I shall be in London Tuesday evening. My address will be
> in care of M. Antoine Bibesco, 114 Grosvenor Road. Kindly let
> me know there when it will be possible to see you....

And on November 3, after his London visit, Copeau wrote again,
this time from Le Limon:

> ...My time has been so taken up by numerous duties since
> my return that I have not yet been able to thank you as I wished
> for the gracious welcome given me by you and Mrs. Gosse. I
> was much moved, I assure you, and I am very affectionately
> grateful for it. All my friends wanted to hear in detail about
> the few hours I had with you, and I had to tell them all about
> your big study at the House of Lords, the Library, and your
> own house. They send you their best wishes.
>
> Your name constantly recurs in our conversation as that of
> an old and tested friend, and we shall be disappointed if we do
> not find you among us a few days hence when all of us go to
> the dress rehearsal of Henri Ghéon's play, *Le Pain.*
>
> Every evening as I work, my wife sits by me reading your
> book about Denmark. Now and then she reads me a passage.

She can't get over being surprised that you know so much about her small country. Soon she will have finished the book and will be writing to thank you....

Winter comes on. I wish you could know how fragrant is my garden, how deep my solitude.... I am going to drown myself in it for long months and work steadily at a new play....

I left *Les Frères Karamazov* with Sir Herbert [Beerbohm Tree], who promised to read it and give me an answer. But I don't rely too much on his initiative. If you get a chance, could you drop him a reminder about it?

Les Frères Karamazov, play in five acts (Nouvelle Revue Française, 1911), was first performed April 6, 1911, at the Théâtre des Arts, Paris. Translated into English in four acts as *The Brothers Karamazov* by Rosalind Ivan (New York, 1919), it was produced January 3, 1927, at the Guild Theatre, New York.

19. GIDE TO GOSSE, *December 31, 1911, from Paris* [?]

BIEN CHER AMI   Voici le dernier jour de l'année; avant de le laisser fuir je me penche encore une fois sur les souvenirs qu'elle me laisse

"While joy recaptures many a province fair [,] flowing, and luminous, and debonair."

Et parmi ce que l'année m'apporta de meilleur, je vois votre amitié me sourire.

Depuis ma dernière lettre, j'ai reçu votre volume de poèmes : presque chaque soir j'en ai lu une ou deux pièces, retrouvant le son de votre voix dans vos vers, d'une *intonation* si grave et tendrement cordiale.

Mais, comme je les prenais le plus souvent à la suite, croiriez-vous que ce n'est qu'avant hier que j'ai découvert la pièce en tête de laquelle vous avez inscrit mon nom! C'était tard dans la nuit; j'étais environné de silence; je n'ai pu retenir mes larmes... Merci de tout mon cœur, cher ami.

Combien je préfère à la photographie de votre portrait par Sargent, l'admirable photographie qui est en tête du *Father and Son* que vous m'avez donné — d'une ressemblance encore si étrangement profonde!

J'ai pu revoir Davray ces jours derniers, — la traduction de Père et Fils était sur sa table, à peu près prête à paraître en volume —

But—I think it is a pity that such a work could not come out in the "*Revue des deux mondes*" formerly, and I cannot understand how Davray doesn't get it, for you as important as you are. I am very ashamed on my national pride and pray you for excusing it.

How are you, dear friend, and Madame Gosse? Je vous prie de bien vouloir lui présenter mes vœux et mes hommages... I take the permission to write in my native language this last sentence, because I noticed the compliments seem always awkward when translated. I dont hope to say in English all that I feel for you in my heart.— How much I wish to see you again! But when? and where?

Votre dévoué ANDRÉ GIDE.

[Here it is the last day of the year. Before I let it slip away I dwell once more on the memories it has left me.

"While joy recaptures many a province fair, flowing, and luminous, and debonair..."

And among the best things the year has brought me I find the blessing of your friendship.

Since my last letter I have received your volume of poems;[1] almost every evening I have read one or two of them, recovering in your lines the sound of your voice, with its depth and gentle warmth of inflection.

But since I have read them mostly in their printed order, could you believe that not until the day before yesterday did I discover the poem at the head of which you have put my name! It was late at night; everything about me was still; I could not keep back my tears. I do thank you with all my heart, my dear friend.

Much better than the photograph of the Sargent portrait[2] of you I like the fine photograph in the front of the *Father and Son* that you gave me, the likeness is still so marvelously close.

I managed to see Davray a few days ago; the translation of
Père et Fils was on his table, nearly ready for book publication.

But—I think it is a pity that such a work could not come out in the
Revue des Deux Mondes[3] *formerly, and I cannot understand how
Davray doesn't get it, for you as important as you are. I am very ashamed
on my national pride and pray you for excusing it.*

How are you, dear friend, and Madame Gosse? Please kindly give
her my regards and best wishes.—*I take the permission to write
in my native language this last sentence, because I noticed the compliments seem always awkward when translated. I dont hope to say in
English all that I feel for you in my heart.—How much I wish to
see you again! But when? and where?*[4]]

[1] *The Collected Poems of Edmund Gosse* was published October, 1911.
The volume contained a ballad in memory of Théodore de Banville
and a poem in memory of Leconte de Lisle. "The Land of France,"
inscribed to Gide (see p. 202), was the next to the last. The couplet
Gide quotes closes the first of four seven-line stanzas, but Gosse
wrote "glowing," not "flowing."

[2] The photograph of the 1885 portrait of Gosse by Sargent was
the frontispiece of the poems; it is also in Charteris at p. 181. The
photograph that Gide preferred shows Gosse as a child with his
father.

[3] Why did Gide suggest, not the *Nouvelle Revue Française* for *Père
et Fils,* but the *Revue des Deux Mondes?* The *N. R. F.* had a declared
preference for the work of young writers; also, one of its canons was
the best in literature.

[4] These are the first and almost the only English sentences that
Gide wrote to Gosse.

20. GIDE TO GOSSE, *January 11, 1912, from Auteuil*

MON CHER AMI   C'est du fond d'Auteuil que je vous écris, et du fond
de mon lit! Une grippe féroce qui rôdait dans les rues de Londres

jeudi dernier, s'est abattue sur moi. Par crainte d'être immobilisé dans une morne chambre d'hôtel, j'ai fait aussitôt mes valises, et Vendredi soir j'échouais au port.

Déjà je vais mieux et vais commencer à me lever tantôt; mais quatre jours durant j'ai eu une assez forte fièvre. Au demeurant je ne suis absolument pas déprimé, et pense que le régime de claustration, qui va m'être imposé d'abord, va plutôt servir à l'achèvement de mon livre.

J'ai pu du moins, quatre jours durant, jouir des délices et convenances de l'Athaeneum [*sic*] — qui a beaucoup fait pour m'apprendre à regretter Londres. Combien je vous suis reconnaissant d'avoir bien voulu m'initier à ce confort! J'espère en pouvoir un jour profiter plus longuement.

Au revoir cher ami. Le temps splendide que nous avons ici me laisse espérer que vous jouissez beaucoup de votre voyage. Veuillez présenter à Madame Gosse mes bien sensibles souvenirs.

Votre ami tout affectueusement dévoué ANDRÉ GIDE.

[I write you from the depths of Auteuil and of my bed! A ravening grippe that was prowling the streets of London last Thursday fell upon me. For fear of being pinned down in a dismal hotel room I quickly packed my bags, and Friday night I was safe in harbor. [1]

I feel better already, and soon I shall try getting up; but for four long days I had a pretty high fever. Anyway, I am not at all bowed down, and I think the confinement, which will be forced on me for a while, will help more than not toward finishing my book. [2]

At least I was able to have four whole days of enjoying the delights and amenities of the Athenaeum[3]—which has gone a long way toward making me miss London. How grateful I am to you for introducing me to this convenience! I hope to be able some day to make use of it for a longer time.

Good-by for now, my dear friend. The fine weather we are having here makes me hope you are greatly enjoying your trip. Please remember me very kindly to Mrs. Gosse.]

¹ Gide, feeling ill, left London Thursday, January 5, before Gosse's return.

² The book that Gide was working on was *Les Caves du Vatican,* completed June 24, 1913.

³ The Athenaeum, founded 1824 to provide a meeting place for writers, artists, scientists, noblemen, and gentlemen, had extended its hospitality to French men of letters before—among them Stendhal, Mérimée, and Taine. (F.Ch.Roe, *Taine et l'Angleterre,* Paris: Champion, 1923, p.12, note 3.) Gosse may have sent a guest card giving Gide the freedom of the Athenaeum.

At the end of Letter 19 Gide speaks of wanting to see Gosse again. A letter seems to be missing.

21. GOSSE TO GIDE, *June 10, 1912, from Lisieux*

MY DEAR GIDE, Is there any chance of seeing you?¹ Mrs. Gosse and I shall arrive at Hotel de France, Rouen, on Wednesday next, for 4 days, returning to London from Le Havre on Sunday night (the 16th). Where is Cuverville? Could we take an autocar to call on you from Rouen? Or come by train? Write to Rouen. I *long* to see you, my dear Friend.   EDMUND GOSSE

¹ The Gosses were on a vacation in Normandy. They liked to wander from town to town. This letter was from the Hôtel du Lion d'Or in Lisieux. (Charteris, *op. cit.,* p.329.)

22. GIDE TO GOSSE, *June 11, 1912, from Cuverville*

CHER AMI   Quelle joie me cause votre carte!

Certainement je viendrai déjeuner *jeudi* avec vous, si vous le voulez bien. J'arriverai vers *11 h* à *l'hôtel de France* de manière à pouvoir faire un tour en ville avec vous avant le repas.

Je suis attendu à Paris jeudi soir et j'y serai retenu Vendredi et Samedi — de sorte que je ne vous invite pas à venir à Cuverville, malgré le plaisir qu'aurait eu ma femme de faire la connaissance de Madame Gosse et la vôtre.

Mais il n'est pas impossible que je vous retrouve Dimanche dans le train qui vous emmenera au Havre et me ramenera à Cuverville.

Je dois voir Davray Samedi matin et pensais précisément lui demander ce que devenait la traduction de *Father and Son?* . . .

Heureux de vous dire: à bientôt. Mes hommages à Madame Gosse je vous prie — Tout amicalement votre   ANDRÉ GIDE.

Les Jean Schlumberger qui naviguent en ce moment entre Cherbourg et le Maroc, vont être désolés de ne pas être au Val Richer (si près de Lisieux) pour vous y recevoir!

[How much pleasure your card gives me!

Indeed I will have luncheon with you Thursday if you like. I will be at the Hôtel de France around eleven, so as to be able to take a walk with you around town before we eat.

I am expected Thursday evening in Paris, and I shall be kept there Friday and Saturday; so that I am not asking you to come to Cuverville, despite the pleasure it would give my wife to meet Mrs. Gosse and you.

But it is possible that I might join you again Sunday on the train that takes you to Le Havre and me back to Cuverville.

I am supposed to see Davray Saturday morning, and I was expressly planning to ask him what was happening about the translation of *Father and Son*.

It is a happiness to be saying *à bientôt*. Please give my regards to Mrs. Gosse.

The Jean Schlumbergers,[1] who right now are at sea between Cherbourg and Morocco, are going to be pained because they are not at Val Richer (next door to Lisieux) to entertain you there.]

[1] Jean Schlumberger, 1877 —— , whom Gosse had met at Pontigny, was a close friend of Gide and a cofounder of the *Nouvelle Revue Française.*

23. GOSSE TO GIDE, *July 20, 1912, from London*

MY DEAR GIDE,   I have been very much in hope of being able to accede to your most kind proposal, and come with you to Pontigny in August. In that case, it would have given me extreme pleasure to accept Vielé-Griffin's[1] kind invitation to Puygivault. But family arrangements make it impossible, to my great regret. I shall not be able to leave London until September.[2]

Will you kindly communicate this melancholy fact, with my warmest greetings of respect, to Vielé-Griffin and to Desjardins?

Why do you not come to London?

Yours ever sincerely   EDMUND GOSSE

[1] F. Vielé-Griffin, 1864-1937, was a symbolist poet born in Virginia. He had written Gosse as early as 1896; they met for the first time at Pontigny in 1911. Vielé-Griffin's summer place, the Château de Puygivault, was near Mérigny, Indre.

[2] Mrs. Gosse's favorite brother, Washington Epps, was gravely ill, and Mrs. Gosse refused to leave him that summer. He died October 12. Gosse had lost, shortly before, another of his brothers-in-law, the painter Sir Lawrence Alma-Tadema (Charteris, *op. cit.,* pp. 336-38), to whose death Paul Desjardins refers in a letter quoted below.

Gosse eventually gave in to Desjardins' insistence. He was a good deal drawn by the program of the *décade*; also, the compliments he received on his book and, curiously, the promise that he should be the only Englishman present won him over.

Paul Desjardins to Edmund Gosse

Abbaye de Pontigny (Yonne)
Wednesday morning, July 24, 1912

MY DEAR AND DISTINGUISHED FRIEND: Let my very first words declare a hope and a wish for the future. The room that you and

Mrs. Gosse occupied last year is all ready, and we are expecting you on the morning of the 21st. You will find the old abbey as peaceful as ever and more eager than ever to add your name once more to the guest list that began with Thomas Becket. I beg you not to abandon us; please do come back. You said that you would if no other English person was to be present. It is a peculiar stipulation, but we want you so much more than we do anybody else that we will adhere to it. For example, we shall not ask Mr. John Galsworthy, who might have been able to come, because you perhaps do not want to encounter him here. Also, we think you must feel committed to us if we exclude others for your sake; and that is what we want.

As you know, we plan to discuss this year the relationship between observation and invention in the novel. Now, the core of this program is eighteenth-century England, the scene of *"the creation, for it can be styled nothing else, of the modern novel"* [quoted in English]. The importance of Richardson and Fielding is unrivaled. Couldn't you bring us some source materials and some thoughts—about Henry Fielding, anyway, since you admire him with surpassing insight? We should like to discuss him for an entire afternoon. If you would like to have put at your disposal some reference books from the Pontigny library, will you kindly let me know what ones?...

The loss of your brother-in-law, whose life was so full of achievements and distinctions, was deeply felt here, and it gave us occasion to realize how much a sorrow of yours inevitably affects us. I have received the translation of *Father and Son*; my wife and I read it aloud for an hour each evening. So, we are in daily contact with your inner self and your intimate memories. All these poignant past experiences will come back to us when next we see you and look into your clear blue eyes. I believe with my friend Vernon Lee that this is one of the undying books of your literature. I am arrested above all by the wonderfully delicate art, visible through a seeming simplicity, that enables you to describe so candidly a diametrically opposed yet revered paternal conscience without ever giving an effect of effrontery. It is a unique document on the psychology of righteous fanaticism and on the law, counterbalancing heredity, that opposes every generation to the preceding. Yes, it is a great book, a major event to those of us whose minds are absorbed in these problems. Also, my dear friend, it makes us value even more highly the honor of having you under our roof....

Jacques Copeau, too, had already written Gosse from Le Limon, pressing him to revisit Pontigny that summer.

Jacques Copeau to Edmund Gosse, July 23, 1912

...André Gide and Paul Desjardins have written you, I know, to urge that you join us this summer at Pontigny. If it is not too officious and if my plea carries any weight, I want to add my voice to theirs and tell you how downcast we should be not to have you with us this year. You are an integral part of our plans, and to lose you would lose them a share of their attractiveness. I think, too, that Paul Desjardins, who has lately undergone unfair and ugly trials, needs more than ever to feel around him the positive affection and trust of friends. He wrote me recently, about you: "I want him here with all my heart."

My dear friend, I am reading *Father and Son* with profound feeling and enthusiasm. I mean to write a little article about it. But, more than anything, how much I should like to talk with you about it!...

24. GIDE TO GOSSE, *August 12, 1912, from Cuverville*

MON CHER AMI   Votre lettre m'emplit d'une grande joie; vraiment nous aurions été trop nombreux à vous regretter, et Pontigny n'eût plus été Pontigny, sans vous. N'était cette décade, je serais déjà en Tunisie, ou en Italie où le sujet de mon livre m'appelle — mais combien je me félicite à présent d'être resté fidèle à cette réunion!

Naturellement nous ferons le voyage ensemble de Paris à Pontigny — et sans doute avec ceux de mes amis que vous avez déjà rencontré [*sic*] l'an passé et qui vont tant se réjouir de vous revoir. Et si je puis dîner avec vous la veille au soir, *le 20*, qu'un mot de vous me dise où je pourrais vous retrouver.

Tous mes hommages à Madame Gosse je vous prie. Bien sincère-
ment votre   ANDRÉ GIDE.

Tant en anglais qu'en français, tout le monde à Cuverville lit ou a lu
Father and son!

[I am overjoyed to have your letter; too many would have
missed you, sadly, and Pontigny would not have been Pontigny
without you. But for these ten days I should now be in Tunisia
or Italy, where the subject matter of my book takes me; but now
I do congratulate myself on having stood by this gathering.[1]
Of course we shall make the trip together from Paris to Pontigny—and probably with those friends of mine whom you
met last year, who will be no end pleased to see you again. And
if we could have dinner together the preceding evening, the
20th, let me have a word to say where I am to join you.
My kindest regards to Mrs. Gosse, please.

In English or in French, everybody in Cuverville is reading or
has read *Father and Son*!]

[1] The letter in which Gosse finally agreed to attend the *décade* is
missing. Gide himself narrowly missed attending. On July 25 he
wrote Claudel: "On my return from Florence I asked Desjardins to
include me no longer among the Pontigny guests; but I am in no
frame of mind to desert him now—although our ways of thinking drift farther and farther apart—inasmuch as the *Indépendance* is
renewing its perfidies and I don't want to seem frightened by their
intimidations." (*Correspondance P. Claudel-Gide*, p. 201; see also pp.
341–42 for a complete account of this literary quarrel.) Gide also
wrote Claudel: "The atmosphere of the Union pour l'action morale
has really become as unbreathable to me as the Protestant atmosphere.
Outside Catholicism I can acknowledge nothing but isolation."
(*Ibid.*, p. 189.)
On August 23 Gosse wrote Robert Ross contentedly from Pontigny: "I am doing here my annual 'retraite.' Nellie is not here, and
I am the only Englishman. Twenty people of varied sex and charm all

reading *Father and Son,* in French at once, is rather an intoxicating phenomenon. Do you know that your poor friend has made quite what they call 'un succès considérable'? Two copies of my book have been sold at Tarbes; and three (but one was returned to the publisher) at Brienon-sur-Armançon. God keeps us humble." (Charteris, *op. cit.,* p.333.) He wrote to another friend a little later: "In Paris, at this moment, I am the celebrated author of the day. Resist the temptation to laugh and make a long nose." (*Ibid.,* p.334.)

Gide wrote in his diary: "The end of the month at Pontigny; rather hybrid ten-day period."

The book to which he refers is again *Les Caves du Vatican.*

25. GOSSE TO GIDE, *August 30, 1912, from London*

MY DEAR GIDE,   The copy of "Critical Kit-Kats"[1] which I gave you was mutilated. I have now obtained a perfect copy of the first edition, which I send to you. I am anxious that you should read the dedication to Hardy[2] and the preface, which are wanting in the Pontigny copy. Please *destroy* the latter. Promise me to do so. I hate the existence of mutilated things.

I have now finished "Paludes"[3] with infinite relish and entertainment. It is a unique book, like nothing else. It seems to have fallen from heaven, perfect, without parentage.

I am always   Yours affectionately EDMUND GOSSE

[1] *Critical Kit-Kats* (London: W.Heinemann, 1894). Two essays had been previously published, the introduction to *Sonnets from the Portuguese* and "The Poetical Works of T.L.Beddoes." The remaining articles were on Keats, FitzGerald, Whitman, Tolstoi, D. G. Rossetti, de Tabley, T.Dutt, Heredia, Pater, and Stevenson. In October, 1896, Henry Davray reviewed the book in the *Mercure de France,* explaining its title and praising its content.

[2] Gosse, in his dedication, adverted to an incident of twenty years before. He and Hardy, on a walk together, were misdirected by a boy; Hardy pointed out that the boy had not *meant* to mislead them; whereupon Gosse hoped that Hardy would be as charitable to his essays, which Gosse was afraid might strike some readers as misguidance. Gosse explained in his preface that he had tried to combine criticism and biography on the principle advocated by the most genial of the great writers, La Fontaine, who had said in the epilogue to his *Contes:*

> Bornons ici cette carrière:
> Les longs ouvrages me font peur;
> Loin d'épuiser une matière,
> On n'en doit prendre que la fleur.

[3] *Paludes* (L'Art Indépendant, 1895), written at La Brévine in the Swiss Jura, to which Gide had been sent by his doctor on his return from Africa in 1894, is a *sotie*, the name that Gide applies to those of his works that Jean Hytier aptly characterized as "enigmatic satires." (J. Hytier, *André Gide,* Paris: Charlot, 1945, p. 93.) The objects of satire are renunciation and resignation, which are sometimes vices mistaken for virtues. "Tityre [the hero] is the idiot, he is I, he is you, he is all of us," says the author, writing simultaneously the story of his book and that of himself, by a device of which he was fond. Gosse in his *Contemporary Review* article had not mentioned *Paludes,* with which he was then unacquainted. In the interim Gide had probably told him about it. Gosse was later to write: "People are fond of repeating that the French have no humor, but *Paludes* is humorous from end to end." (*Portraits and Sketches,* p. 272.)

---

26. GIDE TO GOSSE, *November 28, 1912, from Paris* [?]

BIEN CHER AMI, Que j'ai de mal à renoncer à l'Angleterre. J'ai poussé jusqu'à ces derniers jours l'espoir d'aller vous dire de vive voix la grande joie, et durable — que votre livre m'a causée; il me semblait qu'une lettre n'y suffirait pas —; si bien qu'il me faut une espèce de résignation aujourd'hui pour me contenter de vous écrire; et je l'eusse fait beaucoup plus tôt si j'avais su renoncer plus vite — et encore je ne renonce pas tout à fait.

Oui, j'ai lu votre préface avec l'émotion la plus vive, et peu s'en est fallu que vous me vissiez tout aussitôt accourir. Les additions que vous avez apportées à votre étude sur moi sont excellentes — en particulier ce que vous dites de Paludes. Je suis tout particulièrement heureux que vous aimiez ce livre! dont le ton et l'humour annoncent un peu déjà le roman que j'écris à présent — ce qui me laisse espérer que vous l'aimerez aussi. Et vous ne sauriez croire, cher ami, combien votre approbation me soutient et m'encourage, combien de fois j'ai fait appel à vous lorsque je me sentais excédé... le livre sur lequel je peine, dont je vous ai parlé — est si absurde, si baroque, si en dehors des données admises... J'ai traversé des semaines entières où ma confiance m'échappait presque complètement. Tout va bien de nouveau; déjà j'approche de la fin — et l'impatience où je suis de vous montrer cela m'éperonne.

Cependant le gros dictionnaire étymologique de Skeat encombre mes loisirs. J'ai lu avec délices le Hero and Leander de Marlowe, puis plusieurs chants du Faerie Queene; et à présent je me plonge dans Chaucer. Vous voyez que je mérite de vous revoir! Car c'est un de mes vifs désirs, de lire un peu d'anglais avec [vous], comme cet été vous m'aviez déjà lu du Shelley; si courte qu'ait été cette lecture, je lui dois de sentir mieux aujourd'hui le vers anglais. Combien j'ai joui de ceux de Marlowe et de Spencer [*sic*]!

Vous aurez reçu sans doute les photo de Pontigny; celle où vous vous penchez à la portière du wagon qui vous emporte est sur ma table tandis que je vous écris, et vous me dites "Au revoir."

A bientôt, cher ami qui m'aurez tant aidé à prendre confiance en moi même. Veuillez présenter mes plus souriants hommages à Madame Gosse — je suis bien fidèlement votre reconnaissant

ANDRÉ GIDE.

[It is painful to me to give up England. Up to these last few days I clung to the hope of going over to tell you in person what a great and lasting delight your book gave me;[1] it seemed to me

that a letter was inadequate; so that it calls for a sort of resignation for me to write you today; and I should have done it much
more promptly if I could have managed to do my renouncing
earlier—though it is still only half a renunciation.

Yes, I read your preface with the keenest excitement, and it
was not by much that you missed seeing me arrive posthaste.
The additions to your piece about me are splendid—particularly what you say about *Paludes*. I am especially happy that you
should like this book, whose tone and humor somewhat fore-
shadow the novel I am writing now—a reason for venturing
to hope that you will like it too. And you could not believe, my
dear friend, how much your approval sustains and heartens me,
how many times I have invoked you when I felt at my rope's
end. The book with which I am struggling[2]—I talked to you
about it—is so nonsensical, so fantastic, so far outside the recognized canons—I have gone through weeks on end in which
my faith in myself almost completely evaporated. All goes well
again; I am nearing the end; and my impatience to show it to
you spurs me on.

Even so, Skeat's great etymological dictionary is pre-empting
my spare time.[3] I have delighted in Marlowe's *Hero and Leander,*
and after it several cantos of *The Faerie Queene;* and now I am
plunging into Chaucer. You can see that I deserve to see you
again! For one of my keenest desires is to read a little English
with [you], just as you read Shelley to me last summer; brief as
that reading was, I have it to thank for the improved sense of
English verse that I have now. How much I have enjoyed the
lines of Marlowe and Spenser!

You will doubtless have received the Pontigny photographs;
the one in which you are leaning out of the car window is on my
table as I write, saying "Au revoir" to me.

A bientôt, my dear friend—you who have so helped me gain
confidence in myself. Please give my warmest regards to Mrs.
Gosse.]

¹ The book that gave Gide such delight is *Portraits and Sketches*. Of its thirteen articles, two are about French authors, Vogüé and Gide. Gosse explains in his preface (September, 1912) that he has known the writers studied and is trying to exhibit the personality of each on the principle of Paul Desjardins' phrase about "the cinematography of a bee surprised in the act of honey-making." The eleven-line last paragraph of the preface sums up Gide as "a fascinating writer, still young, who is destined, I believe, to take a place in the very first rank of European writers." The piece about Gide was the only one in the book about a living author; Gosse wanted English readers to be aware of Gide without avoidable delay. The twenty-page essay about him was based on the 1909 article, with which the first three pages were identical; but there was a long new paragraph about *Paludes*. Gosse found it "as difficult to describe *Paludes*... — one of the most exquisite of modern books—as it would be to analyse the charm of *Tristram Shandy*." The critic was delighted to find Gide suddenly poking fun at himself, and he admired the "swift alternations of beauty and fun, of malice and audacity." A four-page study of *Isabelle* was incorporated, and a new closing paragraph said that Gide aimed at "giving a new direction to the art of the novelist," that he was "forever experimenting," and that "he seems to stand alone ... midway between the schools" of modern France. Gosse also detected a "something northern" about Gide's temperament.

² This was *Les Caves du Vatican*.

³ Gide's preoccupation with the English language and its literature can be followed in his *Journal,* November 11–23. He begins at six in the morning, reads Spenser, Conrad, Keats, takes lessons. He delves into Skeat, studies Jusserand's history of English literature, and rereads Keats before going to bed. Then he discovers *Hero and Leander* and is dazzled by its magnificence and passion. On the eighteenth comes a momentary slowdown; he writes that "to get ahead properly with Les Caves, the study of English must be neglected. I have, however, finished the amazing Hero and Leander—and continued the Faerie Queene." Some of his enthusiasm was doubtless ascribable to Gosse's influence.

27. GIDE TO GOSSE, *(undated visiting card), December, 1912, from London*

Si impatient de vous revoir! mais où et quand?

Charing Cross Hotel —

[So impatient to see you again! but where and when?

Charing Cross Hotel—]

28. GIDE TO GOSSE, *December 25, 1912, from London (Charing Cross Hotel)*

CHER AMI   J'accepte avec grand plaisir.

Veuillez déjà présenter mes hommages à Madame Gosse. Combien je me réjouis de vous revoir. A ce soir donc tout votre

ANDRÉ GIDE.

Taine m'avait pourtant bien dit qu'il était très indiscret de venir à Londres au moment de Noël! Excusez-moi.

[I accept with great pleasure.

Please give my regards to Mrs. Gosse forthwith. What a pleasure to see you again! Till this evening, then.[1]

Taine[2] did tell me, though, that it is very tactless to come to London at Christmas time. Do forgive me.]

---

[1] Gosse, from the time of his marriage, punctiliously set down the names of all his guests in the so-called "Book of Gosse," now in the library of Cambridge University. His guests at tea are entered—he was at home every Sunday afternoon—and the names of those who stayed to dinner are underlined. Under "Christmas dinner" in

1912 appear "Mr. Henry James, Mr. André Gide." Farther on we read: "December 30—dinner—Miss Edith Sichel, Mr. George Moore, Mr. André Gide." (The last entertaining registered is a tea on April 22, 1928; fifteen were present, among them Philip Gosse, his son, and Mr. and Mrs. Halévy. On May 16 Gosse died.)

² H. A. Taine, 1828–1893, had been in England many times and knew English usages. When and where did Gide meet him? Gide, when writing *Les Cahiers d'André Walter,* had been Taine's neighbor, near Annecy, but, whether out of shyness or out of reluctance to interrupt his work, he did not then call on Taine. (*Si le Grain ne meurt,* pp. 244–45.)

29. GIDE TO GOSSE, *February 10, 1913 (from ?)*

BIEN CHER AMI   Ne croyez point que j'aie oublié la mission dont vous m'aviez chargé; mais j'ai dû attendre, pour trouver prétexte à revoir les Bonniot, que l'édition de Mallarmé ait paru; telle est la défiance de Madame B. que je n'estimais pas prudent d'aborder de front la question des lettres de Swinburne; c'est par un long détour que j'y suis arrivé. Le voici:

"Ces lettres, ainsi que tous les papiers de Mallarmé, sont à Valvins (où villégiaturait le Faune chaque été) et Madame Bonniot ne pourra s'occuper de les rechercher qu'aux vacances de Pâques. Elle ne répond aucunement de pouvoir les retrouver, car... une crue de la Seine a, paraît-il, inondé leur logement (c'est l'importante inondation d'il y a deux ans) noyant la caisse où se trouvaient ces lettres avec toute la correspondance, qui n'a pu être soignée que quinze jours plus tard — retrouvée dans un état déplorable, — une grande partie de ces papiers a dû être jetée..."

C'est ce que Madame Bonniot m'a prié de vous redire; à force d'insistance et de diplomatie, j'ai obtenu d'elle la promesse que, tout au moins, elle chercherait. Terriblement défiante, et réticente, et butée, elle se réserve par contre de ne livrer ces papiers, (dans le cas où elle les retrouverait) que s'il lui plaît. Je crois avoir convaincu son mari du moins qu'il serait séant et opportun de le faire; et je me propose de revenir à la charge.

Autre chose: Régnier, à qui je racontais ces démarches, m'a aussitôt parlé d'une importante lettre de Swinburne à Héredia [*sic*] — aujourd'hui en sa possession. Je ne crois pas qu'il fasse difficulté pour communiquer le texte de cette lettre; mais je crois qu'il préfère ne pas être pressé.

J'espère que vous aurez fait un heureux voyage, et Madame Gosse à qui vous voudrez bien présenter mes hommages.

Bien amicalement votre ANDRÉ GIDE.

[Don't imagine that I have forgotten the errand you committed to me; but to have an excuse for seeing the Bonniots again I have had to wait for the edition of Mallarmé to come out.[1] Madame B. is so suspicious that I did not think it expedient to tackle the business of Swinburne's letters[2] head on; I got at it by a roundabout route. Here is the way of it:

These letters, along with all Mallarmé's papers, are at Valvins (where *le Faune* used to spend every summer), and Madame B. will not be able to look them up until the Easter holidays. She doesn't at all guarantee that she can recover them, because— a rise of the Seine, it seems, flooded their quarters (this was the big flood of two years back) and submerged the box containing the letters and the whole correspondence, which couldn't be taken care of until two weeks later; it was found in wretched shape, and a large share of the papers had to be thrown out.

That is what Madame Bonniot asked me to convey to you. By persistence and diplomacy I got her to promise that she would at least make a search. Being appallingly distrustful, secretive, and obstinate, she perversely insists that she won't turn over the papers (in the event of her finding them) unless she feels like it. I think I at least convinced her husband that it would be fitting and proper to do it; and I mean to return to the attack.

One other thing: Régnier,[3] to whom I was describing these overtures, promptly told me about an important letter from

Swinburne to Heredia, now in his possession. I don't believe
he will have any objection to giving us a copy of it; but I do
believe he had rather not be pressed about it.

I hope you and Mrs. Gosse had a pleasant trip; please give her
my regards.]

[1] A posthumous, partly original, edition of Mallarmé, *Poésies
complètes,* was published early in 1913 by the Nouvelle Revue Française. Geneviève Bonniot was Mallarmé's only living child; his son
had died.

[2] Gosse was then preparing his *Life of Swinburne* (1917) and, in
collaboration with Thomas J. Wise, an edition of Swinburne's *Complete Works.*

[3] Henri de Régnier, 1864–1936, symbolist poet, had married a
daughter of Heredia. I have not been able to see the letter Gide men-
tions. The papers of both Heredia and Régnier have been given to
the Bibliothèque Nationale, Paris, but access to them is not yet per-
mitted.

30. GOSSE TO GIDE, *February 21, 1913, from London*

MY DEAR GIDE, I have to thank you—and so warmly!—for the
gift of your "Traités"[1] and for your kindness with regard to the
Mallarmé-Swinburne Correspondence. I have been enjoying over
again those beautiful works of your youth: and a new one, which I
read for the first time "El Hadj." Here, too, I rejoice to discover
"Bethsabé," in which, as I read it now, I hear once more the reson-
ance and the aerial harmony of your voice, as you read it by the lamp-
light at Pontigny.

Copeau[2] has been here, but I was not able to see him, for I was ill
in bed. But our dear Jean Schlumberger[3] came to see me, and paid
me a delightful visit in my bed-chamber.

I cannot tell you with what deep solicitude I await your new book.[4] I expect an ecstasy! Let me hear how you progress with it.

We all send you our blessings.

Yours very sincerely, EDMUND GOSSE

My "Portraits and Sketches" has reached 3000 copies, a very unusual sale for a volume of essays with us. I see your name frequently in the journals.

[1] *Le Retour de l'enfant prodigue,* preceded by *Cinq autres traités,* was published by the Nouvelle Revue Française, Marcel Rivière et Cie., 1912. This was the first edition of these works collectively. The book included *Le Traité du Narcisse, théorie du symbole,* dedicated to Paul Valéry (1891); *La Tentative amoureuse, ou Le Traité du vain désir,* dedicated to Francis Jammes (1893); *El Hadj, ou Le Traité du faux prophète,* dedicated to Frédéric Rosenberg (1899); *Philoctète, ou Le Traité des trois morales,* dedicated to Marcel Drouin (1899); and *Bethsabé* (Bibliothèque de l'Occident, 1912), dedicated to Lucie Delarue-Mardrus. *Le Retour de l'enfant prodigue* was printed in *Editions Vers et Prose,* March–May, 1907.

Gide, in an 1890 note to the *Traité du Narcisse,* had said that truth is conveyed by symbols; "we live to demonstrate." The artist's role, then, is to present moral problems well demonstrated. A work of art that does not demonstrate is bad.

[2] Jacques Copeau, in a long article about *Father and Son* published in the *Nouvelle Revue Française* September 1, 1912, just after the Pontigny meeting, had found the documentary part of the book "of the deepest significance" and had praised its naturalness, sincerity, and precision of style. A Frenchman, he said, would have made of this cruel story a more bitter and a more indiscreet book; Gosse had kept it in impeccable taste. Copeau commented on "the son's complete inaptitude in matters of faith" and made a point of the greatness of a father who was "trying to snatch his son away from eternal damnation." Gosse, thanking Copeau, wrote: "How could I but be delighted with your admirable analysis? It was perhaps the most searching, the most complete, which has appeared in any language or country where Father and Son has found a reader.... I found

Thomas Hardy, at Dorchester, in the act of finishing your review, with which he was greatly impressed." (Fragment of a letter sent me by Jacques Copeau's daughter, Mme. Marie-Hélène Dasté.)

[3] Jean Schlumberger was in charge of the theater column of the *Nouvelle Revue Française*. He had reviewed *Portraits and Sketches* on February 1, 1913. He valued especially the essay on Swinburne. About the long article on Gide's works he said nothing: the *N.R.F.* contributors took seriously a rule against advertising one another.

[4] This was *Les Caves du Vatican*.

31. GIDE TO GOSSE, *April 25, 1913, from Italy*

BIEN CHER AMI   Avec quel plaisir je viens vous annoncer l'heureux succès de mon ambassade: j'ai reçu hier, copié par Madame Bonniot (Geneviève Mallarmé) le texte de *cinq* grandes lettres de Swinburne, dont l'intérêt dépasse ce que je pouvais attendre.

Qu'en dois-je faire et où puis-je vous les envoyer... Vous avouerais-je mon vif désir de les voir paraître d'abord à la Nouvelle Revue Française? — Puis-je obtenir *à travers vous* cette autorisation qui m'emplirait de joie? (Le texte de ces lettres est en français.)

Sitôt de retour à Paris, j'insisterai de nouveau auprès d'Henri de Régnier pour obtenir copie des lettres de S. à Heredia.

Madame Bonniot me prie de vous demander... mais pourquoi ne vous communiquerais-je pas sa lettre? Vous y trouverez son adresse, dans le cas où vous voudriez la remercier directement; je crois qu'elle serait sensible à un mot de vous.

Dans le cas où des lettres de Mallarmé à Swinburne seraient retrouvées, vous dirai-je que je serais extrêmement désireux d'en avoir moi-même une copie — précisément puisqu'elles ne doivent point être publiées, pour le moment du moins — Au besoin, j'en pourrais prendre moi-même copie, si c'est à travers moi que vous les faites parvenir à Madame Bonniot — Je viens de lui écrire pour lui exprimer mes remercîments et lui dire que je vous ai transmis sa requête.

Au revoir bien cher ami. Mille souvenirs et hommages à Madame Edmund Gosse. Vous me savez votre reconnaissant et dévoué

ANDRÉ GIDE.

[What a delight to report to you now the lucky outcome of my mission. I received yesterday, in copies made by Madame Bonniot (Geneviève Mallarmé), five long letters of Swinburne,[1] of an interest exceeding anything I could have anticipated.

What am I to do with them, and where can I send them to you? Shall I confess to you my keen desire to see them appear first in the *Nouvelle Revue Française?* Can I get the necessary permission through you? It would make me very happy. (The letters are in French.)

As soon as I am back in Paris I am going to work on Henri de Régnier again for copies of Swinburne's letters to Heredia.

Madame Bonniot wants me to ask you—But why shouldn't I pass her letter along to you? In it you will find her address, should you wish to thank her direct; I think she would be gratified by a word from you.

I am going to tell you that if some of Mallarmé's letters to Swinburne should be recovered, I should dearly love to have copies of them myself—and for the precise reason that they are not to be published, at least for the time being. If necessary I could copy them myself if it were through me that you transmit them to Madame Bonniot. I have just written to her to make my acknowledgments and to say that I sent her request on to you.

Au revoir, my dear friend. Remember me to Mrs. Gosse with warm regards.]

[1] The five Swinburne letters were published in *Letters of Swinburne,* edited by Edmund Gosse and Thomas J. Wise (London: William Heinemann, 1918). The correspondence began when Mallarmé was still little known in France and almost completely unknown in England; it was, in fact, Swinburne's admiration for Mallarmé's trans-

lation of Poe that made the literary elite aware of Mallarmé. The five letters in summary:

1. July 7, 1875. Swinburne thanks Mallarmé for the "magnificent" *Poèmes d'Edgar Poe, texte anglais et français illustrés de cinq dessins de Manet* (Paris: Librairie de l'Eau Forte, 1874). He pays tribute to John Ingram, who "has finally reduced to dust all the lies and calumnies forged or fabricated by this infamous Griswold ... whose name is no better than an emetic," and whom Baudelaire had well characterized as "a blood-sucking pedagogue."

2. January 13, 1876. Swinburne has written a kind of sestina, "Nocturne" (printed in the *République des Lettres* with Swinburne's letter, February 20, 1876), and he is afraid he may have used "some anglicism, some ambiguous or harsh sentence"; ever since "an eminent French critic" had characterized some of his verses as "efforts of a barbaric giant" he had lost confidence in himself. The *envoi* of this melodious "Nocturne" reads:

> Fille de l'onde et mère de l'amour,
> Du haut séjour plein de ta paix profonde
> Sur ce bas monde épands un peu de jour.

3. February 3, 1876. Swinburne has succeeded after sixteen years in translating Villon's "Ballade-Epitaphe" without changing the order of the rhymes. He had long wanted to translate, with Rossetti, all Villon's poems, but "in this virtuous country it is not yet permissible to hymn the beautiful Heaulmière and the fat Margot." Rossetti, however, has achieved superb versions of the "Ballade à la Vierge," "Les Neiges d'antan," and the "Rondeau sur la mort." Swinburne accepts from Mallarmé a changed word in "Nocturne"; "after all, that language so dear to me is not my mother tongue." He speaks of an article on Blake that he is writing and adds that since Baudelaire's death no one but Mallarmé is equipped for the "glorious task" of translating Blake's works.

4. February 14, 1876. Swinburne thanks Mallarmé for his letters and his advice, and says he is awaiting Mallarmé's "drama"—perhaps *Hérodiade*, or *Hamlet et le vent* ? Cf. Jean Noël, "George Moore et Mallarmé," *Revue de littérature comparée*, July–September, 1958, p. 370.

5. June 1, 1876. "A thousand thanks for your marvelous little poem, which is a jewel, so fittingly and delicately set in a case of pearls like a diamond." This little volume, which in *A Rebours* Des Esseintes was wont to touch with delight, was in a white felt cover

stamped in gold and tied with two pink-and-black silk braids. It was the first edition of *L'Après-midi d'un faune, églogue,* illustrated by Manet.

Gosse put the five letters into a privately printed brochure. The next year Swinburne, in *Edgar Poe, A Memorial Volume,* by S. S. Rice (Baltimore: Turnbull Brothers, 1877), was paying tribute to "one of the most remarkable young poets and to one of the most important and powerful painters of France, Mr. Mallarmé and Mr. Manet."

The letter that Gide enclosed for Gosse:

Geneviève Bonniot to André Gide, April 10, 1913,
from 92, Boulevard des Batignolles

Here is a copy of Swinburne's letters to Father that we found at Valvins. There are five of them, beautiful and interesting in more than one respect.

We are going to ask you to present a request to M. Gosse. If he has in his possession some of the letters Father wrote to Swinburne, we should like very much to have a copy of them. If there are any such letters, they must of course not be published in any circumstances.

You know, my dear M. Gide, about Father's strict and un-conditional wish on that subject: he wanted none of his letters made public after his death, and we are seeing to it with filial piety that his request shall be honored....

In the introduction to *The Letters of A. C. Swinburne,* edited by Edmund Gosse and Thomas J. Wise, Gosse wrote: "The letters of Mallarmé to which these [the five Swinburne letters] are replies have disappeared, and were probably destroyed. But even if they were found they would not be published, as Mallarmé left stringent directions that no letter of his, of whatever kind, was to be printed after his death." A curious light is thrown on the processes of that enig-matic character, Thomas J. Wise, by a booklet entitled *Five Letters from Stéphane Mallarmé to Algernon Charles Swinburne,* privately printed (in an edition of thirty copies for private circulation only) by Hazell Watson and Viney, Ltd., for Selwyn and Blount, Ltd., London, 1922, "on behalf of the editor." (One of these copies is in the New York Public Library. See also Henri Mondor, *Propos sur la poésie,* Editions du Rocher, Monaco, 1946.) De V. Payen-Paine says in a prefatory note that Thomas J. Wise gave permission to print these five letters, and that he "possesses most of the letters addressed to Swinburne."

32. GOSSE TO GIDE, *April 28, 1913, from London*

MY DEAR GIDE,   This is quite splendid! You are a famous huntsman, a Nimrod in the service of Apollo! Thank you a thousand times.

Please send the five copied letters at once to me, here. I am all impatience to read them. I believe that I shall be able to get your permission to publish them in the Nouvelle Revue Française. But I must see them first. Send them at once.

When do you return to Paris? Mrs. Gosse and I expect to be there from the 8th to the 24th of May. Shall we see you?

I sent you last week a little edition of Lamb's "Essays of Elia."[1]

Let us hear from you again. How does the great novel[2] progress? I long to read it.

I have written gratefully to Madame Bonniot.

Ever yours sincerely EDMUND GOSSE

[1] Gide had asked Valery Larbaud to send him the *Essays of Elia* in the summer of 1911; cf. Valery Larbaud, *Lettres à André Gide* (Paris: Stols, 1948).

[2] This was *Les Caves du Vatican,* finished June 24.

33. GIDE TO GOSSE, *May 4, 1913, from Rome*

CHER AMI   J'ai mis à la poste, à votre adresse, hier, sous pli recommandé, le texte des lettres de Swinburne. Je vous redis ici le plaisir que vous me feriez, et à ceux de mes amis qui sont devenus les vôtres, si vous pouviez nous obtenir, pour la Nouvelle Revue Française, le droit de première publication, que votre aimable lettre me laisse espérer.

Ghéon est avec moi à Rome qu'il ne connaissait pas encore; l'un et l'autre nous pensons être de retour à Paris vers le milieu du mois — c'est à dire à temps pour vous y voir — et sans doute présenter ma femme à Madame Gosse. Je me réjouis beaucoup de cette conjonction! — Veuillez déjà présenter à Madame Gosse mes hommages — Je suis bien fidèlement   Votre ANDRÉ GIDE.

P. S. C. Ci-joint un mot de M. Bonniot, que je reçois à l'instant. Les scrupules qu'il exprime me paraissent bien exagérés — mais je n'ai pas à me prononcer.

[I mailed to your address yesterday, registered, the copies of Swinburne's letters. I repeat now that you would be giving pleasure both to me and to those friends of mine who have become yours, if you could get for us, in the interest of the *Nouvelle Revue Française,* the first publication rights that your kind letter encourages me to hope for.

Ghéon[1] is with me in Rome, which he did not as yet know; both he and I look forward to being back in Paris by the middle of the month—which means in time to see you there, and doubtless to introduce my wife to Mrs. Gosse. I am greatly delighted with this turn of events. Meanwhile pray give Mrs. Gosse my regards.

P. S. I enclose a note from M. Bonniot, just received. His qualms strike me as a good deal overdone—but it is not for me to say.[2]]

[1] Henri Ghéon, 1875-1944, wrote for the *Revue Blanche,* the *Mercure de France, L'Ermitage,* and the *Nouvelle Revue Française.* He traveled to Algeria, Italy, Turkey, and Greece with Gide, about whom he had published an excellent article in the *Mercure* as early as 1897. His conversion to Catholicism during the war affected the relationship between him and Gide, much to Gide's distress.

[2] This refers to a request of M. Bonniot that a word "a little too harsh" be suppressed in one of Swinburne's letters to Mallarmé. Gosse declined to tamper with the text.

34. GIDE TO GOSSE, *May 18 (Sunday morning), 1913, from Paris*

BIEN CHER AMI   Ceci n'est qu'un petit mot d'amitié — mais je ne me retiens pas de vous l'écrire, puisqu'il me faut attendre jusqu'à Mercredi pour vous revoir.

Fatigue, insomnie et tout le tremblement... voici ce qui m'attendait à Paris! dont je ne songe déjà plus qu'à repartir. Je suis revenu de la rue Servandoni, avant hier soir, avec une pesante tristesse: j'espérais vous voir, et Madame Gosse, et Davray... je n'ai vu qu'un tourbillon de gens de lettres, un cauchemar digne de *Paludes!* *Depuis des années* je n'avais remis les pieds dans une réunion de littérateurs! Et si encore j'avais pu causer avec vous un instant! — J'ai craint de peiner Davray en ne venant pas... Ah! que n'ai-je, au lieu de cela, tout simplement été vous voir rue Saint Roch —! N'importe! A mercredi donc, et dans le calme d'Auteuil notre amitié se sentira plus à l'aise.

Je vois ce soir les Bonniot. Aurez-vous reçu une nouvelle lettre que je vous adressais à Londres au sujet de Swinburne, etc....? Nous en reparlerons Mercredi.

Veuillez dire à Madame Gosse le plaisir qu'aura me femme de vous recevoir tous les deux. Vous savez mon attentive et amicale reconnaissance   ANDRÉ GIDE.

[This is just a friend's little note, but I can't forbear sending it, having to wait for Wednesday to see you again.

Fatigue, sleeplessness, and all the rest of it: that's what was waiting for me in Paris,[1] and already my one thought is to get away from it again. I got back from the rue Servandoni night before last in deep dejection. I was hoping to see you and Mrs. Gosse and Davray, but all I saw was a maelstrom of writing folk—a nightmare worthy of *Paludes!* It was *years* since I had set foot in a swarm of littérateurs. If only I could have got in a minute's talk with you! I was afraid of hurting Davray by not appearing. Why, oh, why didn't I simply go to see you in the rue St. Roch instead? Never mind: I see you Wednesday, and in the peace of Auteuil companionship will be able to breathe.

I am to see the Bonniots this evening. Did you get another letter[2] that I sent you in London about Swinburne and so on? We will come back to that Wednesday.

Please tell Mrs. Gosse how happy my wife will be to have both of you.]

[1] Gide had returned from Italy on May 14.
[2] This refers to Letter 33.

35. GIDE TO GOSSE, *May 20, 1913, from Paris*

Tuesday night

BIEN CHER AMI   Il est trop tard pour vous envoyer un pneumatique, mais cette lettre vous parviendra avant votre départ demain matin. Puis, à défaut de ce mot Griffin vous aurait renseigné, et, à défaut de Griffin, un des trois concierges qui gardent les trois portes de la Villa Montmorency. La villa n'est pas bien loin du quai de Passy; une auto vous amènera en moins de 10 minutes; notre maison est le *18 bis Avenue des Sycomores* en haut de la villa; le concierge, à l'entrée donnera au chauffeur de l'auto l'indication nécessaire pour qu'il vous amène à notre porte; je vous assure que cela est très simple, car la Villa est toute petite. Si par malheur vous vous sentiez trop fatigué pour venir, un mot de vous me ferait accourir n'importe où — mais combien je serais déçu si vous ne pouviez venir; ma femme aussi se réjouit tant de vous voir et Madame Gosse.

A demain donc n'est-ce pas — Croyez à ma profonde amitié

ANDRÉ GIDE.

[It is too late to send you a special delivery, but this letter will reach you before you set out tomorrow morning. If it does not,

Griffin[1] will probably have directed you, or, if not Griffin, one of the three concierges who take care of the three entrances to Villa Montmorency.[2] The villa is not very far from the Quai de Passy; a car will get you to it in less than ten minutes; our house is No. 18 *bis*, Avenue des Sycomores, at the far end of the drive; the concierge will direct your driver to our door. It is all perfectly simple, I assure you, for the driveway is very short. If, unhappily, you should feel too tired to come, a word from you will quickly fetch me to wherever you are—only I should be no end disappointed if you were unable to come, and my wife too is delighted to be seeing you and Mrs. Gosse.

Till tomorrow, then.]

[1] Griffin, when in Paris, lived at 16 Quai de Passy.

[2] Villa Montmorency (cf. note 1, Letter 8) is described by Roger Martin du Gard in *Notes sur André Gide,* p. 23.

36. GOSSE TO GIDE, *June 6, 1913, from London*

MY DEAR GIDE,   Will you do me a great favour? I send you a proof of the little edition (of 20 copies only) which I am preparing of Swinburne's Lettres à Mallarmé. Will you read it carefully, and tell me if you see anything wrong? And send it back?

On page 35, can you (or any other Mallarmé expert) tell me what "merveilleux petit joyau de poésie" it could be which Mallarmé sent to Swinburne on the 1st of June 1876? You see that it was printed, for it had an "éditeur."[1]

Did I tell you I wrote to Mme. Bonniot, thanking her, and telling her that the letters of her Father were destroyed?

I think I shall be able to get you permission to reprint these "Lettres" in the "Nouvelle Revue" as soon as my pamphlet is out.[2]

Do you know why Schlumberger has not made use of the passage from Mallarmé (in my "Questions at Issue") which I sent him?[3] With all kindest messages, I am always yours   EDMUND GOSSE

---

[1] Gide's answer to this letter is missing, but Gosse almost undoubtedly received the information he asked for: his note to Swinburne's letter reads "without any doubt, the first edition of *l'Après-midi d'un faune.*" (Cf. *Letters of A. C. Swinburne.*)

[2] The letters never appeared in the *Nouvelle Revue Française.*

[3] Gosse had published in 1893 the first English article on Mallarmé, "The Symbolism of S. Mallarmé." Mallarmé thanked him, calling his article "a miracle of intuition." (Cf. *Questions at Issue,* London: William Heinemann, 1893. Mallarmé's letter is printed in the appendix.)

37. GOSSE TO GIDE, *June 14, 1913, from London*

MY DEAR GIDE,   Accept my best thanks for so kindly and promptly correcting the proofs. I am grateful for every one of your suggestions.[1]

The portrait of yourself is admirable and precious. It will never leave my writing-table, and will inspire my daily work.

     I am always your devoted EDMUND GOSSE

---

[1] Unfortunately Gide's letter is missing, and we cannot know what suggestions he made.

38. GIDE TO GOSSE, *June 29, 1913, from Cuverville*

MON CHER AMI   Je lis avec intérêt votre discours à *l'English Association.* C'est gentil à vous de me l'avoir envoyé. — Plus d'un passage m'a plongé dans *l'état de discussion* qui m'est cher entre tous; car je ne suis pas sûr d'approuver entièrement ce que vous dites au sujet de l'usure progressive des mots et du rétrécissement de l'inconnu poétique... Il y aurait beaucoup à dire là dessus.

Vous parlez excellemment de Mallarmé, de la "more and more powerful and wide-embracing prose." Et que j'aime ce que vous dites de la littérature anglaise: "never without some dew on the threshing-floor." Excellent!

Mon livre est achevé — enfin! et je vais partir dans quelques jours, le cœur léger, vers Constantinople et Brousse, tandis que Cuverville va s'emplir de cousins et de neveux.

Comment ne pas penser que l'Académie Française a du bon, puisqu'elle sait remarquer un livre comme *Father and Son!* Je m'en suis beaucoup réjoui.

Au revoir. Il me tarde bien de pouvoir vous envoyer mon livre; mais quelques mois s'écouleront encore avant qu'il me soit possible de le donner à imprimer.

Ma femme et moi nous nous rappelons aux meilleurs souvenirs de madame Gosse, à qui veuillez présenter mes hommages —

Votre fidèle et dévoué ANDRÉ GIDE.

[I am reading with interest your lecture before the English Association.[1] Several passages have thrown me into the state of mental ambivalence that I particularly cherish. For I am not sure that I entirely assent to what you say about the way words gradually lose their content and about the shrinkage of the area of poetic mystery. It is a subject on which a lot could be said.

You speak admirably about Mallarmé, about his "more and more powerful and wide-embracing prose." And I do like what you say about English literature—"never without some dew on the threshing-floor." Splendid!

My book is finished—at last!—and in a few days I am setting out lightheartedly for Constantinople[2] and Brusa; meanwhile Cuverville is going to be overrun by cousins and nephews.

How could anyone fail to see that the French Academy has its uses, when it can single out such a book as *Father and Son?*[3] I was very happy about it.

Au revoir. It irks me a good deal that I can't send you my book, but it will be several months yet before I can give it to the printer.

My wife and I want to be remembered most warmly to Mrs. Gosse; please give her my regards.]

[1] The English Association, of which Gosse was president for 1922–1923, published annually various essays and studies by its members and also limited editions of articles or lectures. At the meeting of May 30, 1913, Gosse spoke on "The Future of English Poetry." His lecture, published by the Association as No. 25, discussed the dilemmas that poets of the future would face. Each new school must find a new form of expression; it becomes increasingly difficult to write great poetry, because "all the evident, poignant and simple things have been said"; and the attrition of words makes the task still more complicated. Gosse thought that poetry would survive "the bankruptcy of language" but that it would be exposed to great dangers—primarily those of mannerism and obscurity, from which even Mallarmé's beautiful talent had not been immune.

[2] By July 2 Gide was no longer tempted by the trip to Constantinople. "My imminent departure makes me positively ill; at moments I hope that the situation in the Balkans will become worse so that it will be impossible for me to go." (*Journal,* July 2, 1913.) Instead, he was to go to Italy that year. But he made the trip to Turkey in late April and May, 1914, with Mrs. Mayrisch and Ghéon.

[3] The French Academy had just awarded a prize to Davray's translation of *Father and Son.*

39. GOSSE TO GIDE, *July 2, 1913, from London*

MY DEAR GIDE,   The news that your novel[1] is finished, deeply moves and excites me! For no recent book have I felt so intense an anticipation. And now you start for Constantinople and Broussa [Brusa], —sunlighted names! All luck go with you! I commend you to the care of our Father—Phoebus Apollo.   Always yours, EDMUND GOSSE

¹ The novel was *Les Caves du Vatican,* whose publication Gosse had been impatiently expecting for six months. (Desjardins wrote a long letter from Pontigny on August 8, 1913, urging Gosse to come back that summer, especially since the people from the Nouvelle Revue Française could not be there, being too busy with the new theater.)

40. GOSSE TO GIDE, *January 2, 1914, from London*

MY DEAR GIDE, Conceive the impatience with which, yesterday morning, I tore open the Nouvelle Revue Française and read the opening chapters of "Les Caves du Vatican." ¹

I have awaited this book with unspeakable impatience, with hope and fear mingled. Now all is hope, and joy! Your novel opens with a magnificent originality. I believe this is, perhaps *by far*—the great-est thing you have written. All is your own; no other writer could have written one of these pages; your sign-manual is on them all.

The conversion of Anthime is superb. Nothing could be led up to better, nothing could be more surprising, more brillant, vivid with a more sparkling irony. The characters of the women—so finely contrasted,—the soft, passive Veronique, the more acid, ac-tive and absurd Marguerite. The child Julie promises an admirable character; I see in her a continuation of the force of her grandfather Juste-Agénor. Lafcadio is at present a box of puzzles, anything may come out of him.

There is a singular air of mystery and mystification about these early chapters. I hold my breath in expectation of what that is para-doxical, that is saugrenu, will come out of it all, and I can hardly endure the strain of waiting till February for a continuation.

Bravo! and bravo! This, I am sure, my dear Friend, is a book which will be enormously attacked, widely *discussed, finally immortal.*

Have you forgotten me entirely? Months have passed and you have not given me a sign of your existence. I thought you would have written to me in November, but not a word. You do not realise how much your friendship is to me. I am miserable if I think that you have ceased to think of me with indulgence.

We are well, at last. But both my wife and I had long illnesses since the summer. We were in Paris in August, and then in Wiesbaden for four weeks, ill and unhappy. Since then I have been extremely busy, and much has happened to me. I had the great surprise of a most unexpected and brilliant recognition from the French Government.[2] You did not write. Perhaps you disapproved?

My wife begs to be remembered to Madame Gide and to you. How is everybody? Has the new theater been a success?[3] I hear nothing from any of my French friends—a conspiracy of silence! I wish you would come to London.   Ever sincerely yours, EDMUND GOSSE

[1] Book I of *Les Caves du Vatican,* "Anthime Armand-Dubois," and the first five chapters of Book II, "Julius de Baraglioul," were printed in the January, 1914, *Nouvelle Revue Française.*

[2] Gosse had become an *officier* of the Legion of Honor in November. Henry Davray had been working to that end from 1904. In October, 1913, he wrote Gosse (in English): "Happy to be able to send you a telegram this morning about the big news: you are an Officier in the Legion of Honour in spite of all embassies and regulations." Office errors kept Gosse from receiving the rosette until late November. (Unpublished letters, Davray to Gosse, October 17 and November 14.) Gide's silence had bothered Gosse: he suffered when neglected by his friends. Gide had been ill with a severe otalgia in early November. During the preceding summer and autumn he had been mainly occupied with the translation of *L'Offrande Lyrique,* published December 1, 1913, and he had read less English.

[3] This was the Vieux-Colombier, in which the whole *Nouvelle Revue Française* group took an active part. Copeau directed it. The opening had been announced for October 15; the inaugurating soirée was given November 22. The first bill comprised *Une femme tuée par la douceur,* by Thomas Heywood, and Molière's *L'Amour médecin*; the second, Musset's *Barberine,* and *Les Fils Louverné* by Jean Schlumberger. (Cf. Henri Ghéon, "Au Théâtre du Vieux-Colombier," *Nouvelle Revue Française,* December 12, 1913.)

41. GIDE TO GOSSE, *January 8, 1914, from Paris* [?]

MY DEAR FRIEND   Votre lettre m'emplit de confusion et de joie;
une confusion abondante, mais une joie surabondante! car quel ami
vous faites! et combien je vous aime de ne pas me garder rancune
de ma disparition.

L'espoir d'aller passer à Londres les fêtes de Noël, ainsi que j'avais
fait l'an passé (et quel souvenir exquis, grâce à vous, j'avais remporté
de ce voyage) — a beaucoup prolongé mon silence.

J'aurais eu si grand plaisir à vous souhaiter un heureux Xmas,
et à présenter à Madame Gosse, de vive voix,* tous mes vœux pour
le nouvel an. Un rhume obstiné m'a retenu à Auteuil; mais, durant
des jours et des jours, je balançais: irai-je? n'irai-je pas? Ni n'osant
vous annoncer ma venue, et ni ne prenant mon parti de renoncer
à cette joie.

Je pensais apporter avec moi le texte complet de mes *Caves* —
qu'il me tarde tant que vous connaissiez en entier! surtout à présent
que je sais que le début ne vous a pas déçu… Que de fois j'ai pensé
à vous, en l'écrivant! souhaitant, espérant, *voulant,* que vous puissiez
vous y plaire. Vos éloges bouffissent un peu mon orgueil, mais
m'apportent une force réelle, car je *sais,* maintenant, que mon livre
est réussi.

Désireux, dans cette lettre, de me laver de mes noirceurs, je vous
dirai que, si je ne vous ai pas déjà félicité de votre rosette, c'est pour
la raison que je ne l'ai connue que très tard. Plutôt que de n'être
pas un des premiers à applaudir, mon amour propre, piqué, a préféré n'applaudir plus du tout. Au demeurant, ce n'est pas vous que
j'ai eu envie de féliciter, mais mon brave cher pays de France, d'avoir
su marquer quelque peu de reconnaissance pour la sage et belle amitié que vous lui avez constemment [*sic*] et fidèlement marquée.

---

* et en anglais! (A. G.)

J'étais heureux aussi parce qu'il m'a semblé que par ce geste, la France vous prenait un peu à elle, comme on retient un ami par la veste, et que vous même, après, vous alliez vous sentir encore un peu plus français. — Quelle étrange chose que de n'être pas du même pays! Si nous habitions la même ville, sans doute me sentirais-je un peu moins sauvage. De plus en plus je vis en ours. Pourtant, grâce aux amis du théâtre et de la revue, je ne me sens pas seul. Théâtre du Vieux Colombier et Nouvelle Revue Française, restent le point de rencontre de tant d'amitiés, de dévouements, et de ferveurs! — Oui, le théâtre va bien; beaucoup mieux même qu'on n'avait osé l'espérer; la seule inquiétude vient du terrible surmenage de Copeau, qui n'a pas le droit de se reposer un seul jour, et que le nombre insuffisant des acteurs de la petite troupe, force de jouer lui-même presque tous les soirs.

Rien à vous dire de cet été. Les troubles balkaniques m'ont empêché d'aller à Constantinople et Brousse, ainsi que j'en avais l'intention; je me suis rabattu tout banalement sur l'Italie, puis j'ai regagné la Normandie où ma femme, avec ses frères et ses sœurs, était restée tranquillement à m'attendre. Si seulement j'avais *où* aller en Angleterre, et pu penser vous retrouver sans indiscrétion quelque part, je crois bien que j'aurais passé le Channel. Oui, vraiment, j'y ai pensé sérieusement, et j'ai failli alors vous écrire. Votre lettre me console un peu, en m'apprenant que vous étiez à Wiesbaden à ce moment.

Non, cher ami, ne croyez pas que je vous oublie, ou que mon affection pour vous diminue. Quand vous me reverrez, vous sentirez tout aussitôt que je demeure et demeurerai le même, malgré ces plongées dans le Silence où je perds la conscience du temps. Au revoir. A tout hasard je vous dis: à bientôt. Ma femme se rappelle au bon souvenir de Madame Gosse. Veuillez lui présenter mes hommages et me croire bien fidèlement votre ANDRÉ GIDE.

[Your letter fills me with both embarrassment and delight: embarrassment in quantity, delight in greater quantity. For what a friend you are being! Bless you for not being cross with me for my disappearance.

My hope of getting to London for the Christmas holidays, as I did last year—and, thanks to you, what lovely memories I have of that trip!—has considerably lengthened my silence.

I should have taken such pleasure in wishing you and Mrs. Gosse a Merry Christmas and giving Mrs. Gosse by word of mouth* my best wishes for the New Year. A persistent cold has kept me in Auteuil; but for days and days it was a toss-up: do I go, or do I not go?—with me daring neither to tell you that I would be there nor to make up my mind to forgo the pleasure.

I meant to take with me the whole text of my *Caves*, which I am on tenterhooks to have you know complete—especially now that I know the beginning of it did not disappoint you. How often I thought of you while writing it! wishing, hoping, *willing* that you might be able to find pleasure in it. Your praise [not only] somewhat puffs up my pride, but truly strengthens me, for now I *know* that my book is not a failure.[1]

Wanting in this letter to purge myself of my misdoings, I will tell you that my not having before now congratulated you on your decoration was a consequence of my hearing about it very belatedly. Once I had missed being among the first to applaud, I chose, out of damaged self-esteem, not to applaud at all. And, anyway, it was not so much you that I felt like congratulating as my dear fine France for managing to show recognition of the wise and beautiful friendship you have unceasingly and faithfully shown her. I was happy, too, because it seemed to me that by this gesture France was drawing you a little closer, as one holds a friend back by the coat sleeve, and that you yourself were going to feel, after that, even a little more French. How strange that we are not of the same country! If we lived in the same city, no doubt I should feel a little less shy. I lead a more and more solitary life. Still, thanks to my friends of the theater and of the magazine, I do not feel lonely. The Théâtre du Vieux-Colombier and the *Nouvelle Revue Française* continue to be the focal points of so many friendships and

* and in English! (A. G.)

loyalties and enthusiasms! Yes, the theater is doing well, indeed much better than we had ventured to hope; our only worry is seeing Copeau[2] so dreadfully overworked; he cannot allow himself a single day off, and the shortage of actors in the little company compels him to act himself almost every night.

There is nothing to tell you about last summer. The Balkan troubles kept me from getting to Constantinople and Brusa as I had intended; I just tamely fell back on Italy and then came back to Normandy, where my wife[3] had stayed peacefully with her brothers and sisters, waiting for me. If only I had known *where* in England and could have thought I might join you somewhere without instrusion, I do believe I should have crossed the Channel. Yes, I really did think about it seriously, and I came near writing you at that point.[4] Your letter gives me the consolation of finding that you were in Wiesbaden.

No, my dear friend, don't imagine that I am forgetting you or that my fondness for you lessens. When you see me again you will perceive at once that I remain and shall remain unchanged, despite these lapses into silence in which I lose all awareness of time. Au revoir. I am going to say, whether or no, *à bientôt.* My wife wants to be remembered to Mrs. Gosse. Please give her my regards.]

[1] Gide was in a state to use any praise of *Les Caves du Vatican* that he could get. Jacques Copeau had asked him to rewrite parts of it, and Gide himself, tired and depressed, was not too well satisfied with it. "Odd book; but I am beginning to be fed up with it. I cannot yet realize it is finished and can't stop thinking of it. More than one passage in the first and second books seem to me weak or forced." (*Journal,* June 24, 1913.) On June 26 he wrote: "It seems to me at times that I have never yet written anything serious."

[2] Jacques Copeau, 1879–1949, founder of the Vieux-Colombier, devoted his life to the ideal of restoring poetry and truth to the art of the theater. Wanting students and persons of scanty means to see the performances, he provided three new programs a week out of a wide-ranging repertoire, classic and modern, French and foreign.

To encourage a renaissance of dramatic art he staged the work of young playwrights. Among the classics his principal devotions were to Molière and Shakespeare. The Vieux-Colombier's final season was that of 1923–1924.

³ Mme. André Gide, *née* Madeleine Rondeaux, was her husband's first cousin. She was two years older than he; her sister Jeanne was slightly older than Gide, Valentine a little younger. Her two brothers, Edouard and Georges, were the youngest of the family.

⁴ Gide had indeed thought of going to England at the end of the summer. On September 1 he wrote to Valery Larbaud that he should like to see him again and to "soak" on some beach. (G. Aubry, *op. cit.*, p. 232.)

42. GOSSE TO GIDE, *April 6, 1914, from London*

MY DEAR GIDE,   Your "Souvenirs de la Cour d'Assises"¹ is an exceedingly interesting and valuable divagation from your customary path. My first exclamation (when I saw the first installment in the "Nouvelle Revue") was "What can he have to say about juries and judges and prisoners at the bar?" But I had only to read a couple of pages to see that your profound sincerity, applied to this hackneyed and vulgarised subject, drew it straight up out of the commonplace and gave it style. I read right through the book, page for page, in two sittings, and was at last hungry for more. But you must not indulge this hunger. You have other and larger fish to fry. I am eager to proceed with "Les Caves du Vatican," and I cannot think why the April number has not reached me.

Yours ever sincerely, EDMUND GOSSE

¹ Gide wrote the *Souvenirs de la Cour d'Assises* after a session of the Rouen Court of Assises in which he was a member of the jury, May 13–25, 1912. His observations were published in the November and

December numbers of the *Nouvelle Revue Française*. Only the original edition contains the complete text. The subsequent edition appeared January 6, 1914. Gide was troubled by the perception that "human justice is a doubtful and precarious thing." The distress arising from a sense of responsibility had prompted him to intervene in behalf of one of the accused who he thought had been too summarily convicted. Public opinion was then much exercised over the jury system, and many newspapers published articles about it—the *Journal des Débats, Excelsior, Figaro,* the *Revue Judiciaire, L'Eclair,* and others in October, 1913, alone. *L'Opinion* published (October 25) Gide's statement among others; he deplored the faulty selection of jury members, found the questioning badly conducted, objected to the incompleteness of the information given the jury, and wanted foremen elected instead of appointed.

43. GOSSE TO GIDE, *April 25, 1914, from London*

MY DEAR GIDE, Thank you much for your kind thought in sending me the April number of the N.R.F., for I was exceedingly anxious to finish "Les Caves." It came, however, while I was away in Ireland (following with breathless interest the movements of the Volunteer Army in Ulster).[1] Now at last I have finished your great novel.

It will take me some little time before I can quite clearly put before myself what I think about the book, as a whole. It is extremely amusing, in a very original way, that is, in a way so old that it is quite new! You have gone back to the methods of the 18th century: I see in your book the discipleship of "Gil Blas" and of Fielding.[2]

"Les Caves du Vatican," I should say, is the only *picaresque* novel of our time. It is a gallery of eccentric and violent portraits arranged to excite the imagination by their contrasts. I delight in the rich savour of the style, the humour of the situations, the daring originality of the embroglio. What I cannot just get rid of is a certain disappointment at your having dropped so completely the spiritual and religious element. I was expecting, down to the last page, to hear more about the Pope. However, Geneviève and Lafcadio seem to promise us a new departure. We may yet hear more about the heretics at home.

As soon as the book is published, as a book, I shall carefully read it through again. It is distracting to the critical sense to deal with a great novel in livraisons. And "Les Caves" is a *great* novel,—I am sure of that. I feel an intense curiosity as to its success in France.

Ever sincerely yours, EDMUND GOSSE

[1] The April *Nouvelle Revúe Française* contained the concluding chapters of *Les Caves du Vatican;* Gide sent it to Gosse just before starting for Brusa.

Gosse was recurrently concerned about the Irish problem. He wrote to a friend the following year: "Ireland is now the terrible danger in front of us.... Ulster is most threatening, sullen, provincial, egotistical." (Charteris, *op. cit.,* p. 367.)

[2] For Fielding's robust art, "so healthy and so gay," Gide had the greatest admiration; in *Tom Jones* he saw a masterpiece. French literature was so highly seasoned that he liked, by contrast, "the huge untrimmed gobbets that Fielding and Defoe serve hardly cooked and full of the meat's blood." ("Lettres à Charles Du Bos," *Œuvres complètes d'A. Gide,* X, 541.) Gide's phrasing, by the way, recalls that of Fielding himself: "We shall represent human nature at first to the keen appetite of our reader in that more plain and simple manner in which it is found in the country, and shall, hereafter, hash and ragout it with all the high French and Italian seasoning of affectation and vice." (*Tom Jones,* Book I, chap. i.) Gide stated the same idea in "Voyages dans la littérature anglaise" (*Verve,* Vol. I, No. 2, 1938). Lafcadio, Gide's hero in *Les Caves du Vatican,* is to be sure, a more complex character than Tom Jones, and his "gratuitous" crime excludes him from the company of the true picaros. His story is a satirical novel of adventure—in Gide's classification, a *sotie*.

44. GIDE TO GOSSE, *November 10, 1914, from Cuverville*

MON CHER AMI Pour deux jours à la campagne, où j'installe des réfugiés belges, vite j'en profite pour vous écrire. A Paris je n'ai pas un instant. — J'ai lu vos beaux vers dans le *Times* du 20 octobre, avec l'émotion la plus vive; j'ai découpé le poème, qui, dans mon carnet de poche, depuis ne m'a pas quitté. Je pense à vous souvent. Qu'il sera bon de s'embrasser de l'autre côté du tunnel! Dites à Madame Gosse, je vous prie, mon respectueux et tendre souvenir. Copeau est soldat, dans les bureaux jusqu'à ce jour, mais sans doute bientôt appelé dans l'armée active; Ghéon médecin dans un hôpital militaire. Jacques Rivière prisonnier.

Au revoir, cher ami; n'oubliez pas vos amis de France, qui pensent à vous de tout leur cœur. Votre fidèle ANDRÉ GIDE.

Madame Copeau et ses enfants sont ici auprès de ma femme. Toutes deux me chargent de leurs meilleurs souvenirs.

[Being in the country for two days, settling some Belgian refugees, I snatch at the chance to write you.[1] I never get a minute in Paris. I read your beautiful lines in the *Times*[2] of October 20 with the most poignant emotion; I clipped the poem out, and it has been with me ever since, in my little pocket notebook. I think of you often. How good it will be to exchange embraces when we get to the other end of the tunnel! Please give Mrs. Gosse my humble and solicitous regards. Copeau is a soldier, doing office work so far, but no doubt soon to be on active service. Ghéon is a doctor in a military hospital, Jacques Rivière a prisoner of war.

Au revoir, my dear friend; do not forget your friends in France, who are thinking of you with all warmth.

Madame Copeau and her children are staying here with my wife. Both send their warmest regards.]

¹ This letter is Gide's first to Gosse after the beginning of the war.
² Gosse's poem reads:

TO OUR DEAD

The flame of summer droops and fades and closes
While autumn thins the ember of the copse,
And ever more the violent life of roses
Grows keener as the roseate foliage drops;
O strong young hearts within whose veins was leaping
Love like a fount, hate like a dart shot high,
My heart o'er yours, its dolorous vigil keeping,
Is pierced with sorrow, while in joy you die!

Your ashes o'er the flats of France are scattered,
But hold a fire more hot than flesh of ours;
The stainless flag that flutters, frayed and tattered,
Shall wave and wave, like spring's immortal flowers.
You die, but in your death life glows intenser;
You shall not know the shame of growing old;
In endless joy you swing the holy censer,
And blow the trumpet tho' your lips are cold.

Life was to us a mist of intimations;
Death is a flash that shows us where we trod;
You, falling nobly for the righteous nations,
Reveal the unknown, the unhoped-for face of God.
After long toil, your labours shall not perish,
Through grateful generations yet to come
Your ardent gesture, dying, Love shall cherish,
And like a beacon you shall guide us home.

45. GOSSE TO GIDE, *November 15, 1914, from London*

MY DEAR GIDE, I cannot express to you what pleasure your letter gave me. I had been longing to have news of you, and you give me just what we want. There was a legend that you were seen in England in July: but I knew that it could not be true, for you would not come to London without seeing me.¹

What an extraordinary position we are all in. Year after year we have been saying Germania est delenda! not really believing it to be true: and now all the civilized world is launched upon the formidable adventure!

One beautiful result of the war is the union of hearts. All our political factions and party hatreds are at an end, throughout the Empire. And for you French we feel an affection so close and so fraternal that there has been nothing like it before in our history.

The losses in our own private world are terrible! I know at least twenty families where the son of the house was an officer who has already died in France, fighting side by side with you. When it is over, it will be a new world and an empty world, but it will be *clean:* it will be cleansed of the filthy omnipresent spawn of Prussia.

It makes me very happy to know that you saw my little poem and that it pleased you.

Many friends have been asking me about you,—Henry James and George Moore in particular. My wife and daughters send you their most cordial regards. Our respects, please, to Madame Gide.

I am, my dear friend, Always yours EDMUND GOSSE

We are all well: and London is cheerful and vigorous.

---

[1] Gide had actually started for London in July. He was in Dieppe on July 28 to sail for New Haven, where Valery Larbaud was expecting him. Then came Austria's declaration of war on Servia, general mobilization in France, Germany's declaration of war on France and her invasion of Belgium, and England's declaration of war on Germany. Gide, then forty-five, was not called to military service.

46. GIDE TO GOSSE, *December 29, 1914, from the Foyer Franco-Belge, Paris*

BIEN CHER AMI Je quitte tout pour vous répondre aussitôt — parce qu'un malentendu entre nous est quelque chose que je ne peux pas supporter. Il va sans dire que Gallimard vous a écrit sans me consulter; je crois qu'il ne l'aurait jamais fait en temps ordinaire; il aura craint de me déranger en me parlant de ce dont il m'est impossible de m'occuper pour le moment, car je n'ai pas un instant dont je puisse disposer en dehors de l'œuvre des réfugiés dont je m'occupe. Je lui écris néanmoins une lettre de reproche, car il sait que vous êtes mon ami et n'a pas à agir ici en dehors de moi — qui étais à même de lui donner les renseignements qu'il demande. Maintenant je vous supplie de l'excuser, car le pauvre garçon (que vous avez je crois rencontré à Pontigny) vient d'être très gravement malade et depuis ne sort pas d'un état de neurasthénie noire.

Je suis d'autant plus choqué par la lettre qu'il a pu vous écrire que j'ai, donné par vous, *deux* exemplaires du *Critical Kit Kats,* et que ce volume, ainsi que je vous l'avais écrit dans le temps a été mon *unique* lecture, avec le *Paradise lost,* pendant tout le temps de mon exil dans les Apennins. Je l'ai lu depuis la première jusqu'à la dernière page.

Ah! cher ami quel plaisir j'aurais à vous écrire longuement. Je suis seul à Paris (chez les Van Rysselberghe, 44 rue Laugier) ma femme est toujours à Cuverville avec Madame Copeau et ses enfants. Ghéon va partir ce soir pour Dunkerke (médecin major). Jean Schlumberger s'est engagé (artilleur) — Au revoir. Mille souvenirs et hommages à Madame Gosse — Votre tout dévoué   ANDRÉ GIDE.

Et tous mes vœux de nouvel an —

[I am dropping everything to answer you at once, because a misunderstanding between us is something that I cannot abide. Of course Gallimard[1] wrote you without consulting me; I think he would never have done it in normal times. He was probably afraid of troubling me with mention of something I can't possibly attend to at present, because I haven't a minute that I can spare from the work for the refugees that I am busy with. Nevertheless I am writing him a letter to protest, because he knows that you are a friend of mine, and he had no occasion to do such a thing apart from me—from whom he could have got the information he needed. I now beg that you will forgive him for it, for the poor fellow (whom you met at Pontigny, I believe) is just recovering from a very serious illness, which has left him in a state of black depression.

I am the more upset by such a letter as he may have written you because I have *two* copies of *Critical Kit-Kats* given me by you, and because this book, as I told you at the time, was my *only* reading, along with *Paradise Lost,* in the whole period of my exile in the Apennines. I read it from the first to the last page.

My dear friend, what a pleasure it would be to write you at length! I am alone in Paris (at the Van Rysselberghe's,[2] 44 rue Laugier); my wife is still at Cuverville with Mrs. Copeau and her children. Ghéon starts for Dunkirk this evening (major, medical corps). Jean Schlumberger has enlisted (artilleryman). Au revoir. All remembrances and regards to Mrs. Gosse.

And all best New Year's wishes.

[1] Gosse's letter to which this is the answer is missing. Gaston Gallimard, director of the publishing house of the Nouvelle Revue Française, apparently wrote Gosse asking the loan of a volume of the Pentland edition of Stevenson's works for its typographic interest. Gosse probably believed that Gallimard had asked Gide for information about Stevenson's book and been referred to him, Gosse. Gosse had given Gide his *Critical Kit-Kats,* a chapter of which vividly depicts his friend Stevenson; he had even sent Gide a second copy —"a perfect copy of the first edition." Gosse seems to have believed that Gide had never thoroughly read his book, the chapter on Stevenson being the last.

[2] Théo Van Rysselberghe, the painter, and his wife, Maria (whose pen name is M. Saint-Clair), were perhaps Gide's closest friends. Their daughter Elisabeth was to become, nine years later, the mother of André Gide's only child, Catherine.

47. GOSSE TO GIDE, *May 30, 1915, from London*

MY DEAR GIDE, Miss Stephens[1] has sent me your graceful and touch-ing article, "Les Réfugiés," which I have enjoyed putting into my best colloquial English and sending back to her. How delightful it is, dear and noble friend, for me to be allowed to collaborate with you in your admirable piety! My thoughts go out to you often and often. When shall we meet again? Surely this horror will some day, or some year, be overpast?

Every English heart goes out in warmest union of heart with you in France. But how terrible it is! We have lost, and are daily losing, our most gallant and splendid young men, the very brain and nerve of England, dying on the fields of Flanders.

God bless you and keep you. Mrs. Gosse sends her warmest re-gards to you and to Madame Gide.

Yours very affectionately, EDMUND GOSSE

Do you know that the Marcellus of our age, the most promising of all the young English poets, has fallen in the Dardanelles? This was Rupert Brooke, who lies buried in Tenedos.[2]

---

[1] Winifred Stephens edited in 1915 *The Book of France,* sponsored by an honorary committee, the president of which was Paul Cambon, French ambassador to England. The book, sold for the benefit of the French Relief Committee for the Refugees from the Occupied Provinces, was published by Macmillan in London and by Edouard Champion in Paris. The first page had a cartoon by Abel Faivre, showing a helmeted German officer looking at ruins and saying: "Only a German knows how to make beautiful ruins." The book contained articles by French and English writers—Rosny *aîné*, Anatole France (translated by H. G. Wells), Rémy de Gourmont, Pierre Loti, the Comtesse de Noailles, Maurice Barrès, François de Curel, Kipling, Henry James, Thomas Hardy, Gide (translated by Gosse), and others.

² Rupert Brooke, 1887–1915, died April 17 on the French hospital ship *Duguay-Trouin* and was buried on Skyros.

48. GIDE TO GOSSE, *June 5, 1915, from Paris*

BIEN CHER AMI   Votre proposition est exquise et je vous en remercie de tout mon cœur. J'aime ce rapprochement de nos deux noms et dans aucune occasion elle ne peut me toucher davantage. Je regrette seulement de ne pouvoir vous envoyer rien de mieux, ni de plus digne d'être traduit par vous. Mais déjà ce simple article m'a pris beaucoup de temps et donné beaucoup de mal à écrire — tout occupé à cette œuvre qu'il présente, il me semble que j'ai perdu tout talent d'écrivain; ma plume ne sait plus que signer des billets de subvention et des bons de logements.

Ma femme vient à Paris dimanche, pour quelques jours — car cette guerre cruelle nous maintient séparés, elle à Cuverville où notre vieille maison de famille hospitalise des parents et des amis — moi à Paris, tout seul, mais occupé chaque jour au "Foyer." Je lui transmettrai votre affectueux message et je sais qu'elle y sera très sensible.

J'aime à vous entendre parler ainsi de Rupert Brooke. C'était l'ami de la fille de mes amis Van Rysselberghe, chez qui j'ai vécu ces cinq dernier mois et auprès de qui j'ai appris sa mort. Toute mon attention était tendue vers lui. C'était aussi le plus intime ami de Jacques Raverat (qui a épousé Mlle Darwin) que vous avez rencontré je crois à Pontigny — et ce deuil m'est aussi sensible que si je l'avais connu moi-même.

Oh! combien j'aimerais vous revoir! Je pense à vous souvent. Veuillez présenter à Madame Edmund Gosse mes affectueux et respectueux hommages. Votre ami bien fidèle   ANDRÉ GIDE.

Notre œuvre a changé de domicile; est à présent 63 Avenue des Champs Elysées et non plus 20 rue Royale ainsi qu'il est dit dans mon article. Il serait sans doute bon d'indiquer la modification.

[Your idea is perfect, and I am deeply grateful to you for it.[1] I love this association of my name with yours, and in no connection could it gratify me more. I am only sorry not to be able to send you something better and more worthy of translating. But this little article has already cost me a lot of time and trouble to write. Swamped as I am by the relief work that it describes, I seem to have lost my ability to write; my pen has forgotten how to do anything but sign appropriations and housing permits.

My wife is coming to Paris Sunday for a few days. For this dreadful war is keeping us apart—her in Cuverville, where our old homestead shelters relatives and friends, me in Paris quite alone, but busy every day at the Foyer. I will give her your very kind message, and I know it will mean much to her.

I am gladdened by what you say about Rupert Brooke. He was a friend of the daughter of my friends the Van Rysselberghes, in whose apartment I have been living these five months past; I was with them when I heard of his death. I was most vividly aware of him. He was the most intimate friend, too, of Jacques Raverat,[2] who married Miss Darwin; I believe you met him at Pontigny. This loss affects me as much as if I had known him myself.

How very much I should love to see you again! I think about you often. Please give Mrs. Gosse my affectionately humble regards.

Our enterprise has a new address: it is now at 63 Avenue des Champs-Elysées, not 20 rue Royale, as my article says. No doubt it would be well to show this change.]

---

[1] What was it? It may be that Gide, rushed as he was, had read Gosse's letter overhastily and misunderstood it as referring to some new collaboration. (Cf. Letter 47, first paragraph.)

[2] Gide's friend Jacques Raverat was a painter who lived in England. A spinal complaint kept him from joining the army. He was envious

of his friend Rupert Brooke, who was "lucky to be in the Dardanelles": he could "be·present at the first mass to be celebrated in Saint
Sophia." Raverat sent to Gide his letters from Brooke after the poet's
death.

49. GIDE TO GOSSE, *July 7, 1915, from the Foyer Franco-Belge, Paris*

BIEN CHER AMI   Ces derniers sonnets de Brooke sont admirables;
je les traduirais volontiers — et aussi, sans doute, un choix de ses
poèmes — ce qui, avec une biographie de Rupert B. et quelques
traductions encore d'articles ou de lettres de lui, pourra bientôt
fournir matière d'un volume qu'éditerait la Nouvelle Revue Française. Pour des raisons autant amicales que littéraires nous serions
désireux de soigner tout particulièrement cette édition. Etes vous en
situation, peut-être, de demander pour moi soit à la famille, soit à
l'éditeur le droit de traduction qui me permettrait de commencer
aussitôt ce travail? Je vous en serais extrêmement obligé.

Ma femme est auprès de moi pour quatre jours. (Le *Foyer* va ɪ ̞
retenir à Paris tout l'été, tandis que d'autres soins retiennent ma femme
à Cuverville) — Elle se joint à moi pour vous envoyer, et à Madame
Gosse, nos meilleurs souvenirs.

Croyez à ma bien fidèle affection.   ANDRÉ GIDE.

[These last sonnets of Brooke's are very fine. I should be
glad to translate them,[1] and undoubtedly a selection of his
poems along with them; these, with a biographical sketch of
Rupert B. and translations of a few more articles or letters of
his, would quickly eke out a volume that the Nouvelle Revue
Française would publish. Out of considerations as much sentimental as literary, we should want to take very special pains
with this publication. Are you by any chance in a position to
ask either the family or the publisher for the translation rights in
my behalf, so that I could begin work right away? I should be
most grateful to you.

My wife is with me for four days. (The Foyer will keep me in Paris all summer, while other duties are keeping my wife in Cuverville.) She joins me in sending you and Mrs. Gosse our best regards.]

¹ Brooke's widely read last sonnets had been published in May, 1915, a few weeks after his death. To Gosse the young poet was the embodiment of patriotism, a sort of English Péguy. A very edifying legend took shape about his life, but "he was neither a trumpet nor a torch ... a smiling and attentive spectator, eager to watch every flourish of the pageantry of life." (Gosse, *Some Diversions of a Man of Letters,* p. 269.) The translation proposed by Gide was never made.

50. GIDE TO GOSSE, *July 19, 1915, from the Foyer Franco-Belge, Paris*

CHER AMI J'ai écrit un mot de remercîment à Mʳ. E. Marsh—mais c'est vous surtout que je veux remercier. Est-ce à vous, ou à lui, que je dois l'envoi du petit volume? que déjà je connaissais, mais que je ne possédais pas encore. — Quel prix cette guerre a donné à tout ce que nous chérissons! Il semble qu'*ensuite,* nous saurons vraiment *pourquoi* vivre. Mais vivrons-nous?

Je suis bien fidèlement et tendrement   votre ANDRÉ GIDE.

[I have sent a note of thanks to Mr. E. Marsh, but you are the one I want to thank most of all. Do I owe the gift of the little book to you or to him?¹ I knew it already, but did not as yet own it. — How precious this war has made all the things that we hold dear! It seems that after it we shall really know what we are living for. Only—shall we be living then?]

¹ The little book contained Rupert Brooke's early poems, written in Cambridge and published in 1911. Gide had simultaneously asked

help from Raverat and from Gosse about permission to translate
and publish Brooke. (Cf. Letter 49.) Edward Howard Marsh, secretary to Winston Churchill, 1917–1922, 1924–1929, was the poet's
executor. He knew of Brooke's admiration for Gide, and he favored
the project, but he needed the assent of Brooke's mother. Gide and
Brooke had planned to meet in 1914; the war intervened.

51. GIDE TO GOSSE, *January 23, 1916, from Villa Montmorency*

BIEN CHER AMI, Si vous ne m'oubliez pas plus que je ne vous oublie,
tout va bien! J'aurais plaisir à causer avec vous de bien des choses,
et je ne désespère pas de vous revoir d'ici peu... Qui m'a parlé d'un
voyage probable de vous en France?... En attendant, je veux vous
entretenir de quelque chose de précis.

Par hasard, ou presque, j'ai lu un livre anglais, que vous connaissez
sans doute: *Mark Rutherford.* Ce livre m'a paru assez remarquable
pour me donner un très vif désir de le traduire. Or, de ce livre, je
ne sais à peu près rien — sinon qu'il serait l'œuvre d'un certain
White Hall (?)... mort ou vivant? je l'ignore. — J'ai lu ce livre —
ou plus précisément: ces deux livres *(The autobiography of Mark
Rutherford* et *Mark Rutherford's Deliverance)* dans la petite collection
Hodder and Stoughton (sevenpenny l.) et la Nouvelle Revue Française s'apprête à écrire à cet éditeur pour traiter des conditions...
mais pas avant que je ne vous ai demandé si peut-être vous êtes à
même de m'apporter quelque lumière, quelque conseil peut-être —
quelque recommandation.

Charles Salomon nous a donné de vos nouvelles à un déjeuner
chez Mrs. Wharton où Jacques Copeau et moi avons eu tant de joie
d'entendre un peu parler de vous!...

Au revoir. Ma femme joint aux miens ses meilleurs souvenirs que
vous voudrez bien transmettre à Madame Gosse avec mes respectueux hommages. Croyez à ma fidèle affection.

ANDRÉ GIDE.

[If you are not forgetting me any more than I am forgetting you, all's well! I should be happy to talk with you about any number of things, and I don't despair of seeing you before long. —Who was it that told me about a prospective visit of yours to France?[1]—Meanwhile I want to consult you about a particular matter.

By chance or nearly so, I read an English book that you undoubtedly know: *Mark Rutherford*.[2] This book seemed to me noteworthy enough to give me a very keen wish to translate it. Now, I know next to nothing about the book, except that it would seem to be the work of one White Hall (?)—whether dead or living, I don't know. I have read the book—or, more precisely, the two books *(The Autobiography of Mark Rutherford* and *Mark Rutherford's Deliverance)*—in the little Hodder and Stoughton collection (sevenpenny l.), and the Nouvelle Revue Française is planning to write to this publisher to discuss terms —but not until I have asked you if you are perhaps in a position to give me some enlightenment, advice, or perhaps endorsement.

Charles Salomon[3] gave us news of you at a luncheon at Mrs. Wharton's,[4] and Jacques Copeau and I had the great pleasure of hearing some little talk about you.

Au revoir. My wife joins me in best regards to you and, please, to Mrs. Gosse.]

[1] Henry Davray was behind the plan to have Gosse visit the war zone. Foreign Minister Delcassé had agreed to sign the necessary papers. The English writer was to be the guest of the General Staff, and an officer was to accompany him. Gosse was to collect evidence of the suffering and destruction wrought by the "barbarians."

[2] It was from Arnold Bennett that Gide heard of *Mark Rutherford*. ("How grateful I am to Bennett for having told me about it!" *Journal,* October 8, 1915.) Gide tried to get information from various persons; Bennett sent him from England a bibliography of the works, some pages of which he thought unrivaled for style, and he was pleased by Gide's wanting to translate them. On January 23, 1916, Gide wrote in the *Journal* that he no longer had any justification at

the Foyer and that he didn't like it there, but at the same period he has frequent mention of reading *Rutherford*.

[3] Charles Salomon, 1859–1925 (professor at the lycée Condorcet), was an orientalist who specialized in Russian; he translated some manuscripts of Tolstoi, whom he had known, and in 1922, the *Nouvelle Revue Française* published letters of Tolstoi that he had collected.

[4] Edith Wharton had been introduced to the Foyer Franco-Belge by Charles Du Bos, and she became its president; it became the Foyer Américain. By 1918 it was taking care of 5,000 refugees, four shelters for the aged, and two sanatoria for women and children. (Edith Wharton, *A Backward Glance*, New York: Appleton, 1934, p. 347.)

52. GOSSE TO GIDE, *January 28, 1916, from London*

DEAR GIDE,   The books (there are *six* of them) written under the pseudonym of "Mark Rutherford" were the work of William Hale White (1829–1913).[1] He was the son of "a compositor in a dingy printing office" at Bedford, who became Doorkeeper to the House of Commons.

I have always greatly admired the "Mark Rutherford" novels. They give a most faithful picture of early Liberalism and of provincial Nonconformity in the forties—time of the Reform Bill, etc....

Hale White lived outside all literary society and very few people knew him. He was a thoroughly isolated figure, but extremely admired within a limited circle of readers. I do not at all wonder that you are pleased with his books, for there is much in them that would naturally attract you.

Have you seen my article in the "Mercure de France" for January 16th?[2] It is a translation by Davray of my article in the "Edinburgh Review" for January. I should like you to see what I have said about our entretiens at Pontigny in 1911. Tell me whether you think what I have written is true and just.

Yours always truly, EDMUND GOSSE

¹ William Hale White was forced to leave a Congregationalist seminary because of his unorthodox ideas. He preached in Unitarian chapels and later turned journalist, critic, and novelist. *The Autobiography of Mark Rutherford,* followed by *Mark Rutherford's Deliverance,* had been published by Fisher Unwin in 1885; they chronicle the life of a young man brought up in a puritan family and obsessed by the question of the life hereafter. Like Dostoevski and Gide, he sees Christ as antithetical to Christianity; he hates evil, but disbelieves in a personal devil. The important thing is to save the "immortal truth," a more vital thing in man than our "poor and wretched being." At the end of a life of vicissitudes he attains peace of mind of a sort. Gide valued White's religious honesty and his beautifully simple style. "...admirable autobiography of M.R.," he wrote in *Dostoievsky;* "life eternal not a thing of the future." Gide translated into French: "I finally learned to live in the present when it was almost too late. Crazy, perpetual running after the future, postponement of happiness to a later date"; and "the doctrine of immortality, men have been able to live happily without it." Gide himself was then experiencing a religious crisis and steeping himself in Pascal and the Bible. (*Journal,* January–February, 1916.)

"French Unity" was the article that Davray translated and published. ("L'Unité Française," *Mercure de France,* January 16, 1916.) The critic rejected the concept of a "new France" bruited by English journalists. The so-called frivolity of the French people, he insisted, was superficial, and he cited Ernest Renan, who had long before denounced pedantic Teutonic science, the *Kultur* that renders man neither kinder nor better. Gosse also paid tribute to his "admirable Pontigny friends" who had remained calm and idealistic through the unnerving Agadir crisis. French unity, endangered by the antimilitarism of a minority, had presently been reborn. Gosse totally discountenanced the "impious suggestion" of a France justly punished for her frivolity, and he found her vitality wonderful but not astonishing. Many in France read and liked his article, among them Jean Schlumberger, who read it at the front when bad weather interrupted his duties as an observer with the Thirty-first Company of the Balloon Corps.

53. GIDE TO GOSSE, *February 6, 1916, from Paris*

BIEN CHER AMI   Non, je n'ai pas lu la traduction de votre article, qui, je l'avoue, m'avait échappé dans le *Mercure* — et, vivant à l'écart, très absorbé par mon travail au Foyer, je ne rencontrais aucun de ceux qui eussent pu m'en parler. — Mais, le lendemain du jour où je vous écrivais au sujet de Rutherford (et merci pour les renseignements précieux que vous me donnez) un ami est venu m'apporter la Edinburgh Review, pour mon plus grand plaisir et réconfort.

Je ne vous ai pas récrit aussitôt, parce que je projetais d'abord, pour quelque revue, une note de réponse ouverte en remerciment *français* à votre article... Mais hélas! — fatigue et manque de temps — je ne suis pas en état d'écrire pour le moment.

Du moins je veux vous dire avec quelle *reconnaissance* je vous félicitais de savoir retrouver sous la France nouvelle si admirable, l'ancienne, celle qui n'a jamais cessé d'exister: "not a new France, miraculously created, but the old France, *welded together,* and passed through the fire of affliction." Cela est excellent.

Et je vous sais gré également d'être, pour nos vieux défauts français, plus indulgent que je ne peux l'être. Vous les couvrez généreusement, ces vieux défauts, parce que vous connaissez bien les Français et que vous savez quelle générosité nous emporte et quelle abnégation, jusque dans nos pires erreurs. Nul plus que le Français, en général, ne vit plus pour les autres, ou en fonction des autres, ou par rapport aux autres; de là tout aussi bien sa vanité, sa politesse, son amour de la politique, la prise qu'il offre à l'émulation, la peur du ridicule, le souci de la mode, etc.

En première page du *Petit Journal Illustré,* j'admirais l'autre jour une image (et qui m'exaspérait aussi) représentant la "prise d'armes" d'un soldat grièvement blessé; étendu sur un lit d'hopital, il se redressait à demi, à l'approche du général qui venait pour le décorer, s'écriait (ainsi que le rapportait la légende): "La croix de guerre, mon général, ça se reçoit debout" — puis retombait mort, exténué

par cet effort de parade. C'est admirable, et c'est absurde — bien dans
la tradition qui déjà faisait dire à Bossuet: "Les maximes du faux honneur, qui ont fait périr tant de monde parmi nous..."

Cher ami, combien j'aime vous entendre dire: "If France has of
late laughed less, her smile has on occasion been more beautiful than
ever."

Au revoir. Bien amicalement ANDRÉ GIDE.

Excellent le passage sur Péguy, sur Pontigny — tout l'article —

[No, I haven't read the translation of your article; I confess I
missed seeing it in the *Mercure,* and, living aloof and buried in
my work at the Foyer, I ran into none of the ones who might
have mentioned it to me. But the day after I wrote you about
Rutherford—and thank you for the valuable information that
you give me—a friend brought me the *Edinburgh Review,* to my
infinite pleasure and gratification.[1]

I did not write you again forthwith because I was planning to
write first, for some magazine, an open letter of response by
way of a *French* acknowledgment of your article. But, alas, what
with fatigue and lack of time, I am in no shape to do writing
for the time being.

At least I want to tell you how gratefully I was congratulating
you on being able to rediscover, underneath this wonderful new
France, the old France that has never ceased to exist—"not a
new France, miraculously created, but the old France, *welded
together,* and passed through the fire of affliction." That is admirable.

And I am no less grateful to you for being more charitable to
our chronic French shortcomings than I myself can be. You gen-
erously condone these chronic shortcomings, because you know
the French people well, and you understand what generosity
actuates us and what spirit of self-sacrifice, even through our
worst mistakes. No one ordinarily outdoes the Frenchman in
living for others, or in relation to others; hence his vanity, his
politeness, his fondness for politics, the store he sets on sur-

passing his fellows, his dread of ridicule, his deference to fashion, and so on.

There is a picture on the first page of the *Petit Journal Illustré* that I was admiring the other day and being irritated by, too: it shows the *prise d'armes* of a soldier with a serious wound, stretched out on a hospital bed but struggling to draw himself up at the approach of the general coming to confer a decoration; he exclaims (as the caption has it): "General, sir, the Croix de Guerre is received standing," and falls back dead, finished by the strain of showing off. That is admirable, and it is ridiculous —exactly in the tradition that produced Bossuet's saying about "the mottoes of false pride that have destroyed so many of us."

My dear friend, I do love your saying: "If France has of late laughed less, her smile has on occasion been more beautiful than ever."

Au revoir.

Splendid, the passage about Péguy, about Pontigny—the whole piece.]

[1] On February 2 Gide wrote in the *Journal:* "Tried to write Gosse in reply to his article on France. I spent the better part of the morning on it and produced nothing worth while." The *Journal* shows a seriously disturbed Gide. He is upset by the way the Foyer is functioning; he is in the midst of religious doubts; small complications are exacerbating him. (*Journal,* February 4.) On February 5 he copies into the *Journal* the greater part of his letter to Gosse.

Gide abandoned the idea of translating *Mark Rutherford*. In his *Voyage au Congo* (1927) he wrote: "...the interest I have in it is a little too particular." Religious questions did not now engage him as formerly; he had been rereading these books in the desert, but presently he was preferring Part II of *Faust*. His *Journal* often shows his annoyance at French faults—negligence, unsteadiness, lack of foresight. During this February he often quotes Bossuet; he is re-reading the *Elévations sur les mystères* and thinking of writing a counterpart of *Les Nourritures terrestres,* a book of "meditations and aspirations."

54. GIDE TO GOSSE, *July 3, 1916, from Cuverville*

MON CHER AMI   Je vais vous donner quelques nouvelles de nous
dans l'espoir d'en obtenir de vous quelques autres. Quel long silence! Pourtant je pense à vous souvent, très souvent — chaque fois
que je pense à l'Angleterre, c'est à dire chaque jour. Je soupçonne
ma dernière lettre* de ne vous être jamais parvenue — où je vous
parlais longuement de votre bel article de la Edinb. Rev. que je
venais de lire avec une émotion si vive. Depuis, diverses raisons,
d'ordre moral, psychologique, ou ... économique, nous ont forcé
de quitter Paris, et c'est à Cuverville que ma femme et moi venons
de passer ces trois derniers mois. J'y ai travaillé de mon mieux, à
ce que j'appelle mes "œuvres posthumes" — c'est à dire sans aucun
souci de publication; mais on a la tête et le cœur accaparés par l'idée
de la guerre, et par ce qu'il faut appeler: l'angoisse de l'espérance.
Si distants que nous soyons du front, croiriez vous qu'à l'écho de la
canonnade anglaise notre vieille maison tremble toute! C'est un roule-
ment ininterrompu, depuis douze jours; et l'on pense: comme nos
amis travaillent bien! Ah! puisse le triomphe ne pas leur être trop
cruel!

Agnès Copeau et ses deux plus jeunes enfants sont auprès de nous;
Jacques et sa fille ainée viennent aujourd'hui même la rejoindre, pour
la remmener bientôt au Limon. Peut-être aurez-vous appris que Copeau vient de faire une "tournée" à Genève où il était convié à venir
monter Barberine, la Femme tuée par la douceur, et le Pain de ménage; il semble avoir remporté un vrai succès.

Il fait là-bas quelques pressantes démarches pour obtenir le trans-
fert en Suisse de notre ami Jacques Rivière, qui, depuis Octobre
1914 est prisonnier là bas, et nous semblait à bout de résistance.
Mais une lettre de lui nous prie de renoncer à toutes démarches, disant

---

* du 5 février! qu'il y a longtemps déjà! (A. G.)

qu'il *veut* supporter jusqu'au bout son épreuve, et qu'il ne se pardon-
nerait pas d'avoir fait quoi que ce soit pour l'alléger.

Marcel Drouin, mon beau-frère, travaille depuis un mois, à Belfort, ainsi que Jean Schlumberger, auprès de l'Etat Major — leur
rôle est de prendre connaissance de tous les journaux allemands et
d'écrire quotidiennement un résumé de la situation intérieure et, si
j'ose dire, une carte de l'état des esprits — à l'usage de nos chefs mi-
litaires. Le travail est très absorbant mais des plus intéressants, di-
sent-ils.

Dominique Drouin, mon neveu, s'est engagé et fait son in-
struction de dragon à Saumur. L'élan, l'enthousiasme de ces jeunes
est admirable; j'ai pu croire d'abord qu'il entrait un peu d'ostentation
dans ce déploiement d'héroïsme, mais non, l'enthousiasme est réel,
profond, grave, et c'est dans toute la sincérité de leur cœur qu'ils
souhaitent s'offrir au danger, et s'impatientent de ne pouvoir aller
sur le front tout de suite.

De même tous nos petits soldats de Cuverville — je veux dire les
enfants des paysans d'ici — sont héroïques; déjà plus d'un est tombé,
et l'on s'attend à de nouveaux deuils car la gloire que nous préparons
à Verdun est sanglante — mais tout de même nos amis immédiats
n'ont pas été trop éprouvés ces derniers temps.

Cher ami, vous m'écrirez, n'est-ce pas? Ne fût-ce qu'un mot, il me
ferait tant de plaisir!

Ma femme se rappelle au meilleur souvenir de Madame Gosse, à
qui vous voudrez bien présenter mes hommages. Agnès Copeau
joint aux nôtres ses plus affectueux messages. Je suis bien fidèlement
votre ami.

ANDRÉ GIDE.

[I am going to give you some news of us in the hope of receiving some of you.[1] What a long silence! Just the same, I
think of you often, very often—every time I think of England,
and that means every day. I suspect that my last letter* never
reached you—one in which I wrote at length about your fine

* of February 5 — what a time ago! (A. G.)

Edinburgh Review article, which I had just read with such great emotion.[2] Since then various considerations of a moral, mental or—economic sort have compelled us to leave Paris, and it is at Cuverville that my wife and I have spent these three months past. I have been working here as best I could at what I call my posthumous works—that is, without any concern for publication; but one's mind and heart are monopolized by the thought of the war and by what I can only call the agony of hope. Far as we are from the front, under the reverberation of English gunfire this old house of ours, if you can believe it, shudders bodily. There has been an incessant thundering for the twelve days past, and we think: What fine work our friends are doing! Oh, may victory not be too hard on them!

Agnès Copeau and her two youngest children are here with us; Jacques and his elder daughter get here this very day to join her and take her back shortly to the Limon.[3] You may have heard that Copeau has just been "on tour" to Geneva, where he had been asked to go to stage *Barberine, La femme tuée par la douceur,* and *Le Pain de ménage;* he seems to have scored a real success.

While there he made some energetic attempts to effect the transfer to Switzerland of our friend Jacques Rivière,[4] who has been a prisoner ever since October, 1914, and seemed to us at the end of his endurance. But a letter from him begged us to give up all attempts: he *wants* to undergo his trial to the end, and he could not forgive himself for doing anything to lighten it.

Marcel Drouin,[5] my brother-in-law, has been working for the past month at Belfort, as Jean Schlumberger has, at General Headquarters. Their job is to follow all the German newspapers and write a daily summary of the internal situation and, if I dare say so, a chart of the German state of mind, for the use of our military chiefs. Their work is very demanding but most interesting, they say.

Dominique Drouin, my nephew, has enlisted and is taking his cavalry training at Saumur. The dash, the ardor of these youngsters is wonderful; I couldn't help thinking at first that there was a bit of showing off in this parade of heroism. But not so: their enthusiasm is real, deep, sober; it is in all simplicity of heart that they yearn to give themselves up to danger, and they chafe at not being able to get to the front immediately.

In the same way all our little Cuverville soldiers—I mean the peasants' sons of the region—are heroic; more than one has already fallen, and we foresee more losses, for the glory that we have in the making at Verdun is a bloody one. Still, none of our very close friends has been too hard pressed on these latest occasions.

My dear friend, you will write to me, won't you? Even if it were just a note, it would give me so much pleasure!

My wife wants to be warmly remembered to Mrs. Gosse, to whom please give my regards. Agnès Copeau adds her most affectionate greetings to ours.]

[1] The Gides left Paris on March 27 to settle down in Cuverville, where Gide stayed until early July, except for three days in Paris with Ghéon, on leave April 13–17.

[2] The *Journal* for March 3 says: "Written to Mrs. Wharton, to Gosse and to a journalist." This March letter to Gosse is missing. Since Letter 54 identifies his preceding one as that of February 5, he may not have sent the letter mentioned in the *Journal*. On March 16 again: "Written to Mrs. Wharton, to Ghéon and to Gosse." This letter to Gosse is also missing. On June 16 there is a hiatus; Gide wrote on June 15: "I have torn out about twenty pages of this notebook;... I feel an immense upset.... The pages I tore up seemed like pages written by a madman." On September 5 he records a terrible crisis for which he blames "Em." (Mme. Gide).

[3] "Le Limon" was Jacques Copeau's country house in Seine-et-Marne. There, in 1913, Copeau had assembled a company to rehearse and to prepare for the opening of the Vieux-Colombier. Copeau added the following postscript to Gide's letter:

Jacques Copeau to Edmund Gosse [Cuverville, July 3, 1916]

MY DEAR FRIEND, I want to add a few words to Gide's letter, to let you know that I too am thinking of you. I have wanted many times to write you. I have not done so because we have spent the past two years in suspense and torment; we have lost the inclination, the wish, almost the power, to speak. But I remember you steadfastly, and let me thank you—as doubtless many before me have done—for your beautiful *Edinburgh Review* article.

Like all of us who have not the honor of fighting for France, of serving France, I strive as best I can to turn our sublime ordeal to the preparation of a better future for ourselves and for those who are to follow us—for our children growing up. There has begun the fighting in unison that is to lead to victory. This in itself should suffice to persuade you that never before have we thought of our English friends with more warmth.

An affectionate handshake to you.   J. COPEAU

⁴ Jacques Rivière was a prisoner in the Königsberg and Hülseberg camps. The prisoners organized discussions in which each talked about what he knew best. Rivière had decided "to speak about God." During his imprisonment he wrote *A la Trace de Dieu* and *Journal de Captivité* (1915). When he was freed, Gide went to Engelberg in Switzerland to meet him.

⁵ Marcel Drouin, whose pen name was Michel Arnaud, had met Gide through Pierre Louÿs. Drouin married Mme. Gide's sister Jeanne. Gide wrote in the *Journal* in 1891: "M. Drouin is perhaps the person I like best in the world." Dominique Drouin, his son, enlisted at seventeen and was sent to the battlefront in March, 1918. During Gide's later years Dominique was for some time his secretary.

55. GOSSE TO GIDE, *July 12, 1916, from London*

MY DEAR GIDE,   I was rejoiced to get your letter, and learn your news. We live here in a great excitement.¹ The War seems to have developed to a pitch beyond which human endurance can scarcely be strained. The diabolic strength of Germany is horrible to contemplate, but all our hopes are lively. Whatever happens, the blazon of glorious France will fill the world for ever.

I sent you a long letter of thanks for your very charming letter some months ago, but it seems never to have reached you.[2] Now I am sending you my new book, my War Essays collected.[3] Let me hear that it reaches you.

We have Maurice Barrès[4] here. I entertain him at dinner tomorrow night, to meet some representative men.

We are very busy. It is the only way to forget the strain of the war. Our son[5] is at Béthune, at the front. Imagine what we go through! He has been out there for just a year, and had men killed on each side of him, but he lives still.

Give Mme. Gide and all our kind dear friends our love. It is a wonderful thing to be alive in such a world. But all the honour, all the glory, concentrates on France. Good-bye, my dear Gide. Do write to me.

Ever yours sincerely, EDMUND GOSSE

[1] The great excitement was the Battle of the Somme, July 1–November 18.

[2] The letter is missing.

[3] Gosse's war essays were entitled *Inter Arma*. The volume contained pieces already printed in the *Edinburgh Review,* most of them about France; the article mentioned in Letter 52 was among them.

[4] Maurice Barrès turns up in the "Book of Gosse" for July 13: "Dinner at Ritz.—M. Maurice Barrès, Lord Haldane, Mr. Harold Cox, Mr. Antonio Cippico, Sir George Frampton, Mr. E. Gye, Sir Ray Lankester, Mr. Thorold, W. Heinemann, Sir Maurice de Bunsen, Captain Philip Millet." On July 20 Barrès went to the Gosses' for tea. Gosse had known him for many years. Barrès had been invited by the British government to spend a few days in England that he might give the French people a more circumstantial realization of the English war effort. He visited camps, arsenals, industrial plants, and colleges. On July 12 he gave a lecture in London, which Gosse attended. He was entertained by Asquith and Lloyd George. (Barrès, *Voyage en Angleterre, L'Ame Française et la guerre,* Paris: Emile-Paul, 1919, X, 15–26.)

⁵ Gosse's only son, Philip (1879———), had enlisted in 1914. A medical man, he had been assigned to the Sixty-ninth War Ambulance Corps. He served first on the Somme; in September, 1917, in India, and later in Salonika. (Philip Gosse, *Memoirs of a Camp Follower,* London: Wyman and Son, 1934.)

56. GIDE TO GOSSE, *July 27, 1916, from Cuverville* [?]

BIEN CHER AMI   Cette longue lettre de vous perdue me désole. Je sais que vous m'y parliez d'une manière qui m'eût fait tant de bien à entendre... Du moins j'ai bien reçu votre dernière, et votre livre, dans lequel aussitôt je me suis plongé, car je ne connaissais qu'un seul des articles. Le sujet est passionnant. Il me plaît que vous ayez senti le besoin de rajouter un postscriptum au premier article; mais ce que j'aime dans votre livre tout entier, c'est, à côté de son enthousiasme latent, sa prudence. Ce que vous y dites est vrai, et *restera* vrai; et repose de tant de choses qu'on écrit aujourd'hui et qui ne sont vraies qu'en fonction d'un état d'esprit de circonstance.

La constatation des rapports avec 70 (ou plutôt: de l'absence de rapports) est des plus instructifs. "...a suspension, not a determination." Evidemment là est la grande différence. La tape qui en 70 nous a tout à coup assis par terre, est restée pour ainsi dire extérieure à la France. L'admirable aujourd'hui, c'est que le coup de clairon du 2 Août ait retenti au cœur même de la patrie. — Aujourd'hui l'on peut chercher en France quel homme de lettres n'aura pas écrit "sur la guerre"; je crois aussi qu'il y cherche une excuse de ne pas être sous les drapeaux. Certains auteurs néanmoins trouvent le moyen de combattre et d'écrire tout à la fois. A mon avis les écrits datés du front tranchent nettement sur ceux de l'arrière; l'accent en est tout autre, et je crois qu'une sage critique devra se garder, plus tard, de les assimiler. Pour un peu je dirais qu'il n'y a que ces derniers qui comptent — je parle des poèmes, naturellement — et je songe en particulier au dernier livre de Ghéon, que vous aurez reçu et dont l'*authenticité* vous aura frappé sans nul doute (en particulier la partie du livre intitulée "Prières").

Pour moi je suis tout étonné encore de m'être remis à travailler; oui; depuis quatre mois; le Foyer dont je m'occupais depuis octobre 1914 fonctionne à présent d'une manière toute administrative et ma présence y était devenue peu nécessaire; tant que je m'en occupais j'y donnais tout mon temps, j'ai préféré m'en retirer complètement — et depuis quatre mois je me donne complètement au travail. (Mais je crois que je vous disais déjà tout cela dans ma dernière lettre...)

Au revoir cher ami; je pense à vous souvent. Les dernières semaines ont été pour l'Angleterre glorieuses et cruelles — puissent votre famille et vos amis n'avoir pas été trop directement éprouvés!

Veuillez me rappeler au meilleur souvenir de Madame Gosse et lui présenter mes hommages — et croire à mon amitié fidèle

ANDRÉ GIDE.

[I am distressed by the loss of that long letter of yours. I know that in it you were talking to me in a vein that it would have done me no end of good to hear. Anyway, I have duly received your latest letter; also your book,[1] which I plunged into right away, for I knew only one of the articles. The subject is a stirring one. I am glad that you felt the need to add a post-script to the first article.[2] But what I love in your whole book, over and above the underlying fervor, is its wisdom. What you say is true, and it will *stay* true; and that in spite of a lot of things being written these days that are true only as matching a transient mood.

Your exposition of the analogies with 1870—or rather of the lack of analogies—is uncommonly illuminating. "...*a suspension, not a determination*"—clearly, that is the great difference. The blow that suddenly struck us down in 1870, one might say, left France untouched. What is inspiriting today is that the bugle call of August 2 reverberated in the very heart of our country. You can comb France in vain today for the man of letters who has not written "on the war"; indeed, I think the man of letters tries to find in his writing a justification for not being with the colors. Nevertheless some writers are managing to fight and at the same time to write. To my mind, the writing from the front shows a sharp contrast with that done behind the battle zone; it has an altogether different ring, and I think informed criticism will have to take care later on not to confuse the two. I would almost go so far as to say that only the second kind matters—I am speaking of poems of course,—and I have particularly in mind Ghéon's latest book;[3] which you will have received; you will doubtless have been impressed by its *genuineness* (especially the section called "Prayers").

As for me, I keep on being astonished to find myself back at work. Yes, these four months! The Foyer, with which I was busied from October, 1914, is now entirely a matter of administration, and I had come to be not much needed in it any more. Since, as long as I was working at it, I gave it all my time, I preferred to withdraw from it altogether, and for four months now I have been applying myself entirely to my own work. (But I believe I told you all this in my previous letter.)

Good-by for now, my dear friend. You are often in my thoughts. These past weeks have been glorious ones for England; dreadful ones, too. I hope your own family and your friends have escaped being too directly afflicted.

Please remember me kindly to Mrs. Gosse and give her my regards.]

---

[1] The book was *Inter Arma.* "War and Literature," its opening article, of October, 1914, examined how writers had been affected by the war. In England it had forced them out of their "lethargy of dilettantism." In Belgium a young and brilliant literature had been brought to a standstill; the learned Germans had deliberately destroyed libraries and works of art. But "our beloved France," an indispensable part of the spiritual wealth of the world, could not die. Gosse expressed the prophetic sentiment that even if all France were to be invaded, Roland's horn would be heard and the country delivered from her enemies and God's. The critic harked back to the

Franco-Prussian War, after which writers had resumed their literary activity as early as June, 1871.

² The postscript, added in April, 1915, discussed the effect of the war on French writing: England's writers were still at work, but France had been too deeply wounded, and almost no one continued productive.

³ Ghéon's *Foi en la France,* war poems dedicated to the French soldiers, was published by the Nouvelle Revue Française in 1916. It contained:

I. *Prelude de la Paix,* 1909–1914, patriotic poems.

II. *Hymnes et Chants,* 1915, a poem on Paul Déroulède, one on Verhaeren, and a long and beautiful Round of the Communion of Men, from which the German people was excluded until it should become worthy.

III. *Feuillets,* poems of religious intimation.

IV. *Prières,* dedicated to the memory of Lieutenant Commander P. Dupouey, killed on the Yser on Easter Eve, April 3, 1915, expressive of a deep and pervasive emotion—

> Ami, vous êtes ma pensée
>
> . . . . .
>
> Et c'est votre image qui luit
> Au ciel que j'aime et dont je doute.
>
> (May 7, 1915)

V. *Discours Lyriques,* to the memory of Charles Péguy, killed in action September 5, 1914, written in a manner reminiscent of Péguy's highly individual poetic style.

> O paysan, ô maître d'école, ô poète
> Et avant tout, de naissance troupier!
> Petit troupier, cher troupier, qui aime les routes,
> Les routes plates, les routes longues,
> les routes infinies de Beauce.

57. GOSSE TO GIDE, *September 16, 1916, from London*

MY DEAR GIDE, I am coming to Paris, next Tuesday (the 19th).¹ I have been invited by M. Briand as the guest of the French Government.

Of course, I have accepted, but with great apprehension, for I am getting old (I shall be 67 next week) and I am not in good health. However, I must obey. M. Briand's invitation was the most flattering that any one could receive. I am to be taken to Reims. If only I shall be inspired to write something ever so infinitesimally useful to France,—my adored and adorable France!

Every day I pray that I may live to see the final and glorious victory of France. How slow history is, and how rapidly life ebbs away!

I suppose I shall not see you, alas! I have written for René Doumic's "Revue des Deux Mondes," an article on the literary entente.[2] Very stupid—and I don't like my own style in a different language. But— I had to accede to Doumic's wish. I took pleasure in hauling in *your* name, my dear! à propos de bottes!

Ghéon's poems were sent to me by the publishers. I read them with great emotion, and wrote him at once a long letter. Ask him whether he received it: I should like a post-card from him.

Our son, after nearly 14 months at the front, is still unwounded: but we live in the constant anguish of anxiety.

In Paris, I believe I am to be put up by the Government at the Hotel Crillon.

                              Ever your affectionate Friend EDMUND GOSSE

My wife joins me in all best messages.

---

[1] On September 28, 1915, Gosse wrote his friend Earl Spencer about his approaching November trip to France: "A fortnight ago I received a wholly unexpected invitation from M. Delcassé, through the Embassy, to go to France as the guest of the French Government and describe the state of things behind the front. I telegraphed back I must refuse so great an honour on account of my health. But Delcassé would not take my refusal and an emissary of his—a very interesting M. Leyret, who was Waldeck-Rousseau's private secretary—called here on Monday and would not go until I consented. I cannot see the utility of it to them, and I told him so. They declare they want a statement from me, 'sentimental and intellectual'! I feel dreadfully unfitted for the task, and ready to weep with apprehension,

but I could not continue to refuse. It is a tremendous compliment, but like being slain with gold pieces." (Charteris, *op. cit.,* p. 382.) Administrative slowness had delayed the trip. After the Delcassé cabinet fell, Aristide Briand renewed the invitation. For further details see the two letters of Henry Davray, below.

Henry Davray to Edmund Gosse, September 15, 1915, from Waldorf Hotel, Aldwych, W.C. (In English after the salutation)

CHER MAITRE ET GRAND AMI,   Here is the news I was eagerly looking for. I am in a position to let you know confidentially that the Ministre des Affaires Etrangères, Mr. Delcassé, has been pleased to approve and sign the proposition concerning your visit to France, our dear France. You will be the guest of our General Staff; a distinguished officer will take you wherever you like, in a comfortable closed motor, and you need not fear any trouble, any danger, nor the slightest difficulty. You will be officially informed of the fact through the embassy but, meanwhile, I have been asked to arrange with you as to the approximate date of your going over to the front.

I know what it means for you, I perfectly conceive you may be afraid of the fatigue for your health, that you may dread the consequence for your "verte vieillesse"; but I assure you there are no hardships to face, no particularly youthful energy to display. Whenever you have a day out in the zone des armées you may come back to your quarters and rest as long as you like. Be confident that everything will be managed so that you are very much tempted and that you desire, in your inner heart, to pay that visit to the country you have been the faithful friend of so long! You may even feel it a duty to go and bear witness to her sufferings and also to her glory. What you shall see, you will tell, and you will be heard not only at the present time, in your own country, our ally, but in these countries, the Scandinavian and the American where your name is honored among the best and it is for the times to come we all want witnesses against the Barbarians, so that the race of brutes who have killed innocent and inoffensive women and children, dishonoured our women folk, wantonly destroyed peaceful homes and time respected monuments of beauty have to bear the burden of their crimes, the mark of infamy. The France you have known happy and smiling in her welcome to her friend you will see in her ordeal sad, proud, and unflinching. She wants you to come in her dire hour; friends are welcome at such moments and her smile will have a keenness and a gravity that will make you love her more.

What you will tell the world will be unlike all others have said, because no other like you has gone, no one knows the spirit, the soul of France, no one is familiar with so many parts of the country. Your testimonial will remain and be a link between your country and mine, a living commentary on history in the making . . . .

Henry Davray to Edmund Gosse, September 19, 1916, from London

DEAR SIR AND FRIEND,   It was not without regret that I saw you set out . . . without me, just a little while ago; but I know you are in safe hands. Everybody will be watching over you, and you will realize that I am not alone in cherishing you. If you should have any sort of message to be conveyed, do not hesitate to ask Millet to have it telephoned to me, and I will relay it. Also, give your mail to Millet; it will arrive promptly by way of the King's messenger, and I will forward it. Millet is to arrange a luncheon to which Vallette, Dumur, Vielé-Griffin, Gide etc. will come. Ask him to invite all the young friends and admirers you wish to see. If you need some copies of *Père et Fils,* please ask Vallette for them, for he will be happy to give them to you. I wish you an agreeable and interesting stay.   H.-D. DAVRAY

² The *Revue des Deux Mondes* published on October 1, 1916, a translation of Gosse's article "La France et l'Angleterre, l'avenir de leurs relations intellectuelles," in which the critic discussed the spiritual aspects of the war and the necessity of discerning more clearly the defects and dangers of German culture and of forming closer postwar ties between France and England. Gosse deplored the French neglect of great writers such as Meredith, Henry James, and Thomas Hardy, in contrast to the popularity of Kipling and Wells. English readers were more familiar with French novelists; MM. Bourget, Gide, Bazin, and Prévost had enthusiastic admirers. The French example would help English imaginative literature ac-

quire form and a better sense of proportion; France was the guide, the beacon light of the Allies, and her influence would speed the rebuilding of the traditional European civilization.

On October 9 Gide confided to his *Journal* that Gosse was "playing on words, confusing European culture with European literature," and he wrote no congratulations to his English friend. He may have been not too pleased to find himself bracketed with Bourget, Bazin, and Prévost. At any rate, Gosse himself was not overpleased with the piece. (Cf. Letter 57.)

58. GIDE TO GOSSE, *September 20, 1916, from Paris*[1]

BIEN CHER AMI, J'accours de Cuverville où j'ai reçu votre lettre avant-hier. Je ne puis supporter l'idée que vous veniez en France et que je ne vous verrais pas.

Si "officiel" que soit votre voyage, tout de même vous saurez bien trouver, j'en suis sûr, un petit instant à donner à l'amitié. Déjà j'irais ce soir vous attendre à l'arrivée du train si je ne pensais que quelqu'un soit là pour vous recevoir.

A tout hasard je viendrai ici, demain matin, vers onze heures, vous demander — et, si ce moment ne convient pas, un mot de vous peut-être saura m'en indiquer un autre. Je ne suis à Paris que pour vous revoir.

Votre ANDRÉ GIDE.

Ne fût-ce qu'un petit instant.

Comme c'est bien à vous de venir! Quel brave ami vous faites... je veux dire ami de la France et que je suis heureux d'être Français!

[I come posthaste from Cuverville, where I got your letter day before yesterday. I can't endure the thought of your coming to France without my seeing you.

However official your trip may be, you will nevertheless manage, I am sure, to find a moment to give to friendship. I should already be waiting for you on the arrival of your train this evening if I did not think someone will be there to welcome you.

In any event I shall come here tomorrow morning around eleven to inquire for you; and if that is not convenient, maybe you could leave a note naming some other time? I am in Paris for no reason but to see you again.

Even if it were for but a moment. How good of you to have come! What a grand friend you are—I mean, friend of France; and how happy I am to be a Frenchman!]

[1] Gide left this note at the Crillon Hotel on September 20. His *Journal,* September 19, says: "This evening I am going to Paris; my pretext is to meet Gosse, whom Briand has invited here. I shall be extremely happy to see him again and I am not doing anything worth while here." Gide was still extremely depressed, and he believed that evil, the devil himself, had hold of him. He hated himself. Any excuse to leave Cuverville was welcome. The substance of his moral crisis is recorded in *Et nunc manet in te.*

59. GOSSE TO GIDE, *September 20, 1916, from the Crillon, Paris*

Only this evening, dearest Gide, I arrived, to find you had so kindly called and left a letter.

Tomorrow I go with Maurice Barrès to Reims.

I have asked Capt. Philip Millet[1] to let me ask you and Vielé-Griffin to déjeuner here one day.[2] It is difficult to fix, because M. Briand will have me go some day to him. Millet will arrange it.

It is *wonderful* to be in France again! Ever your devoted

EDMUND GOSSE

¹ Philippe Millet was a young journalist and writer. When drafted, he was attached to the Maison de la Presse. After the war he became colonial editor of *Le Temps* and foreign affairs editor of *Paris-Midi,* in which he published an article on Edmund Gosse's seventieth birthday. He was assigned to accompany the critic because of his command of English. He had accompanied Maurice Barrès during Barrès' English tour two months before.

² On September 22 Gide was Gosse's guest at the Crillon, and that evening he wrote in his *Journal:* "This morning, lunch with Gosse at the Crillon. More wearing than pleasurable. The conversation exhausts me. Gosse is exquisitely cordial. Nevertheless I felt, two or three times, that perhaps I was approaching a bit too closely." On October 3, back in Cuverville, he described the encounter at greater length and with more candor: "I had gone to meet Gosse at the Hotel Crillon, where the Propaganda Ministry had reserved a very pleasant apartment of three rooms for him. He was expecting me. I was taken up; it was on the third floor. I found the same old Gosse barely a bit older-looking; slightly shriveled, thinned out in spots. As in the past, his movements seemed to me prompted perhaps a bit more by his mind than by his heart, or at least by a sort of self-respect. Intelligence, which with him always has a weather-eye, intervenes and checks him on the slope of surrender. He begins to catch himself at the moment when I was beginning to like him. Moreover, it is perhaps not so much me as himself that he distrusts.

"As soon as I come in, effusion; our four hands are joined for some time; then I sit down. And he, after a very brief silence, which seemed intended to catch his breath, as if yielding to an irresistible impulse (yet it was a trifle put on):

" 'Ah, dear friend, let us embrace once more.'

"Seeing an invitation in these words, I rise from my chair and, rushing toward him, apply to both his flabby cheeks two big kisses in the French manner. He jumped a bit, drew back almost imperceptibly with a slight grimace immediately hidden, but from which I recognized that he intended to remain master of the situation and tell me just how far to go and no farther, that by taking literally his 'let us embrace' I was forgetting that he spoke French only half well and that, in short, for the English, so chary of demonstrations, a prolonged handshake was better than any embrace. I can imagine Gosse later on asking Millet, his guide, or someone else: 'But tell me, sir, when you want to shake someone's hand in the middle of a conversation, how do you say this in good French? Just imagine that the other day, having had the imprudence to say to Gide: "Let us embrace," I find him actually embracing me! It was absurd.'"

To Osbert Sitwell this incident was simply part of the "cat-and-mouse technique" that Gosse had made his own. "He wished Gide to come a modified cropper, and to be left in consequence with a slight and rankling sense of inferiority in social experience and usage: in which design he evidently succeeded." (*Noble Essences,* London: Macmillan, 1950, p. 62.) Other English writers have mentioned Gosse's biting humor and his malice; Somerset Maugham, for example, said: "For many years Gosse had been acquainted with eminent persons. I think he was a vain man and he had observed their absurdities with satisfaction." (*The Summing Up,* New York: Doubleday, Doran and Company, 1938, p. 5.) It seems to me that the words "once more" indicate simply that Gosse wanted to shake hands again with the friend he had not seen for so long, and that he was really surprised and annoyed by the double kiss. As Gide says, he did not speak French with ease.

60. GOSSE TO GIDE, *Sunday, September 24, 1916, from the Crillon, Paris*

MY DEAR GIDE,   P. Millet tells me that he has arranged with you to see me to Havre on Tuesday evening.[1] How charming of you, and how delightful for me. P. M. will make all the dispositions for us.

I had 4 (quatre!) hours with M. Briand yesterday.[2] Epatant! Quel homme de génie!

Ever your affectionate EDMUND GOSSE

[1] Gide's return to Cuverville on the train that took Gosse to Le Havre on September 26 did not occur: Gide stayed in Paris until September 29.

[2] On September 25 Gosse wrote again to his friend Earl Spencer: "I wait for the tootling of M. Briand's motor, which is in a few min-

utes to take me—a long day's adventure—over the whole battle-field of the Marne. It is hopeless to give you an impression of my wonderful week—doubtless the most wonderful of my life. I have seen Reims, I have been taken along the Champagne front, where at Cernay I was suddenly and unexpectedly under fire for a few minutes (an enchanting experience in dram-drinking!). I have been (what I believe no other Englishman has ever been) entertained at dinner by the Académie Française. Perhaps most interesting of all I have seen M. Briand in the intimacy of his house, and I have had several hours of his conversation.

"The French are the most glorious people in the world. I always suspected and now I know it.

But adieu! I shall be back in England almost before this reaches you." (Charteris, *op. cit.,* p. 396.)

Gosse does not mention here his visit with Gide, which was no part of his official trip.

61. GIDE TO GOSSE, *December 21, 1916, from Cuverville*

BIEN CHER AMI Je vous aurais écrit plus tôt, et je vous écrirais mieux aujourd'hui, si je n'étais repris depuis quelque temps par cette fatigue de tête qui m'a déjà si souvent empêché dans la vie... Mais si imparfait que doive être ce mot, il vaudra mieux pourtant que le silence.

Je pense que la mort de Verhaeren vous aura beaucoup affecté, car il avait pour vous une affection très vive. La guerre m'avait beaucoup rapproché de lui, et comme son ami le plus intime, Théo Van Rysselberghe, était condamné au repos à la suite d'une petite opération, c'est à moi qu'est revenu le triste soin de prévenir Madame Verhaeren et de la soutenir durant ces premières journées de deuil. Vous savez déjà que c'est à La Panne que repose à présent notre ami. Ce que fut ce pèlerinage sur ce lambeau de terre encore belge, je vous laisse l'imaginer. Durant tout le voyage et la funèbre cérémonie la beauté, la noblesse, l'héroïsme l'emportaient de loin sur la tristesse — ainsi qu'il convenait pour Verhaeren. Si affreuse qu'ait été cette mort, je songe qu'on pourrait dire à son sujet ce que Pater écrivait au sujet de celle de Winkelmann [*sic*]: "It seemed as if the gods had given him a death which, for its swiftness and its opportunity, he might well have desired." — Mais depuis que je ne le sais plus là, il me semble que le ciel s'est un peu refroidi.

Quel regret qu'il n'ait pu venir à ce déjeuner à l'hôtel Crillon...! J'ai bien reçu votre tiré à part — et combien je vous en remercie. J'ai lu *Reims revisited,* avec l'émotion la plus vive — et peut-être plus encore la description des rues de la ville que celle-même de la cathédrale. La *qualité* de votre sympathie est exquise et tout le temps que je vous lisais je me sentais heureux d'être votre ami.

Au revoir. J'espère que vous n'avez que de bonnes nouvelles de votre fils et que vous et Madame Gosse êtes en bonne santé, malgré de si constantes tristesses... Veuillez lui présenter mes hommages. Ma femme me demande de la rappeler à votre bon souvenir à tous deux. Je suis votre bien dévoué

ANDRÉ GIDE.

[I should have written you sooner, and I should be doing it better now, but for being overtaken by one of those prolonged headaches that have so often put me out of commission.[1] But this note, whatever its deficiencies, will be better than nothing.

I think Verhaeren's death[2] must have shaken you a good deal, for he had great fondness for you. The war had brought me much closer to him, and because his most intimate friend, Theo Van Rysselberghe, was having to lie low after a minor operation, there devolved on me the painful task of breaking the news to Madame Verhaeren and of standing by her through those first days of her grief. You already know that our friend now lies at La Panne.[3] What the pilgrimage was like to that strip of land that is still Belgian, I leave to your imagination. Throughout the trip and the funeral observances, beauty, exaltation, and courage altogether triumphed over sadness, as befitted Verhaeren. Dreadful as his death was, I feel that we can say of it what Pater wrote of Winckelmann's: "*It seemed as if the gods had given him a death which, for its swiftness and its opportunity, he might well have desired.*" But ever since I have known that he is no longer with us it has seemed to me that the sky has grown a little colder.

What a pity that he could not come to that luncheon at the Crillon!—I have indeed received your offprint, and how grateful I am to you for it. I read *Reims Revisited*[4] with very deep feeling—more, perhaps, for the description of the city streets than for that of the cathedral itself. The *quality* of your sympathy is beautiful, and all through my reading I was feeling happy to be a friend of yours.

Au revoir. I hope you have none but good news from your son and that you and Mrs. Gosse are in good health despite all the recurrent sorrows. Please give her my regards. My wife wants me to remember her kindly to both of you.]

[1] Gide's *Journal* continues to bear testimony to his moral distress and to his fatigue. For private reasons he found 1916 a particularly hard year. On December 21, ending his notebook, he wrote: "Oh! not to be able to liquidate all that past this last day of the year of disgrace 1916!"

[2] Emile Verhaeren, 1855–1916, was killed by a locomotive at the railroad station of Arras in December, 1916. Gosse, at first disturbed by the bold novelty of his poetry, had become an admirer. He had introduced Verhaeren's work to the English in 1902.

Gosse, as vice-president of the Royal Society of Literature, organized an impressive London ceremony in memory of Verhaeren on March 3, 1917. In 1915 he had received from Gide the following subscription bulletin:

> The friends of Emile Verhaeren have decided to give to the Luxembourg Museum a portrait of the great poet of Flanders which his compatriot Théo Van Rysselberghe has just finished painting. The friends of the Museum will join with them, and also all those who wish to see the establishment of a close union between France and "bleeding Belgium." Subscriptions will be accepted at the Galerie Druet, 20 rue Royale [seat *pro tem.* of the Foyer Franco-Belge]. The portrait will remain on exhibition

July 1–25. The list of subscriptions will be printed in the August
number of the *Mercure de France.*   Paris, June 1915

³ La Panne, a small Belgian resort, was then in the small unoccupied
part of the country. Gide records (*Journal,* December, 1916): "Suddenly Verhaeren's death called me to Rouen, then taken as far as La
Panne. Amazing trip, but one that I do not feel in a mood to relate."
But in some "Detached Pages" of his *Journal* for 1918 one finds,
under the heading "In an album … to the memory of Emil Verhaeren" (February), a half-page tribute to the author and to his
small peace-loving country, so flagrantly attacked. In 1918 Gide
wrote also an "Eloge" to the poet, in which he commented on his
work and its considerable importance in literary history. (*Eloges,
Ides et Calendes,* Neuchâtel, 1948, pp. 37–48.)

⁴ "Reims Revisited" was printed in November, 1916, in the *Fortnightly Review.* Gosse had twenty copies privately printed, one of
which he sent to Gide.

---

62. GIDE TO GOSSE, *December 23, 1916, from Cuverville*

CHER AMI   Sitôt après vous avoir quitté avant hier, j'ai pu lire
l'admirable, l'enthousiasmant discours de Lloyd George. L'Angleterre et la France sont vraiment dignes l'une de l'autre, et dignes de
vaincre toutes deux.

Un bon Noël, bien cher ami. Je songe à celui que vous m'invitiez
à fêter avec Henry James, près de vous.

Bien fidèlement ANDRÉ GIDE.

[Directly after leaving you day before yesterday¹ I had a
chance to read Lloyd George's fine and thrilling speech.² England and France are truly worthy of each other and worthy of
victory, both of them.

A good Christmas to you, my dear friend. I am thinking of
the one you asked me to celebrate with Henry James at your
house.]

[1] This is a reference to the preceding Letter 61.

[2] David Lloyd George became prime minister December 6. His speech to the House of Commons on December 19 rejected, jointly with France and Russia, the German chancellor's proposal for a peace conference; the conditions for peace would be complete restitution, total reparations, and real guarantees. Lloyd George asked great sacrifices of the nation, proposed an imperial conference with the Dominions and intensified unity of action with the Allies, and pledged continuation of the fight to deliver humanity from Prussian oppression.

63. GIDE TO GOSSE, *October 26, 1917, from Cuverville*

BIEN CHER AMI Votre admirable livre attendait ici mon retour. Quelle joie de trouver hier ce somptueux présent sur ma table! Et je voyais votre main tendue, votre affectueux sourire; il me semblait être accueilli par vous. Je ne puis vous dire à quel point votre attention me touche et combien je suis sensible à cet honneur que vous me faites de me compter au nombre de ces rares élus. Et je vais vous dire un secret: ma femme a été très particulièrement touchée de voir, à côté de mon nom cette indication: *Cuverville,* de préférence à: Paris, car ici je suis chez elle, plus à elle que n'importe où ailleurs. M'y voici de retour, et pour tout l'hiver je suppose, souhaitant que rien ne me dérange plus du travail dont je me suis trop longtemps distrait depuis l'été. Ce que j'écris à présent (je vous l'ai dit je crois dans ma dernière lettre) c'est un peu mon *Father and Son.* J'ai compris que je ne parviendrais à expliquer ma position vis à vis de certains problèmes religieux et moraux, jamais mieux qu'en en racontant l'histoire. Non point l'histoire de ces problèmes; mais l'histoire de ma position — si j'ose dire. Entre temps je poursuis la traduction d'Antoine et Cléopatre, que veut jouer Ida Rubinstein aussitôt après la fin de la guerre. Je prends le plaisir et l'intérêt le plus vif à ce travail — comme à tout ce qui me rapproche de l'Angleterre.

Le passage de votre préface où vous parlez de cette habitude de Swinburne "of allowing miscellaneous material to gather on his table, until a moment came when he could bear the pressure of it no longer" — m'a beaucoup amusé, car c'est une manie que mes amis me reprochent. Permettez-moi de souhaiter qu'un jour prochain, à la faveur des temps, nous soient livrées également ces pièces, ces "very bad songs" à quoi vous faites illusion; et que leur éditeur soit vous-même. Oui, vraiment, il faut que ce soit vous.

Je plonge avec ravissement dans ce beau livre. Vous parlez excellemment des *border ballads* et votre louange du *Death of Sir John-Franklin* ne me paraît point exagérée. Certains vers, à la lueur tragique de cette guerre, brillent d'un bien étrange éclat: "Was this not worth the pain wherein he died?"

Quelles belles et nobles joies je vous dois, cher ami! Je vous en remercie de tout mon cœur. — Ma femme se rappelle au bon souvenir de Madame Gosse, à qui je vous prie de présenter mes hommages. Croyez moi votre reconnaissant et dévoué

ANDRÉ GIDE.

Lady Rothermere vient de traduire mon Prométhée mal enchaîné qui paraîtra prochainement — chez Chatto and Windus probablement — à moins que d'abord dans une revue ... mais laquelle?? —

Votre carte me parvient à l'instant. Excusez le retard de cette lettre. Je vous signale deux petites erreurs qui se sont glissées dans les vers français: "ix," pour "if" p. 131 v. 2; et "*la* chèvrefeuille" pour "*le* chèvrefeuille."

[Your admirable book[1] was here awaiting my return. What a delight to find this lavish gift on my table yesterday! and I saw you, hand outstretched, warmly smiling; I had the feeling of being welcomed home by you. I cannot tell how moved I am by your considerateness or how much I value the honor you do me by counting me among the happy few. And I am going to tell you a secret: My wife was especially touched to find beside my name the inscription "Cuverville" rather than "Paris"; for here I am in her house and more hers than I am anywhere else.

Here I am, back again,[2] and I presume for the whole winter, for I want nothing to distract me from the work that I have let be too long interrupted—since last summer. What I am writing now—I told you this, I think, in my last letter—is more or less my *Father and Son*.[3] I realized that I should never manage to explain my postures toward sundry religious and moral problems better than I could by telling the story of them; not the story of the problems but that of my own postures, if I may venture to put it so. Meanwhile I am going on with my translation of *Antony and Cleopatra*,[4] which Ida Rubinstein wants to play as soon as the war is over. I am taking the liveliest pleasure and interest in this task, as I do in everything that brings me closer to England.

The passage in your preface[5] in which you speak of Swinburne's habit of *"allowing miscellaneous material to gather on his table, until a moment came when he could bear the pressure of it no longer"* amused me a good deal, for it is an aberration for which my friends take me to task. Let me hope that someday soon, when occasion serves, we shall likewise be given those poems, the "very bad songs" to which you refer, and that their editor will be yourself. Yes, to be sure, you must be the one.

I am delving enchantedly into this fine book. You write splendidly about the *border ballads,* and your tribute to "The Death of Sir John Franklin" does not strike me as at all overstated. Particular lines, under the tragic illumination of this war, shine forth with an uncanny radiance. *"Was this not worth the pain wherein he died?"*

What beautiful and exalted pleasures I owe to you, my dear friend! I thank you for them from the bottom of my heart. My wife wants to be remembered kindly to Mrs. Gosse, to whom please give my regards.

Lady Rothermere[6] has just finished translating my *Prométhée mal enchaîné,* and it will be published soon, by Chatto and Windus, probably—unless in a magazine first; but which??—

I just received your card.[7] Excuse me for writing so late. I point out for you two small errors[8] that slipped into the French poems: "ix" for "if," p. 131, v. 2; and "*la* chèvrefeuille" for "*le* chèvrefeuille."]

[1] This was Swinburne's *Posthumous Poems,* edited by Gosse and Thomas J. Wise (London: Heinemann, 1917).

[2] Gide had just spent three weeks, October 1–22, in Paris.

[3] The reminiscences were eventually entitled *Si le Grain ne meurt.*

[4] Gide's translation of *Antony and Cleopatra* was first printed in the *Nouvelle Revue Française,* July–September, 1920. The volume was published by Lucien Vogel in 1921. There were five performances in June, 1920, at the Paris Opéra, with music by Florent Schmitt. De Max played Antony, Ida Rubinstein played Cleopatra. Gide was much disappointed at the first rehearsal of the six-act prose drama in May: the actors did not sufficiently perceive "the beauty of words in themselves," he wrote; "I am once more convinced of the impossibility of making a play a work of art." (*Journal,* May 11, 1920.)

[5] The long preface to the *Posthumous Poems* was the work of Gosse. The "very bad songs" had been so-called by Swinburne's professor at Oxford, Benjamin Jowett, who had heard Swinburne sing one evening. Gosse thought they should not yet be published. The "Border Ballads" had been written about 1862–1863. Gosse thought that Swinburne had not published them because his friends Rossetti and William Morris found them "naked and savage." The 1917 volume contained eleven of them; Gosse thought Swinburne had destroyed the others. "The Death of Sir John Franklin" was written in 1858 in competition for the Newdigate Prize in poetry; the assigned subject was "The Discovery of the North-West Passage." Swinburne did not win the prize, and he wanted to destroy the poem, but his father rescued it. Gosse felt that it deserved to be published for its purity of style, its lofty sentiment, and the harmony of the verse, free of any Pre-Raphaelite influence. Gide quotes line 22 of stanza 6.

[6] Lady Rothermere's translation was done, with the help of Paul Méral, under the title *The Prometheus Illbound*; it was the first English rendering of a book by Gide.

⁷ Gide did not mention one that could not now be mended, Swinburne's rhyming of *prés* with *cyprès*; nor did he call attention to *la* [for *le*] *roseau*. (P. 135.)

⁸ Gosse's card to Gide is missing.

64. GIDE TO GOSSE, *June 10, 1918, from Paris*¹

MON CHER AMI   Un immense désir de revoir l'Angleterre, d'entendre de l'anglais, de *vous* revoir ... me tourmente depuis longtemps. Je n'y tiens plus. Je profite d'un prétexte de jeune neveu à conduire à Cambridge pour cross the channel et espère pouvoir vous embrasser dans les premiers jours de la semaine prochaine. Je dis "j'espère" car les formalités pour l'obtention des papiers sont de plus en plus difficiles et si je vous écris aujourd'hui, au lieu de tomber chez vous on a sudden [*sic*] et inopinément comme je me le proposais d'abord, c'est que je crois qu'une petite lettre de vous, sur papier le plus officiel possible — "bibliothèque de la Ch. des lords" par exemple, me rendrait le plus grand service en montrant que vous me connaissez, souhaitez me revoir, m'attendez. Et si vous y ajoutez que tout est prêt pour recevoir le jeune Marc Allégret à Cambridge et faciliter ses études (ce qui est vrai) ce serait parfait. Mais je vous serais bien obligé de m'envoyer cette lettre en toute hâte. Excusez je vous prie l'indiscrétion de cette insistance [*sic*] et veuillez n'y voir qu'une grande impatience de me sentir près de vous. Ah! puissé-je n'avoir que de bonnes nouvelles à vous apprendre, et à apprendre de vous et des vôtres. Tous mes hommages à Madame Gosse je vous prie —

Fidèlement votre ANDRÉ GIDE.

Votre father and son que je donne à lire à ceux qui en sont dignes vient de BOULEVERSER la mère du jeune Allégret qui m'accompagne. Elle même fille et sœur de pasteur, épouse d'un missionnaire; elle m'écrit assez longuement au sujet de votre livre; une très curieuse lettre, que je vous communiquerai.

[A great longing to see England again, to hear some English, to see *you* again has been tormenting me for a long time.[2] I can't bear it any longer. I take advantage of the pretext of escorting a young nephew to Cambridge, and I am hoping to be able to embrace you early next week. I say "am hoping" because the formalities of getting the necessary papers are more and more troublesome, and my writing you today instead of falling upon you *on a sudden* and unexpectedly, as I meant to do at first, means that I think a note from you on the most official stationery possible—"Library of the House of Lords," for example—would be of the greatest help to me by showing that you know me, want to see me again, and are expecting me. And if to so much you were to add that all arrangements are made to admit young Marc Allégret to Cambridge and to facilitate his studies (which is true), that would be perfect. But I should be much obliged to you for sending me this letter with all speed. Please do excuse the tactlessness of my urgency and see in it nothing but my great impatience to find myself near you again. And, oh, may I have only good news to tell you and to hear about you and yours. My best regards to Mrs. Gosse, please.

Your *Father and Son,* which I lend to such as are worthy of it, has just OVERWHELMED the mother of my young traveling companion Allégret. She herself is the daughter and sister of ministers and the wife of a missionary; she wrote me at some length about your book—a very odd letter, which I will show you.]

[1] Gide was writing from 14 rue Claude Lorrain, the address of the Van Rysselberghes.

[2] Gide had actually been thinking about such a visit for more than a year past. Raverat, who lived between Cambridge and London, was helping with preparatory errands. Administrative obstacles prompted Gide to ask Gosse's intervention. A week later he was able to start from Cuverville.

Gide's 1918 visit to England was the occasion of an extremely serious quarrel with his wife. The *Journal* for June 18 says: "I am

leaving France in a state of inexpressible anguish. It seems to me
that I am saying farewell to my whole past."

65. GIDE TO GOSSE, *July 31, 1918, from Cambridge*

BIEN CHER AMI   J'ai enfin reçu votre livre et je n'attends pas de
l'avoir achevé pour vous en remercier, car je lis très lentement ce qui
m'intéresse.

Depuis longtemps la figure de La Rochefoucauld m'occupe très
particulièrement et j'aime vous voir faire si grand cas de ce petit
livre des Maximes. Le portrait que vous tracez de lui est excellent —
amicalement dessiné, si j'ose dire — et j'admire la beauté des traductions que vous donnez de lui. Je suis particulièrement sensible à ces
pages du début où vous montrez à quel point l'esprit anglais demeure
réfractaire à son genre de cynisme psychologique... mais vous
avouerai-je que je me sens terriblement anglais sur ce point! —

Peut-être eussé-je souhaité (mais cela débordait votre sujet) qu'à
la fin de cette belle étude vous montriez à quel point l'esprit français,
émancipé d'abord par les Maximes, est demeuré par la suite esclave
de cette misérable façon de voir. Moralistes et romanciers n'ont plus
admis d'autre ressort que l'égoïsme et ont soumis toutes les passions
à sa loi. Ils ont méconnu profondément le besoin parallèle qu'il y a
dans l'homme, de se détruire, besoin qui selon les cas peut conduire
au vice le plus absurde ou à la plus sublime vertu. Je crois qu'aujourd'hui toute découverte psychologique ne peut être faite qu'en
prenant pour ainsi dire le contrepied de La Rochefoucauld.

J'ai quitté Londres trop brusquement pour pouvoir profiter de
votre recommandation au directeur du Zoo, et j'ai dû remettre à
plus tard cette visite; par contre, grâce à votre amicale lettre, j'ai
trouvé le plus aimable accueil auprès du Vice Chancellor de Christ's
College —

J'ai pu trouver à m'installer assez confortablement à Grantchester,
tout près du Old Vicarage où vivait Rupert Brooke. Cambridge est

merveilleux, enthousiasmant; j'y rencontre quantité de gens char-
mants — mais surtout j'y écoute les voix du passé. Comme j'aime
vous y sentir près de moi, je vous écoute à présent me parler de John
Donne, ayant sur ma table votre admirable publication. C'est pour
vous lire que je vous quitte.

Au revoir. Présentez je vous prie mes respectueux hommages à
Madame Gosse et veuillez me croire votre reconnaissant et affectueusement dévoué

ANDRÉ GIDE.

[I finally received your book,[1] and I am not waiting to get
through reading it before thanking you, because I read very
slowly anything that interests me.

For a good while the figure of La Rochefoucauld[2] has been
uncommonly absorbing to me, and I am happy to find that you
set such store by his little book of *Maxims*. The portrait you draw
of him is admirable—limned by the hand of a friend, if I may
venture to say so—and I marvel at the beauty of the translations
of him that you supply. I am particularly impressed by those
early pages in which you show how very resistant is the English
mind to his species of psychological cynicism—only let me confess
to you that I feel dreadfully English myself on that score!

I might perhaps have wished (only it was beyond the scope
of your subject) that in the closing part of this fine study you
had shown how very completely the French mind, liberated to
begin with by the *Maxims,* presently remained enslaved by that
pitiful way of looking at things. Moralists and novelists stopped
recognizing any alternative to egoism and have subjected all
human impulses to its sway. They have radically misprized the
parallel human need for self-immolation—a need that on occasion can lead to the most fantastic vice or to the most sublime
virtue. It is my belief that no discovery about the mind can be
made today except by starting from what may be called the op-
posite premise to La Rochefoucauld's.

I left London too suddenly to be able to make use of your introduction to the director of the Zoo, and I have had to post-

pone that visit; on the other hand, thanks to your friendly letter, I was received most graciously by the Vice-Chancellor of Christ's College.[3]

I have been able to find myself a rather comfortable lodging at Grantchester,[4] very near to the Old Vicarage where Rupert Brooke used to live. Cambridge is wonderful, thrilling; I meet any number of delightful persons here; but above all I listen here to voices out of the past. Liking as I do to feel that you are near, I hear you just now talking to me about John Donne; for I have your fine book on my table.[5] It is to read you that I go away from you!

Au revoir. Please give my warm regards to Mrs. Gosse.]

[1] This was *Three French Moralists* (London: Heinemann, 1918), to which had been added "The Gallantry of France," first printed July, 1917, in the *Edinburgh Review*. The studies of La Rochefoucauld, La Bruyère, and Vauvenargues, prepared as lectures at the Royal Institute, had been revised and expanded.

[2] Gide, in his *Feuillets* of this same year, observes that La Rochefoucauld, when he "simply nipped in the bud any approach to a more venturesome inquiry," fell back on the expedient of "reducing the heart's impulsions to the promptings of self-esteem." He also said: "Dostoevski's greatness lies in the fact that he never reduced the world to a theory." To La Rochefoucauld Gide preferred Saint-Evremond, who perceived that man is "wicked, virtuous, equitable, unjust, humane, and cruel." So much remained to be discovered in the human heart! But by September 30, 1921, Gide felt that he had been unfair to La Rochefoucauld; he had been wrong in trying to "assimilate what he calls 'amour-propre' to egotism."

[3] Gide's reception perhaps owed something to the circumstance that Gosse was a lecturer in English literature at Trinity College, Cambridge, 1884–1889.

[4] Gide, while he was staying at Grantchester, met in Cambridge Lytton Strachey's sister, Dorothy Bussy, who was to translate many of his books. He had been given a letter of introduction to her family by a friend, Auguste Bréal. Mrs. Bussy began by giving him lessons in English; he bicycled to her house every morning, punc-

tually prepared his written assignments, and memorized English poetry. He was now speaking English haltingly, but reading it with great ease.

He met, besides the Strachey group, A. E. Housman, John Drinkwater, and that indefatigable collector of personages, Lady Ottoline Morrell. With Aldous Huxley, Gide found little in common. Cambridge in the summer holidays was half emptied of undergraduates and half filled with wounded soldiers, and not at its best. (Cf. Dorothy Bussy, "Quelques Souvenirs," in *Hommage à Gide,* Paris: Nouvelle Revue Française, November, 1951, p. 37.)

⁵ Gosse's *Life and Letters of John Donne, Dean of St. Paul's* (1899) is still consulted and respected.

66. GIDE TO GOSSE, *August 9, 1918, from Cambridge (Grape House, Grantchester)*

MON CHER AMI   Voici le triste mot que Marcel Drouin recevait de Paul Desjardins, et que me renvoie ma femme ce matin.

Pour Gide et pour vous —

Paris 29 juillet —

CHER MONSIEUR ET AMI

Quand nous avons déjeuné ensemble l'autre Samedi, Michel n'était déjà plus vivant. Il a été tué le matin du jeudi 18, d'une balle au front, comme il entraînait sa section à l'assaut. Son corps est resté dans les lignes ennemies. Sa fin a été brève et belle. C'était un matin de victoire, et il le pressentait. Il est pleuré de ses hommes.

Puisse votre Domi être épargné!

Je retourne à Pontigny demain.

Je crois que Michel Desjardins n'avait pas encore 20 ans — Je me souviens du mot que vous m'écriviez — (y a-t-il déjà deux ans de cela?) "All our gallant youth"... Je vous transmets cette triste nouvelle le cœur plein de larmes...

Bien amicalement votre ANDRÉ GIDE.

[Here is the sad word that Marcel Drouin received from Paul Desjardins; my wife forwarded it to me this morning:

For Gide and you

Paris, July 29

DEAR SIR AND DEAR FRIEND,

When we were having luncheon together last Saturday Michel[1] was already dead. He was killed the morning of Thursday the 18th by a bullet in the forehead while leading his platoon to the attack. His body remained inside the enemy lines. His end was sudden and beautiful. It happened on the morning of a victory, of which he had a presentiment. He is mourned by his men.

May your Domi be spared!

I go back to Pontigny tomorrow.

I believe Michel Desjardins was not yet twenty. I remember the lines you wrote me—can it already be two years ago?—"All our gallant youth . . . ." I send you this sad message from a heart overflowing.]

[1] Paul Desjardins' only son.

67. GIDE TO GOSSE, *August 25, 1918, from Cambridge*[1]

CHER AMI Combien je vous remercie de votre obligeance! Je savais bien que par vous ne pouvait advenir que le meilleur. Si maintenant Marc Allégret n'est pas accepté, du moins cette affreuse pensée ne me tourmentera point: Ah! si j'avais écrit à Edmund Gosse!

Oui, j'aimerais beaucoup vous revoir. J'ai cette fatuité de penser que le livre que je prépare est de nature à vous intéresser; il me plairait aussi que vous le connaissiez un peu avant "les autres." J'espérais l'achever ici, mais je comptais sans l'amabilité des Cambridgiens et sans le charme de Cambridge. Au revoir. A bientôt, j'espère.

Bien amicalement votre ANDRÉ GIDE.

[Thank you so much for your helpfulness! I knew that through you nothing could happen but the best. If Marc Allégret is not accepted now, I shall at least not be hounded by the frightful thought, Oh, if only I had written to Edmund Gosse!

Yes, I should dearly love to see you again. I have the fatuity to think that the book I am working on will be of a sort to interest you;[2] it would please me, too, to have you know it a little ahead of "the others." I was hoping to finish it here, but I was not reckoning with the kindness of the Cantabrigians and the charm of Cambridge. Au revoir. *A bientôt,* I hope.]

[1] Merton House, Queen's Road, from which this letter was written, was a comfortable residence lent Gide by a friend. Living in Cambridge saved him the daily trip for his lessons in English. (*Journal,* September 2, 1918.)

[2] This was *La Symphonie pastorale,* first printed October–November in the *Nouvelle Revue Française* and published as a book at the close of the year.

68. GIDE TO GOSSE, *August 30, 1918, from Cambridge*

CHER AMI Je reçois votre lettre et celle de Sir M. B. C. qu'elle contient. Vous êtes exquis de me proposer à nouveau votre aide; mais je ne suis pas à même de savoir ni quelles autorités il serait souhaitable d'atteindre, ni ceux que vous connaissez dans la partie. — Mais comprenez bien, cher ami, que je ne voudrais rien demander ni obtenir, que de normal et de régulier; il me déplairait de faire appel ici à quelque faveur spéciale ou à quelque "passe-droit." Lorsque Marc a été faire sa déclaration au consulat français, on lui a dit en souriant: "Ils vont vouloir vous prendre dans l'armée anglaise!" et quelques phrases lui ont montré qu'il ne lui serait pas impossible de s'y engager. Au même moment j'ai reçu de Madame Allégret, sa mère,

une lettre m'invitant à examiner sérieusement la question d'un en-
gagement possible ici.

Au bureau de recrutement de Cambridge, où Marc Allégret a dé-
posé sa demande, rien ne lui a été dit qui fût de nature à le décourager;
on lui a déjà fait subir un certain nombre d'épreuves, d'où il semble
être sorti à son honneur; — en tout cas il est appelé à continuer. Il
me semble que s'il y avait une raison péremptoire, de principes ou
autre, qui s'opposât à son admission, on le lui aurait *déjà* fait savoir.
C'est ce qui m'encourage à continuer, et qui fait que j'espère encore.
C'est ce qui me fait croire aussi que quelque mot d'appui de tel ou
tel personnage bien placé peut être, en l'espèce, d'un grand secours
— et c'est ce qui m'a poussé à vous écrire.

Je pense aller à Londres dans quelques jours et j'espère bien avoir
le plaisir de vous y voir.

Votre reconnaissant et dévoué ANDRÉ GIDE.

[I have your letter with Sir M.B.C.'s enclosed.[1] It is grand
of you to offer me your further help; but I am not in a position
to know either what officials it would be desirable to approach
or what ones you are acquainted with in those quarters. But do
understand, my dear friend, that I should not want either to
ask or to get anything but what is normal and regular; I should
dislike resorting in this matter to some special favor or some
dubious short cut. When Marc went to register at the French
consulate, they said to him with a smile: "They will want you to
enlist in the British army!" and something they said showed him
that it would not be impossible for him to do so. At the same
time I had a letter from Madame Allégret, his mother, asking me
to look seriously into the possibility of enlistment here.[2]

At the Cambridge recruiting office where Marc filed his application, nothing was said to him of a sort to discourage the
idea. He has already been put through a number of tests, which
he seems to have passed creditably—anyway he has been asked
to keep on. It seems to me that if there were a decisive reason—
a matter of principle or what not—against his admission, they
would *already* have let him know. That is what encourages me

to persist and why I continue hopeful. That is also why I think a word of recommendation from one or another important person might be, in the circumstances, of great help, and that is what impelled me to write you.

I mean to go to London in a few days, and I hope to have the pleasure of seeing you there.[3]]

[1] Probably Sir Maurice Bonham-Carter, 1880 ——, who had been secretary to Herbert Asquith, 1910–1916, while Asquith was prime minister. (The two letters are missing.)

[2] Marc Allégret's mother already had three sons in the French army, and she did not want this boy to enlist so young. He took his military training in England, but the war ended before he saw service.

[3] Gide's name does not appear, however, in the "Book of Gosse" in this period.

69. GIDE TO GOSSE, *September 4, 1918, from Cambridge*

DEAR FRIEND Je reçois votre lettre et j'écris tout aussitôt aux parents de Marc. Sa tante, Mademoiselle Allégret, est directrice du Lycée Victor Duruy, où précisément sont installés les bureaux du recrutement militaire, de sorte qu'elle est en relation constante et directe avec les autorités que précisément il importe d'atteindre. Elle fera son possible pour appuyer la demande de son neveu. Je suis heureux d'apprendre que, du côté anglais, les oppositions sont levées — grâce à vous. Je vous remercie encore et suis

votre bien reconnaissant et dévoué ANDRÉ GIDE.

[I have your letter,[1] and I am writing immediately to Marc's parents. His aunt, Mademoiselle Allégret, is the principal of the Lycée Victor Duruy, in the very building where the military recruiting offices have been set up, so that she is in regular and direct contact with just the officials it is important to reach. She will do what she can to support her nephew's application. I am happy to hear that, on the English side, the obstructions have been removed—thanks to you. Thank you again.]

¹ Gosse's letter is missing, like the preceding ones.

70. GOSSE TO GIDE, *August 15, 1920, from London*

MY DEAR GIDE,   Thank you for the gift of your "Symphonie Pastorale." I have read it with the deepest emotion and admiration! I am about to review it, and therefore will say no more today.[1]

How long,—how long, it is since I saw you or heard from you![2] I hunger for the pressure of your hand, my dear, exquisite friend! I wish you would write to me. We are passing through dreadful days,[3] in which the pillars of the world seem to be shaken and all in front of us seems to be darkness and hopelessness. It is much harder to bear than the War was, because there is no longer the unity which sustained us nor the nobility which inspired hope and determination. What is to come of the angry, distracted world? I feel very old and very helpless.

Do write me a good, long letter. I think of you constantly.

                    Your affectionate friend, EDMUND GOSSE

¹ Gosse's article about *La Symphonie pastorale* appeared first in the *Sunday Times*; it was collected in *Books on the Table* (1912). There was, he said, no more exquisite talent in Europe; yet, save for a style, he was hard put to it to find any singleness of purpose in Gide's works. This book was in the vein that Gosse preferred, that of *La Porte étroite* and *Isabelle*; but he wished that Gide would rewrite and alter the ending. The truth was that Gide had found it difficult to resume work after his summer in England. "Today, I have the greatest

difficulty getting interested again in the state of mind of my minister, and I fear that the end of the book may suffer from this." (*Journal,* October 16, 1918.) He added on October 19: "I am somewhat worried to see myself reach so quickly the end of my Symphonie Pastorale." Later he wrote a preface to this last project of his youth, which he had to consummate for the freeing of his mind; but it had been hard to finish a work so remote from what he then wanted to write. ("A propos de la Symphonie Pastorale," *Hommage à Gide,* p. 308.) Paul Claudel wrote to Gide August 7, 1920: "Thank you, my dear Gide, for your beautiful book, in which I recognize what is best in yourself." (Claudel–Gide, *Correspondance,* p. 237.)

[2] Gosse and Gide had not written each other for two years, so it seems. For Gide, 1919 was pervaded with gloom. Soon after his return in November, 1918, Mme. Gide confessed that she had destroyed all his once cherished letters under the pressure of her suffering when he left her to go to England. To Gide this disclosure was a terrible blow. The gentlest cadences in the symphony of his works collectively would be forever unheard. He was as downcast as if he had lost a child; sad, withal, for the unhappiness he had brought upon one whom he still deeply loved. (*Journal Intime,* pp. 18–25.)

[3] England was plagued by strikes and unemployment. Gosse was dejected about the postwar situation, and he anticipated a German *revanche* a decade later. (Charteris, *op. cit.,* p. 459.)

71. GIDE TO GOSSE, *August 23, 1920, from Llamberis*

BIEN CHER AMI, Mon cœur fond d'affection et de joie en lisant votre excellente lettre. Ma femme me la renvoie de Cuverville et c'est dans le fond du Carnarvonsh que je la reçois. Je n'ai fait que traverser Londres à l'aller, mais, avant huit jours, j'ai l'espoir d'être près de vous (si vous êtes à Londres).

Veuillez présenter mes hommages à Madame Gosse je vous prie et me croire votre dévoué

ANDRÉ GIDE.

Mon adresse à Londres sera: 51 Gordon Square W.C.1.

[My heart melts with affection and joy in reading your fine letter. My wife forwarded it from Cuverville, and I have just received it deep in Caernarvonshire. I merely went through London without stopping, but inside a week I hope to be in your vicinity (if you are in London).[1]

Please give my regards to Mrs. Gosse.

My address in London will be 51 Gordon Square, W.C.1.]

[1] Gide, on his return from Wales, stopped in London and was Gosse's guest. The "Book of Gosse" records: "September 3. Mrs. Asquith (tea), M. André Gide (dinner)." A few days before, Gide and young Allégret had been Arnold Bennett's guests on his yacht at Comarques, Thorpe-le-Soken. (*Journal of Arnold Bennett,* New York, p. 711.)

72. GIDE TO GOSSE, *January 16. 1921, from Cuverville*

MON CHER AMI Me permettrez-vous de venir vous importuner au sujet de ceci, qui ne laissera pas de vous intéresser vous aussi.

Nous voudrions publier à la Nouvelle Revue Française une traduction du *Mayor of Casterbridge.* Le Dr. Neel que nous chargeons de ce travail vient de nous donner une traduction de *Under Western eyes,* que Conrad lui-même tient pour excellente; je lui fais confiance et crois que Thomas Hardy ne pourra être que satisfait et de son traducteur et de nous. Mais Hardy, qui ne connaît ni l'un ni l'autre, et qui peut-être se défie, a laissé sans réponse la lettre où le Dr. Neel sollicitait son autorisation. Le Dr. N. — et moi — pensons que peut-être un mot de vous à celui que je sais votre ami pourrait le décider, en l'éclairant sur la bonne qualité de notre admiration et de nos intentions. Seriez-vous assez aimable pour nous prêter ici votre appui?

Au surplus voici la lettre de Monsieur Neel. Vous y verrez qu'il propose de récrire à Hardy une lettre, qu'il vous enverrait et que peut-être vous voudriez bien faire parvenir en y rajoutant quelques lignes de vous — mais il ne sera fait que s'il vous convient...

Veuillez présenter à Madame Edmund Gosse mes hommages et les meilleurs souvenirs de ma femme, et croire à mon amitié bien fidèle.   Votre dévoué ANDRÉ GIDE.

[Allow me to beg a favor of you about a matter that can hardly fail to interest you too.

We at the Nouvelle Revue Française should like to publish a translation of *The Mayor of Casterbridge*.[1] Dr. Neel, to whom we are entrusting the work, has just given us a translation of *Under Western Eyes* that Conrad himself thinks admirable; I have confidence in him, and I think Thomas Hardy could not be less than satisfied with his translator and with us. But Hardy, knowing neither the one nor the other and perhaps feeling some distrust, has left unanswered a letter from Dr. Neel requesting permission. Dr. Neel and I think that a few lines from you to Hardy—who I know is a friend of yours—might persuade him by convincing him of the genuineness of our admiration and of our intentions. Would you be so kind as to lend us your support in this matter?

For good measure here is M. Neel's letter. You will see that he means to write another letter to Hardy—one that he would send you and that you would perhaps care to forward with the addition of a few lines of your own; but this will be done only if it is agreeable to you.

Please give Mrs. Gosse my regards and my wife's best wishes.]

---

[1] The translation by Philippe Neel was published in 1922 by the Nouvelle Revue Française.

73. GOSSE TO GIDE, *August 25, 1924, from London*

MY DEAR GIDE, For a long time past I have been intending to thank you for the gift of your "Incidences,"[1] but I have been prevented by the mass of work which I have had in hand, and by a certain indolence which creeps over my old age.[2] I will delay no longer.

In reading "Incidences" I have once more found myself listening to the voice which (almost more than any other) fascinates and allures me. Many of the little essays I have read before in the N.R.F. but they gain a new accent, a fresh significance in re-reading. Your mind is excessively limpid. I see strange and beautiful things moving in its depths, as in the hyaline of a pacific sea.

I will not specify more particularly what pleases me than to say that no one has written so well (*nearly* so well) on Proust as you have. "Si désintéressée, si gratuite," nothing could be more excellent. Your article on Gautier interests me very much, because, when I was quite young, about 1873, his prose and verse exercised a violent influence over me, which a little later, the preface to "Les Fleurs du Mal" accentuated. Now I cannot read Gautier any more; Theodore de Banville[3] has faded for me also but not nearly so much as Gautier. It is like the pleasure one takes in Fragonard's pictures: the thing may not be very well worth doing, but no one does it better than Banville. But all through "Incidences" I enjoy your line of thought: it goes *leaping* along, with great *jumps*, and I joyously jump with it.

You did not send me "Corydon,"[4] so I had to buy it. Perhaps you thought I should be "shocked." But that is not my way. There is nothing in the whole diversity of life which serious men can not seriously discuss. I think you show great courage in writing this book, although I do not quite know *why* you wrote it. But that is your business, and I read with sympathy and respect everything you choose to write. No doubt, in fifty years, this particular subject will

cease to surprise any one, and how many people in the past might
wish to have lived in 1974.

You will have seen that we have lost Conrad,[5] a beautiful figure.
But he had said all he had to say, and went on writing in order to
make money. He will live in half a dozen of his early books. Here in
England, literature is in a deplorable state, dying of collectivism and
emptiness. Well, well! I wish you would write to me, but at least I
am glad that you have not forgotten me. I am always

Sincerely yours, EDMUND GOSSE

[1] A volume of criticism made up of twenty-three articles, most of
them already printed 1914–1923 in the *Nouvelle Revue Française*. Noteworthy among them is "A propos de Marcel Proust," a tribute to
a writer whose works are "so disinterested and so gratuitous" at a
time when everybody else seems to be preoccupied with nothing
but utility. In the article about Gautier, part of a lecture given at
the Vieux-Colombier in April, 1914, Gide found Baudelaire's admiration for Gautier excessive.

[2] Gosse was only a month away from his seventy-fifth birthday.

[3] Gosse's youthful discipleship to Banville expressed itself in a
ballade to the memory of "the last joyful poet." (Gosse, *Collected
Poems,* p. 284.)

[4] Gide had been working on *Corydon* since 1910. The original
edition, *C. R. D. N.,* appeared in 1911, but only twenty-one copies
were printed. The names of author and publisher and the place of
publication were suppressed. (Bruges: St. Catherine Press, Ltd.) This
first edition comprised only the first two dialogues and the beginning
of the third. The second edition bore the title *Corydon,* but was still
anonymous. (Bruges, 1920; twenty-one copies.) The half title was
"Corydon: quatre dialogues socratiques." The preface said that the
author had decided to publish the volume because to him nothing
was so pernicious as falsehood. The third edition (*Corydon,* Nouvelle
Revue Française, 1924), the first available to the public, was put on
sale in May, 1924. Gide wrote a new preface to explain why he had
withheld the book—chiefly because of considerate affection for
persons whom he shrank from saddening. But he felt that the time
for publication had come. " 'Here is something that, I fear, will

bring grist to your mill,' Rivière said to me the other day, speaking
of Freud's little book on sexual development. I should say! It is
high time to publish Corydon." (*Journal,* February 4, 1922.)

⁵ It was Claudel who first spoke of Joseph Conrad to Gide. This
was in 1905, before any of Conrad's works had been translated. Gide
translated *Typhoon,* published in French in 1918; and he borrowed
two sentences from *Lord Jim* as an epigraph for Chapter V of *Les
Caves du Vatican.* Gide wanted to translate *Youth* and *Heart of Darkness,* but never did so. On December 1, 1924, Gide published an
"Eloge à Conrad" in the *Nouvelle Revue Française.* ("Among my elders
I liked and knew only him." *Eloges,* p. 20; the volume contains
éloges to Conrad, Bennett, Verhaeren, and others.)

74. GIDE TO GOSSE, *September 12, 1924, from Cuverville*

MON CHER EDMUND GOSSE,   Combien votre exquise lettre me touche!
et que je vous sais gré de m'écrire ainsi . . . . Mes longs silences n'ont
donc pas diminué votre attentive sympathie, qui m'est précieuse
entre toutes. Ce que vous me dites de mes *Incidences* me ravit.

Si vous n'avez pas reçu *Corydon,* c'est que je ne l'ai envoyé à personne. Mais l'eussé-je fait, il me faut bien vous avouer que vous
êtes un de mes amis à qui je n'aurais pas osé le donner. C'est pourquoi
je suis particulièrement sensible à vos quelques phrases au sujet de
ce petit livre. Des incompréhensions lamentables, de tragiques mal-
entendus, dont j'ai vu souffrir cruellement, m'ont poussé à l'écrire.
D'autres raisons encore que vous comprendrez, je le souhaite, lorsque vous lirez au complet "Si le grain ne meurt," — au printemps
prochain sans doute. — Ce livre également, je me propose de ne l'envoyer à *personne . . .* à vous pourtant j'en donnerai un exemplaire, en
gage de ma grande reconnaissance et de ma respectueuse et bien
fidèle amitié.

ANDRÉ GIDE.

P. S. Dent m'avait demandé une préface pour une nouvelle édition de *Tom Jones;* par admiration pour Fielding j'avais accepté avec enthousiasme. Hélas! la traduction proposée s'est trouvée si mauvaise qu'il a fallu abandonner ce beau projet. Chaque fois que je m'éprends d'un auteur anglais, il se trouve qu'il a été étudié, préfacé ou commenté par vous. Quel amical plaisir de vous retrouver à tous les coins de ma bibliothèque!

[I am greatly warmed by your fine letter and no end gratified that you should write to me in such terms. My long silences, it seems, have not lessened your sympathetic awareness, which I value above all things. What you tell me about my *Incidences* enchants me.

Your not receiving *Corydon* means that I did not send it to anyone. But if I had done so, I really must confess to you that you are one of my friends to whom I should not have dared give it. That is why I am especially moved by your few lines about this little book. Various deplorable misconceptions and calamitous misunderstandings that have cost a good deal of pain were what drove me to write it; also other considerations that you will understand, or so I hope, when you read the completion of *Si le Grain ne meurt*[1] (next spring, probably). This is another book that I mean to send to *no one*—only I shall give you a copy of it as witness to my gratitude and my deferential and steadfast friendship.

P. S. Dent had asked me for an introduction to the new edition of *Tom Jones;* I admire Fielding so much that I had assented with enthusiasm. Alas, the proposed translation was discovered to be so wretched that this splendid undertaking had to be given up. Every time I am captivated by an English author it turns out that he is the subject of an essay, introduction, or analysis of yours.[2] What a genial arrangement, this coming upon you again in every corner of my library!]

[1] Excerpts from these memoirs had appeared in the *Nouvelle Revue Française* in February, March, May, November, and December, 1920, January, 1921, and 1924. Champion published these excerpts in 1924. The first complete edition was published in 1924 in three volumes, but was not on sale until October, 1926.

[2] Gosse had written in 1898 an introduction to Fielding's works. ("Henry Fielding: An Essay," London: A. Constable and Company, 1898.)

75. GOSSE TO GIDE, *October 23, 1924, from London*

MY DEAR GIDE, At a council Meeting of the Royal Society of Literature[1]—(our nearest approach to an Academy of Letters), yesterday, I presiding—you were unanimously elected to be an Honorary Fellow in the place of Anatole France,[2] who had held that position for many years.

You will hear in due course from the Secretary. There is nothing to pay and nothing to do!

Ever sincerely yours, EDMUND GOSSE

[1] The Royal Society of Literature, founded 1825, had four hundred members. Joseph Conrad, Austin Dobson, John Galsworthy, Gosse, Thomas Hardy, Max Beerbohm, Henry James, Gilbert Murray, Henry Newbolt, Sir Arthur Pinero, Bernard Shaw, and W. B. Yeats were or had been members of the Academic Committee. There were fortnightly meetings and an annual June meeting. The Society published, through the Oxford University Press, essays or "transactions." Volume IV, New Series, had been edited by Gosse, who wrote the introduction, in May 1924; he discussed the "paradox" of criticism.

[2] Gide succeeded Anatole France in the Royal Society of Literature; Paul Valéry succeeded Anatole France the following year (November 19, 1925) as a member of the French Academy. Later,

when Gide joined the Communist party, the Royal Society of Literature crossed him off, an unprecedented occurence. In 1939, when he was known to have long since renounced Communism, the Society wanted to make reparation by having him as guest of honor at a banquet, but he would not attend. (C. Mauriac, *Conversations avec André Gide*, Paris: A. Michel, 1951, p. 117.)

76. GIDE TO GOSSE, *October 26, 1924, from Cuverville*

MON CHER EDMUND GOSSE   Il ne me vient de vous rien que d'exquis. J'allais vous remercier de la biographie de Congrève — et voici votre lettre m'annonçant l'unique honneur qui m'échoit. Je sens de reste que je le dois beaucoup moins à mes mérites qu'à votre appui et à l'affectueux zèle que vous m'avez toujours témoigné; je n'en suis pas moins flatté, délicieusement — et voici qui me soutient et me fortifie. C'est la revanche des attaques dont je suis l'objet depuis quelque temps: un parti de "néothomistes" me prête une figure d'antéchrist et me désigne à l'indignation des nationalistes. Je me garde de répondre autrement qu'en continuant tranquillement mon travail. Il me tarde que vous puissiez lire mon prochain livre; il est assez long et je suis loin de l'avoir achevé, mais la Nouvelle Revue Française en donnera prochainement la première partie, qui déjà remplit un volume. Puisse-t-il ne pas décevoir les espoirs que vous voulez bien poser sur moi!

Vous me dites, au sujet de cette élection: "nothing to pay and nothing to do." Il y a pourtant lieu de remercier d'autres encore que vous-même, sans doute. J'attends des instructions...

Et ce beau titre que me donne ce vote, ne sera-t-il pas décent d'en user, de l'inscrire au-dessous de mon nom, dans le petit volume que prépare, à l'usage des classes, le Oxford U.P. avec des fragments de mon "Si le grain ne meurt"...?

Je lis votre livre avec un intérêt très vif, ayant depuis longtemps une grande admiration pour Congrève. Je poussais même Co-

peau à tâcher de porter une de ses pièces sur la scène du Vieux Colombier. Mais, pour un temps, Copeau se retire et va travailler loin
de Paris. Je compte moi-même partir dans quelques mois pour un
lointain voyage en Afrique Equatoriale — mon roman fini, je l'espère,
car je ne pense pas pouvoir beaucoup écrire là-bas.

Au revoir, cher ami. Ma femme s'est montrée extrêmement sensible
à la nouvelle dont votre lettre nous fait part et me demande de vous
exprimer sa gratitude particulière. Elle voudrait que vous la rappeliez
au bon souvenir de Madame Gosse, à qui je vous prie de présenter
tous mes hommages.

Croyez à la profonde et respectueuse amitié de votre dévoué

ANDRÉ GIDE.

[Nothing ever comes to me from you but what is perfect. I was
about to thank you for the life of Congreve[1]—and here is your
letter telling me about the exceptional honor bestowed on me.[2]
I quite realize that I owe it much less to my own deserts than
to your advocacy and to the affectionate enthusiasm for me that
you have always shown; I am none the less flattered for that—
delightfully so. And what has happened gives me real aid and
comfort. It is a requital for the attacks to which I have been
subjected for some time:[3] a neo-Thomist faction will have it
that I am Antichrist and holds me up to nationalist wrath. I deny
myself any retort except that of keeping peacefully on with my
work. I am impatient to have you read my next book;[4] it is
rather long, and I am a good way short of the end of it, but the
Nouvelle Revue Française will shortly bring out Part I, which runs
to a full volume. May it not disappoint the hopes you have been
good enough to vest in me.

You tell me as to this election of mine: "nothing to pay and
nothing to do." There is doubtless occasion, though, to thank
others than yourself. I look to you for guidance.

And this fine honorific that has been voted me—wouldn't it
be fitting to make use of it by adding it to my signature in the
little book being prepared for classroom use by the Oxford
U.P., containing excerpts from my *Si le grain ne meurt*?[5]

I am reading your book with very keen interest, having long had a great admiration for Congreve. I was even urging Copeau to try putting on one of his plays at the Vieux-Colombier. But Copeau is withdrawing from the theater for a while and will be working away from Paris.[6] I too plan to go away in a few months, on a long journey in Equatorial Africa—with my book finished, I hope, because I don't think I can manage to write much down there.[7]

Au revoir, my dear friend. My wife took boundless pleasure in the news your letter brought us, and she asks me to express to you her special thanks. She would like you to remember her kindly to Mrs. Gosse, to whom please give my own best regards.]

[1] Gosse's *Life of William Congreve* (London: W. Heinemann, 1924) had just appeared in a second edition, revised and enlarged.

[2] The Royal Society of Literature asked Gide in 1926 what titles or honorifics were to follow his name on the list of honorary fellows soon to appear. He replied: "Honors began by fleeing me. Later I fled honors. On the list of Honorary Fellows of the Royal Society my name is not to be followed by any title. The F.R.S.L. will only stand out better." (*Journal,* August 23, 1926.) Oxford University gave Gide the degree of Doctor Honoris Causa in 1946, and in 1947 he received the Nobel Prize in Literature. He never belonged to the French Academy.

[3] Gide refers principally to Henri Massis' articles in the *Revue Universelle,* November 1 and 15, 1923. *Les Caves du Vatican* and *Dostoievsky* were the books that Massis singled out.

[4] *Les Faux-Monnayeurs.* Part I was published in the *Nouvelle Revue Française,* March 1, 1925, and the book appeared in February, 1926.

[5] A "classical English edition" of excerpts from *Si le Grain ne meurt,* edited by V.F. Boyson, was published at Oxford by the Clarendon Press in 1925.

[6] Jacques Copeau left Paris, after closing the Vieux-Colombier, for his country residence at Pernand-Vergelesse in Burgundy. There he recovered his Catholic faith; indeed, most of Gide's intimate friends became converted to Catholicism.

[7] Two *Journal* entries: June 8, 1925, "Finished *les Faux-Monnayeurs*"; July 14, 1925, "Departure for the Congo."

77. GIDE TO GOSSE, *January 15, 1925, from Cuverville*

BIEN CHER AMI,   Je viens d'être assez malade; d'abord une inter-
minable grippe, puis aussitôt après, une crise d'appendicite; on dé-
couvre, en m'ouvrant le ventre que, sans m'en douter, j'en souffrais
depuis des années! C'est-à-dire que l'opération n'a pas été des plus
simples. Quittant enfin la clinique, je rentre à la villa et reprends
contact avec le monde des vivants et des lettres, pour apprendre,
avec quelle joie! votre nouveau titre.

J'aime cette expression "rendre des honneurs" à quelqu'un; cela
implique vraiment qu'ils sont *dûs*. Voici qui va achever de me guérir.
Permettez-moi de joindre mes félicitations à celles de vos proches et
de vos intimes. Vous savez de quel cœur je m'associe à ce qui vous
touche.

Veuillez présenter, je vous prie, mes plus sensibles hommages à
Lady Gosse et me croire votre très fidèle, très reconnaissant et très
dévoué

ANDRÉ GIDE.

[I have been pretty ill of late—first an obstinate grippe, and
right afterward a siege of appendicitis; they found on operating
that I had been a victim of it for years! Which meant that the
operation was not exactly a simple one. Out of hospital at last,
I come home and regain contact with the world of life and letters, and hear—with what delight!—about your new title.[1]

I like the expression "pay honor" to someone: it really signi-
fies that honor is due. This is something that will speed me back
to health. Let me add my congratulations to those of your nearest
and dearest. You know how deeply I feel myself identified with
everything that concerns you.

Please give Lady Gosse my most cordial regards.]

¹ Gide left the hospital January 10. Earlier that month Gosse had been knighted. *Le Temps* published the fact January 9; a major reason for the distinction was the critic's fifty years of devoted promotion of Anglo-French literary relations.

78. GIDE TO GOSSE, *October 25, 1925, from Bangui*

MON CHER GRAND AMI   Il est temps que je vous écrive si je veux que cette carte vous arrive à temps pour vous souhaiter, à vous et aux vôtres, heureux Noël et bonne année. La grande distance qui nous sépare (me voici presque au centre de l'Afrique, et d'ici peu je m'y enfoncerai plus avant encore) ne diminue en rien la profonde affection que je vous garde, et ma grande reconnaissance. Alors que presque personne encore ne me considérait, en France, vous m'avez bien voulu *prendre au sérieux*. Je compte bien le raconter un jour.

Croyez-moi, bien respectueusement

Votre fidèle et dévoué ANDRÉ GIDE.

[It is time I wrote you if I expect this card to reach you in time to wish you—you and your family—a Merry Christmas and a Happy New Year. The great distance between us (here am I, near the middle of Africa and shortly to penetrate even deeper)¹ does not in the least lessen my deep affection for you or my great gratitude. At a time when almost no one was aware of me in France, you were disposed to *believe in me*. I certainly mean to tell the story of it someday.²]

¹ Gide, accompanied by Marc Allégret, was to have left Bangui on October 26 in a Ford. He made the trip much more arduous by refusing to take the customary route to the Chad and following an itinerary through the bush that lengthened the trip by two months.

Bangui
25 Oct. 25 —

Mon cher grand ami

Il est temps que je vous écrive si je veux
que cette carte vous arrive à temps pour vous
souhaiter, à vous et aux vôtres, heureux Noël
et bonne année. La grande distance qui
nous sépare (me voici bientôt au centre de
l'Afrique, et d'ici peu je m'y enfoncerai plus
avant encore) ne diminue en rien la

profonde affection que je vous garde, et ma
grande reconnaissance. Alors que presque
personne encore ne me considérait, en France,
vous m'avez bien voulu prendre au sérieux.
Je compte bien le raconter un jour...

Croyez-moi, bien respectueusement

votre fidèle et dévoué

André Gide

He published his journal of it, *Voyage au Congo,* in 1927, and its sequel, *Le Retour du Tchad,* in 1928. The first is dedicated to the memory of Joseph Conrad, whose *Heart of Darkness* Gide often quotes; he traversed its very region.

² Gide did not write an *éloge* of Edmund Gosse when Gosse died, as he did of Conrad and Bennett. But on March 11, 1930, he wrote Philip Gosse expressing his gratitude and his admiration for the understanding generosity of Gosse's criticism, and he declared a wish that his letter be published. (See pp. 203–205.)

79. GIDE TO GOSSE, *July 27, 1926, from Cuverville*

MON CHER AMI   J'ai appris, à mon retour en France, que vous veniez de visiter Paris — ce qui m'a rendu quelque peu jaloux de ceux qui avaient pu vous voir et vous fêter. Je ne vous ai écrit qu'une fois, au cours de mon long voyage, aux approches de Christmas, et ne suis encore pas bien sûr que vous ayez reçu ma lettre, car il en est un certain nombre qui se sont égarées. Quant à celles qui m'étaient adressées là-bas, il en est beaucoup (le plus grand nombre) que je n'ai reçu qu'à Paris, ou qu'à Cuverville, a fortnight ago, — certaines datées d'octobre, et même de septembre 25. Voilà ce que c'est que de s'en aller si loin.

J'ai poussé jusqu'au Tchad; et j'ai même traversé cet affreux lac. On ne dira jamais la monotonie sans grandeur de cet immense pays, l'informité du paysage; mais l'intérêt des questions humaines, sociales, morales etc. qui se lèvent à chaque pas devant vous, dépasse tout ce que je pouvais attendre, et compense amplement la déception que la nature peut vous causer. J'espère qu'il en paraîtra quelque reflet dans le récit de voyage que je compte donner bientôt.

Le retour par le Cameroun, à pied et à cheval deux mois durant, par une chaleur torride, m'a passablement fatigué, et je vais partir dans deux jours pour le midi de la France, chercher un repos que je n'ai pu trouver encore.

Ce mot n'est qu'un signe d'affection, en passant — pour vous dire les sentiments très fidèles de votre reconnaissant et dévoué

ANDRÉ GIDE.

[I heard on my return to France that you had just been in Paris,[1] and that made me no little envious of those who could see you and entertain you. I wrote you only once in the course of my long journey, when Christmas was coming on, and I am still not entirely sure that you got my letter, for a certain number of them went astray; and of the ones that were mailed to me out there a large number—the majority—did not reach me until I was in Paris, or Cuverville, a fortnight ago—some of them dated October and even September, 1925. Such is the price of going so far away.

I went as far as the Chad, and I even crossed that horrible lake. I shall never be able to convey the trivial monotony of that vast land, the shapelessness of its landscape; but the fascination of the human, social, moral, and other problems that confront you every step of the way exceeds anything I could anticipate, and it is ample compensation for the disappointment produced by nature. I am hoping that some impression of it will emerge from the account of my journey that I mean to give shortly. The return trip by way of the Cameroons,[2] walking and horseback riding for two months in a scorching heat, wore me down quite a little, and I am starting in a couple of days for the Midi in search of the rest that I haven't managed to get so far.

These few lines are only an incidental token of affection.]

[1] On November 27, 1925, Gosse had received an honorary doctorate at the Sorbonne. A luncheon was given for him on November 26 by the France-Grande Bretagne Association, M. Emile Legouis, professor of English Literature at the Sorbonne, presiding. This visit was the occasion of an engaging letter:

Henry Davray to Edmund Gosse, November 20, 1925
(The italicized matter is in English)

HONORED SIR AND DEAR FRIEND, I admit that it was rather *flippant* of me to speak of the Folies Bergères in such a way, but it is the fault of the excellent Bellows. That is my way of responding to his austere and *dour* personality. Otherwise my natural sympathy would get the better of me, and I should finally become a convert to Quakerism, and that would produce a scandal, which the Holy Scriptures discountenance.

Be that as it may, he is taking you to a hotel at which you will not encounter any distasteful persons except provincial representatives, perhaps inflamed by the current debates. For the so-called Hôtel de Bourgogne is right behind the Palais Bourbon, where the people's representatives meet!... I am acquainted with only the outside of it, but I suppose *that it is up to the idea of comfort a self-denying Quaker* can entertain. This evening I am sending another batch of notes to the press, of the same kind as those you must have seen in l'*Intransigeant*. I shall send you a copy. Among the guests next Thursday you will find Vielé-Griffin, back from his Périgord castle and rejoiced to see you again. We will go together to the reopening session at the Sorbonne, and we shall be there for the conferring of degrees, so as to add our applause to that of the enthusiastic audience when yours is conferred!

As to your Commander's cravat, it was our friend Philippe Berthelot who *did the trick,* if I may put it so, with the complicity of Aristide Briand; I had been nothing but the go-between. I am sure that Philippe Berthelot would be extremely delighted if he got from you a little confidential note confessing your suspicion that he had had a finger in the scheme; but it had better go to his house, 126 *bis* Boulevard du Montparnasse, 14ième. And if you are still in Paris on Sunday, a day on which he always has many friends in to tea, we can go and see him together under Bellows' tutelary guardianship.

All of us are very happy to be seeing you again; meanwhile I am, with all seriousness and very affectionately, your humble and devoted disciple, HENRY-D. DAVRAY

[2] An aftermath of the trip to Africa, about which Gide had been thinking for years in a desultory way, was a report of his findings that he brought back for the Colonial Department. (During the trip he somehow became *chargé de mission.*) The sight of poverty-stricken

and ill-treated Negroes had outraged his deep sense of justice and his "sympathy." A scandal about the "big concessions" broke out and was investigated by the Chamber of Deputies. According to Gide, the natives were brutally exploited and some were killed by employers for refusing to obey orders. Gide was chiefly engaged by the social phenomena observed, but not to the neglect of the land and its flora and fauna. The return trip through the Cameroons lasted from February 20 to May 14, the day when Gide sailed from Douala. He, Allégret, and their convoy had sailed up the Logone, with Allégret filming scenes of the native life and the landscape. On March 20 they left the Logone to cross the bush with eighty porters and four horses. Gide quickly tired of horseback riding and preferred to walk; sometimes he used the *tipoye* (system of native bearers).   Much of his exhaustion was due to the heat.

80. GOSSE TO GIDE, *August 22, 1926, from London*

MY DEAR GIDE, It gave me great pleasure to receive your letter from Cuverville. I did get your earlier letter from central Africa, but did not know how to respond to it, as you seemed moving across incalculable deserts over pathless sands! But I welcome you back in France, and I hope you will give us impressions of your strange adventures such as you, alone, are capable of doing.

You must write them soon, if you please, for if you delay too long, I shall not be here to welcome them. In a few days I shall complete my 77 years, and although I am not conscious as yet of any mental infirmity, my body gets more and more "crawxy" (as we say). I shall certainly never come to France again,[1] but I hope to see you in London.

I read everything you publish, and always with admiration of your sincerity and your courage. I do not always agree with you, but that is another thing. I admire extremely your rectitude, and it is all the more marked because most of contemporary literature seems to me to be cowardly and conventional.[2] It all tends to be standardised and the only salvation for us is to specialise,—to say clearly and boldly what we, individually, believe and feel. I should like you to know that I sympathise deeply with your determination to see things as they are to you.

May I venture to wish, however, that you would try to release yourself from your bondage to the Russians, and particularly to Dostoevski?[3] We have all in time been subjected to the magic of this epileptic monster. But his genius has only led us astray, as I should say to any young writer of merit who appealed to me. Read what you like, only don't waste your time reading D. He is the cocaine and morphine of modern literature.

Do not be long before writing to me again. Tell me what works you are projecting and what use you are going to make of your African travels. Will you not come over to London; say towards the end of October? I should like to organise a public dejeuner in your honour. Will not that tempt you?

Your affectionate Friend, EDMUND GOSSE

[1] But see pp. 28.

[2] As early as 1893 Gosse had pointed out (in *Questions at Issue*) the jeopardy in which the English novel stood because writers were adhering to obsolete conventions. At the same time, however, Gosse distrusted the influence of various convention-defying books. Taine in his latter years made pronouncements to the same purport: e.g., "The effect of certain reading matter—books by Swinburne, Rossetti, Daudet, and Bourget—was that of hashish and morphine." (*Correspondance de Taine,* IV, 237.)

[3] Gosse is referring to *Les Faux-Monnayeurs.* He had been disappointed by the book, as Gide feared he would be. During Gide's trip to the Congo, Gosse wrote about *The Coiners* in the *Sunday Times* column "The World of Books." (March 21, 1926.) He frankly disliked it, though he praised its style; and without really condemning its author, he deplored his enslavement to Dostoevski's perversities.

81. GOSSE TO GIDE, *December 19, 1926, from London*

MY DEAR GIDE, I am very angry with you! You have published a book ("Le Grain ne meurt") which all the world is talking about. You have not sent it to me,—your earliest and most loyal admirer.[1] Pfui! I know all about it and I must read it. Send it to me *at once:* if you do not, I shall know that you have no confidence in my discretion or my indulgence.

Ever sincerely yours, EDMUND GOSSE

[1] Gide had promised (see Letter 74) to send Gosse *Si le Grain ne meurt,* but his courage had failed him.

82. GIDE TO GOSSE, *December 22, 1926, from* [?]

MON CHER EDMUND GOSSE, Non, ne vous étonnez pas de n'avoir point reçu "Si le grain ne meurt." Je ne l'ai envoyé à *personne* et n'ai laissé la N.R.F. faire aucun "service."

Mais vous me demandez ce livre d'une façon si cordiale, si exquise, que je ferai pour vous une exception, sitôt que la grippe me permettra de sortir et d'aller en prendre un exemplaire à la N.R.F.

Je vous ai fait adresser récemment un mirifique exemplaire du *Journal des Faux-Monnayeurs,* qui, j'espère, ne se sera pas égaré car dès à présent il est devenu rare et très recherché. Mes amis les plus intimes se sont vivement opposés à la publication de *Si le grain ne meurt;* c'est ce qui m'a amené à ne point le leur envoyer et, du même coup, à le refuser à chacun et à tous. Je ne parviens pas, néanmoins, à me persuader que j'.ai eu tort de le laisser paraître — et aujourd'hui déjà, certains des plus opposés commencent à revenir sur leur première opinion.

Tous mes meilleurs vœux de nouvelle année pour vous et les vôtres.

Croyez à ma bien fidèle et reconnaissante amitié   ANDRÉ GIDE.

[No, don't be disconcerted at not having received *Si le Grain ne meurt*. I did not send it to *anyone,* and I have not let the N.R.F. distribute any review copies.[1]

But you ask me for the book in so warmhearted and irresistible a way that I am going to make an exception in your favor as soon as an attack of grippe will let me get out to pick up a copy at the N.R.F.

I sent you just lately a superfine copy of the *Journal des Faux-Monnayeurs.* and I hope it hasn't gone astray, for the book has now come to be very rare and hard to find.[2] — My most intimate friends protested emphatically against publishing *Si le Grain ne meurt;*[3] that is what led me not to send it to them and, at the same time, to withhold it from all and sundry. Just the same, I can't manage to persuade myself that I was wrong to have it come out—and some of the most opposed have already begun to change their original opinion.

All best wishes for the New Year to you and yours.]

[1] It was a fact that Gide had not given the publisher permission to distribute any review copies of *Si le Grain ne meurt,* but, anomalously and rather surprisingly, in October, 1926, he had authorized the sale of the book. The inconsistency is very characteristic of Gide. The personae in his novels go in their actions to the logical extremes of their opinions: Gide himself, who so wished to be perfectly sincere, was inhibited mostly by dread of hurting persons he loved and often remained well within the limits of what he would have liked to do.

[2] The original edition of *Le Journal des faux-monnayeurs* was published in 1926. There were two copies on Japanese vellum, twenty-five on tinted Holland (Dutch) paper, and 535 on white Dutch paper.

³ Roger Martin du Gard had vainly tried to stop Gide from publishing the book; he was convinced of the "pathetic uselessness of scandal." Jacques Copeau was of the same opinion, and he blamed Gide for indulging himself in the "nostalgic appeal to martyrdom." Martin du Gard felt that, as Gosse had recently remarked, Gide was suffering from a "Slavic intoxication." (Martin du Gard, *op. cit.*, pp. 44–46.)

83. GOSSE TO GIDE, *December 26, 1926, from London*

MY DEAR GIDE,   It was very neglectful of me not to thank you at once for "Le Journal des Faux-Monnayeurs," which I read with great interest, and prize. You will perhaps be intrigued to hear that we have at this moment a case of a closely parallel kind. A Club of school-boys has been discovered by the fact that they forced one of their number to commit suicide.¹ The circumstances were very much like what you describe in your novel. They called themselves the Red Avengers! The ringleaders (boys of 14 to 16) are now to be tried for murder.

I look forward with keen anticipation to your gift of "Si le Grain ne meurt." I regard you as the most important artist now writing in France and I cannot afford to miss any movement of your mind.

I hope la grippe is better. My Wife joins me in warmest greetings.

Yours always EDMUND GOSSE

¹ A suicide similar to that of little Boris in *Les Faux-Monnayeurs* had actually happened in the Clermont-Ferrand lycée in 1909. It had taken place in circumstances very like those cited by Gosse.

26.12.26

My dear Gide

It was very neglectful
of me not to thank you at once
for "Le Journal des Faux-Monnayeurs",
which I read with great interest,
and prize.   You will perhaps
be intrigued to hear that we
have at this moment a case of
a closely parallel kind.   A
club of school-boys has been
discovered by the fact that they
forced one of their number to commit suicide.   The circumstances
were very much like what you
describe in your novel.   They called

themselves the Red Avengers! The
ringleaders (boys of 14 to 16)
are now to be tried for murder.

I look forward with
keen anticipation to your gift
of " Si le Grain ne meurt." I
regard you as the most important artist now writing
in France, and I cannot
afford to miss any movement
of your mind.

I hope la grippe
is better. My Wife joins me
in warmest greetings.

Yours always
Edmund Gosse

84. GIDE TO GOSSE, *December 30, 1926, from Cuverville*

CHER GRAND AMI   Savez-vous que j'ai failli très *"mal prendre"* votre lettre...

Eh quoi! vous me demandez si je connais "Father and Son" — !!! un livre que j'ai lu et relu, et fait lire je ne sais combien de fois; un livre avec qui j'ai vécu, que j'ai senti écrit *pour moi* et qui put réveiller les échos les plus indiscrets dans mon cœur. Dans le temps j'ai dû vous en parler longuement, m'efforçant de prendre un peu le parti de votre père contre vous — mais il y a déjà longtemps de cela; c'était avant la guerre.

Vous trouverez, si vous continuez la lecture (ah! je souhaite presque que vous l'interrompiez) de "Si le grain ne meurt" un trait commun avec votre livre, plus important que le Kaleidoscope: c'est l'émerveillement devant la faune et la flore marine — dont je me souviens que vous parlez admirablement dans F. and S. Mon livre soulève de l'enthousiasme et de l'indignation. Je crois qu'il mérite l'un et l'autre; mais déjà je vous dis que si, après l'avoir achevé, vous deviez me retirer votre estime et votre amitié, ce serait un des gros chagrins de ma vie. Fidèlement votre

ANDRÉ GIDE.

Ma femme vous demande de bien vouloir présenter à Madame Gosse ses souvenirs et ses vœux les meilleurs — J'y joins les miens, de tout mon cœur.

[Do you know, I came near to being put "out of sorts" by your letter.[1]

So you ask me if I know *Father and Son!!!* — a book that I read and reread and made others read, I don't know how many times; a book that I have lived with and felt was written *for me,* one with the power to stir up the most intrusive echoes. In my time I must have discussed it with you at length and tried to take in some sort your father's side against you. But that was a long time ago—before the war.

You will find if you keep on reading *Si le Grain ne meurt*—and oh, I almost wish you would stop it short—one feature in common with your book, one more important than the kaleidoscope; and that is the wonderment in the presence of the marine fauna and flora that, I remember, you describe superbly in *Father and Son*. My own book evokes both enthusiasm and resentment.[2] I believe it deserves both; but I tell you now that if, after you had finished reading it, you were to revoke your respect and your friendship, it would be one of the great regrets of my life.

My wife asks you please to give Mrs. Gosse her regards and best wishes. To them I add mine, most cordially.]

[1] The letter that annoyed Gide is missing.

[2] Roger Martin du Gard sees in Gide's inveterate need for explaining, defending, and justifying himself a betrayal of the "moral reflexes" that he owes to his puritanical ancestry.

85. GOSSE TO GIDE, *January 7, 1927, from London*

MY DEAR GIDE, I have now read "Si le grain ne meurt" very carefully to the end. I have already read much of it twice. Up to page 44 of Tome III I have nothing but admiration of your art, your originality, your exquisite manner of writing. There are passages here which will bear comparison with the best modern literature.[1]

But when I read the "Deuxième Partie" I am confronted by an immense difficulty. What can I say? Yet I must not leave what I feel unsaid. I pray you to bear with me.

The *facts* here related offer me no surprise, since I divined the truth when I read "L'Immoraliste" more than twenty years ago, while later publications have confirmed my knowledge. This has not affected my feeling, personal or literary, since I have never allowed the idiosyncrasies of my friends to blind me to their qualities. I am not a critic of temperaments, nor so ignorant as to believe myself fitted to be a judge.

But now you have gone much further, and I cannot help asking myself, in the face of this narrative.—Was it wise? Was it necessary? Is it useful? I am incapable of answering these questions, which leaves me in a very painful perplexity.

Heaven forbid that I should be such a prig as to put my instinct in the matter before yours. You have acted not without reflection, certainly not without a marvellous courage. You possess so unusual a genius that perhaps it may claim to be a law to itself. But *why* have you done it, and what advantages to any one can accrue from it?

If you think that my old (and undiminished) affection gives me a right to ask you this question, I beg you to send me a full and clear reply. I do not ask it from curiosity, or in a priggish or dictatorial spirit; I ask it in deep sympathy and in an earnest wish to comprehend your position.

I am, my dear Gide, now as ever,

Your attached friend, EDMUND GOSSE

[1] About the first part of *Si le Grain ne meurt* Gosse agrees with many persons of taste. Arnold Bennett went so far as to declare it Gide's best book—an opinion shared by Léon-Paul Fargue. (*Journal of Arnold Bennett,* p. 936.)

86. GIDE TO GOSSE, *January 16, 1927, from Roquebrune-Cap Martin*

MON CHER EDMUND GOSSE   Quelle excellente lettre je reçois de vous, et combien profondément elle me touche!

Pourquoi j'ai écrit ce livre? — Parce que j'ai cru que je *devais* l'écrire.

Ce que j'en attends? — Rien que de très fâcheux pour moi (et pas seulement pour moi, hélas!). Et certes il a fallu que cette obligation morale fût bien impérative pour me faire passer outre; mais, vraîment, il m'eût paru lâche de me laisser arrêter par la considération de cette peine et du danger. Je sentais que je ne pourrais mourir satisfait si j'avais gardé tout cela sur le cœur.

Cher ami, j'ai le mensonge en horreur. Je ne puis prendre mon parti de ce camouflage conventionnel qui travestit systématiquement l'œuvre de X, de Y, et de tant d'autres. J'ai écrit ce livre pour "créer un précédent," donner un exemple de franchise, éclairer quelques uns, en rassurer d'autres, forcer l'opinion à tenir compte de ce que l'on ignore ou que l'on affecte d'ignorer — au grand dam de la psychologie, de la morale, de l'art ... et de la société.

J'ai écrit ce livre parce que je préfère être haï, qu'aimé pour ce que je ne suis pas. "Je reviendrais volontiers de l'autre monde, pour démentir celuy qui me formerait aultre que je n'étais, fût-ce pour m'honorer," disait Montaigne.

J'ajoute que je n'ai tiré de ce livre qu'une édition vite épuisée, et qu'il n'est pas dans mes intentions de le laisser réimprimer — d'ici longtemps du moins — sinon en faisant tomber tout ce qui peut prêter à redire. Mais je voulais ne pas mourir sans pouvoir sentir qu'*il est là*.

Je vous parle sans effort et sans crainte, et même je suis heureux de vous parler. Veuillez voir dans tout ce que je vous dis un témoignage de ma grande estime et de mon amitié profonde. Votre reconnaissant et dévoué

ANDRÉ GIDE.

[What a fine letter I have from you, and how deeply I am moved by it!

Why did I write this book? Because I thought I *had* to write it.[1]

What advantages do I expect from it? I expect nothing but consequence painful to me (and not only to me, alas).[2] And of course the moral obligation had to be more than a little imperious

to make me persist; but in truth it would have seemed to me
cowardly to let myself be stopped by contemplation of the
distress, or of the risk. I had the feeling that I could not have
died in peace if I had kept all this locked up in me.

My dear friend, I abominate falsehood. I can't endure having
a share in the customary camouflage that deliberately belies the
writing of X, Y, and many another.[3] I wrote this book to "create
a precedent," to set an example of candor; to enlighten some persons, hearten others, and compel public opinion to reckon
with something of which it is oblivious or pretends to be, to
the immense impairment of psychology, morality, art—and
society.

I wrote this book because I had rather be hated than be beloved for what I am not. "I would willingly come from the
other world, to give him the lie, that should frame me other than
I had beene: were it he meant to honour mee," Montaigne said.[4]

I will add that I printed but one quickly exhausted edition
of the book and that I am not minded to have it reprinted—at
least, for a long time to come—except with the elimination of
everything censurable. But I did not want to die without knowing that it is *there*.

I am talking to you without strain and without fear, and I
am actually happy to be talking to you. Please do see in all I
am telling you a testimony to my deep respect and steadfast
friendship.]

[1] For ten years Gide had been expressing the same thoughts in his
Journal. "I am not writing these Memoirs to defend myself. I am not
called on to defend myself since I am not accused, I am writing them
before being accused. I am writing them in order to be accused."
(*Journal*, January 19 and 21, 1917.) "...it seems to me that everything remains to be said and that, up to now, I have merely prepared
the way." Roger Martin du Gard had urged him to tell more than
he had at first dared; he reproached Gide for having "scamped the
question." But Martin du Gard was opposed to publication while
Gide was living.

² In a conversation with the French critic Léon Pierre-Quint, Gide admitted responsibility for his wife's unhappiness; it had been a mistake for him to marry. The last pages of *Si le Grain ne meurt,* in which he tells why he married, have been very adversely criticized. (Léon Pierre-Quint, *André Gide,* Paris: Stock, 1952, p. 390.)

³ Gide refers to Wilde and Proust, among others. (*Journal,* October 1, 1927.)

⁴ Montaigne, *Essays,* III, 9., trans. John Florio.

87. GOSSE TO GIDE, *June 4, 1927, from London*

MY DEAR GIDE,   A M. Pigon?¹ has written to me (3 times!) to insist that I should write for some book of his an eloge of your writings. I have refused, because I never join in these combinations, and besides have no leisure to do it. But if you should hear of the matter I want you to be quite sure that I rejoice in any honour that is done you, although I decline to be one of the geese that applaud you in the Capitol!   Ever sincerely yours, EDMUND GOSSE

¹ G. Pigon was director of the Editions du Capitole, Paris; he was preparing the book *Hommage à Gide,* published in 1928 in the series "Les Contemporains." On April 14 Gide wrote in his *Journal:* "I almost asked [Bernstein] yesterday for a defense of *Les Faux-Monnayeurs* for the book the Capitole is preparing." There is indeed an article by Bernstein; it opens the volume.

88. GIDE TO GOSSE, *April 8, 1928, from* [?]

CHER GRAND AMI,   Votre dernière lettre m'émeut, comme toutes celles que je reçois de vous, d'une cordialité toujours si chaude et si exquise; mais davantage encore, car, tandis que les années s'écoulent, je sens toujours et toujours mieux, le prix, la rareté d'une sympathie comme la vôtre.

Vous êtes aujourd'hui mon seul ami aîné; aussi, de quel cœur je vous écoute! Mais une phrase de votre lettre m'attriste, me consterne: Vous n'avez pas reçu l'an dernier mon *Voyage au Congo*. J'ai, tout aussitôt, consulté ma liste d'envois, pour constater que, non seulement je vous l'avais envoyé, mais encore un exemplaire sur papier "de luxe"!!! Quantité d'envois de ce livre se sont égarés, détournés sans doute par un employé infidèle qui, depuis, a été congédié. Ce qui a facilité ces escamotages, c'est le fait que tous ces livres ont été expédiés sans dédicaces, mais seulement avec ma carte de visite, car j'étais, comme il en advient souvent, "en voyage." J'inscris donc aussitôt votre nom sur un nouvel exemplaire (mais, hélas! un papier ordinaire cette fois, car les "luxe" sont épuisés) ainsi que sur le "Retour du Tchad" qui y fait suite. Vous recevrez les deux volumes en même temps, dans quelques jours.

Non, je n'ai fait appel à aucun étranger pour le livre du Capitole; et, de toute manière, je me serais fait scrupule de solliciter de vous quelque nouvel article; mais ce que vous me dites de ce projet d'écrire encore quelques pages à mon sujet, m'emplit de joie. Il se trouve que l'édition américaine des *Counterfeiters* remporte un certain succès, ce qui encourage Knopf, mon éditeur, à lancer une édition anglaise. Et sans doute fera-t-il de même pour *Les Caves du Vatican,* dont il m'a demandé de changer le titre scandaleux! et qui paraît maintenant comme "Lafcadio's Adventures."

Le traduction de mon *Voyage au Congo* doit également paraître bientôt. Enfin, Heyneman [*sic*] m'a fait l'honneur de choisir ma *Symphonie Pastorale*, pour figurer dans le second volume des "*Great short stories of the World.*" Je m'en réjouis en raison de ma grande sympathie pour l'Angleterre. Mais persuadez-vous que les élogieuses phrases de votre chère lettre me touchent bien davantage, et que votre goût m'importe bien plus que celui du "grand public." N'importe: il est possible que je donne à la langue anglaise la primeur de *L'Ecole des Femmes,* le court roman que je suis en train d'écrire et qui sera achevé, j'espère, dans quelques mois. C'est une façon de marquer ma reconnaissance.

Au revoir, cher grand ami. Veuillez présenter mes respectueux hommages à Lady Gosse et croire à la bien fidèle et profonde affection de votre dévoué et reconnaissant   ANDRÉ GIDE.

[Your last letter[1] moves me, like all the letters I get from you, its cordiality is so warm and so exquisite; and the more so because, as the years slip away, I am more and more sensible of the value, the rarity, of an understanding such as yours.

You are now my one elder friend;[2] how gladly, then, do I listen to you! But one sentence in your letter depresses and upsets me: you did not receive last year my *Voyage au Congo*. I quickly looked up my list of presentation copies and found not only that I had sent you the book, but also that it was one of the de luxe copies on special paper!!! Many presentation copies of that book were lost—pilfered without doubt by an untrustworthy employee who has since been discharged. What made these thieveries the easier was that all these books were sent out without inscriptions and with nothing but my card, since I was then traveling, as I often am. I write your name, then, in a fresh copy right away—only, alas, of the ordinary trade edition this time, because the de luxe copies are all gone—and also in the *Retour du Tchad,* which is a continuation of it. You will get both books together in a few days.

No, I did not call on any foreigner for the Capitole book;[3] and anyway I should have had qualms about begging any new article of you; but what you tell me about your plan to write some additional pages about me leaves me overjoyed.[4] It seems that the American edition of *The Counterfeiters* is doing fairly well, and that encourages Knopf,[5] my publisher, to put out an English edition. And he will doubtless do the same for *Les Caves du Vatican,* the title of which he asked me to change as being offensive! and which is now appearing as *Lafcadio's Adventures.*

The translation of my *Voyage au Congo* is likewise to appear soon. Finally, Heinemann has done me the honor to choose my

Symphonie Pastorale for inclusion in the second volume of *Great Short Stories of the World*. I am gladdened by this because of my great affection for England. But be assured that the words of praise in your valued letter affect me a good deal more and that your taste matters much more to me than that of the "general public." Never mind: I may give the English language first publication of *L'Ecole des femmes,* the short novel I am writing now, which will be finished, I am hoping, in a few months. It is one way of showing my gratitude.

Au revoir, *cher grand ami.* Please give my respectful regards to Lady Gosse, and believe in the faithful and deep affection of your devoted and grateful					ANDRÉ GIDE.]

¹ Unfortunately this is missing.

² Gide was then fifty-nine; Gosse seventy-nine.

³ This is *Hommage à Gide, Etudes, Souvenirs, Témoignages.* The printing was finished September 10, 1928, four months after the death of Edmund Gosse. There were articles by twenty-two writers, among them Paul Valéry, Albert Thibaudet, François Mauriac, Jacques Copeau, Jean Schlumberger, and Roger Martin du Gard.

⁴ Gosse's last printed mention of Gide is, as far as I know, that in the *Sunday Times* article of November 14, 1927.

⁵ *Voyage au Congo* and *Le Retour du Tchad,* translated by Dorothy Bussy, were published together as *Travels in the Congo* (New York and London: Alfred A. Knopf, 1929). *L'Ecole des femmes* (*Nouvelle Revue Française,* 1929), translated by Mrs. Bussy as *The School for Wives,* was published by Knopf in the same year. *Les Faux-Monnayeurs,* also translated by Dorothy Bussy, was published by Knopf in New York in 1927 under the title *The Counterfeiters.* *Les Caves du Vatican* was first given the English title *The Vatican Swindle* (Knopf, 1925); it was republished in 1927 as *Lafcadio's Adventures.* *La Symphonie pastorale,* translated by Dorothy Bussy, was published in English (1931) with *Isabelle* under the title *Two Symphonies.*

APPENDIX

A GOSSE CHRONOLOGY, 1849–1928

1849   Edmund Gosse was born September 21 at Hackney, a sub-
urb of London. His parents, who married late, belonged to
the puritanical sect of the Plymouth Brethren. Philip Gosse,
Edmund's father, of Huguenot ancestry, was a naturalist of
distinction. His ˏmother, Emily Bowes, had Bostonian parents; Gosse did not learn of his American ancestry until
1888. His mother had a conspicuous literary gift but wrote
only devotional works; she thought novels sinful.

1856   Mrs. Gosse died of cancer.

1858   Philip Gosse with his son settled in Devonshire. The young
boy was fascinated by the sea and became deeply interested
in his father's researches. He was given an extremely strict
and puritanical education.

1859   Edmund was publicly baptized—to him, the capital event of
his childhood.

1861   Sent to school for the first time, he acquired a little French and
German.

1862   Philip Gosse married Eliza Brightwen. (Edmund had and
retained for the rest of his life a great affection for his step-
mother.)

1863   He was sent to boarding school.

1867   He became a clerk in the cataloguing section of the British
Museum; he lived at the house of two elderly spinsters who
belonged to the Plymouth Brethren. He taught Sunday school;
he also taught himself the Scandinavian languages.

1870   The 1870 war making it impossible for him to go to France,
he took a trip to the Hebrides. He met Stevenson, later his
intimate friend.

1871   His first article was printed in *Fraser's Magazine*. He traveled
to the Lofoten Islands. An article of his about Ibsen, the first
to appear in England, was printed in the *Spectator*. His friendship with Swinburne began.

1872 On a trip to Denmark he met Andersen and the poet Paludan-Müller.

1873 Gosse wrote for the *Academy* and published his first volume of verse, *On Viol and Flute;* Robert Browning praised it. Gosse now became spiritually free from his father.

1874 On a second trip to Denmark the young critic preached "a gospel of intellectual emancipation," with the poems of Baudelaire and Swinburne as text.

1875 He became a translator to the Board of Trade. In August he married Nelly Epps. He wrote, at the suggestion of Georg Brandes, a long article on the poetry of Swinburne; it was translated into Danish, Swedish, German, and Dutch. Gosse met Mallarmé in London.

1876 He had the signal experience of reading "L'Après-midi d'un faune."

1878 He visited Paris.

1879 His first volume of criticism, *Studies in the Literature of Northern Europe,* was published. His son Philip was born.

1880 His reputation as critic was growing; he had many friends in the London literary world.

1881 He met Oscar Wilde; he was sent to Paris by the *Pall Mall Gazette* to write articles about the salons.

1882 He saw with excitement the cathedrals of Amiens, Noyon, Laon, and Reims. He wrote further articles on French salons.

1884 He was appointed Clark Lecturer at Cambridge University. On a trip to the United States he lectured for a few weeks, but refused a chair of English literature at Johns Hopkins University.

1886 His Cambridge appointment was renewed for three years.

1887 Reading *Crime and Punishment* in French, he found Dostoevski a remarkable psychologist.

1888 His father died.

1889 He published many articles and gave numerous lectures. He became a member of the National Club, a vehemently anti-popish Protestant group.

1891 His absorption in French literature steadily increased.

1893 "Symbolism and Mr. S. Mallarmé" was printed in the *Academy*. In April Gosse spent a week in Paris to gather information about the symbolist poets; he met Jean Moréas and Verlaine. *Questions at Issue* was published; two of its articles dealt with the novel in France and in England. Gosse defended Zola, accused of having written nothing but "filth and crimes." Back in London, he again saw Verlaine.

1894 A little poem by Verlaine dedicated to Gosse was published in the *Athenaeum*. Gosse entertained Mallarmé, who lectured in England, and he published an article on Heredia in the *Contemporary Review*.

1895 He lectured in the West End; he became president of the (London) Norwegian Club.

1896 Five long articles of his on French contemporary writing were printed in *Cosmopolis*.

1898 *Cosmopolis* having been discontinued, Gosse found an outlet for "Some Recent Literature in France" in the *Contemporary Review*.

1901 He summered in Dieppe. (From now on he spent a few weeks in France almost every year.) He published an unsigned article about Queen Victoria, who had just died; he wrote of her, rather audaciously for those days, not as an idol but simply as a woman.

1902 He spent a vacation in the southwest of France, the region of his paternal origins. He prepared an edition of twenty nineteenth-century French novels in English translation.

1904 A banquet was given for him in Paris; he lectured to a Paris audience on the influence of French poetry in England; he was appointed Librarian to the House of Lords; and he began his correspondence with André Gide.

1905 *French Profiles* was published.

1906 He became director of the Literary Supplement of the *Daily Mail*. (It lasted, however, only eighteen months.)

1907 He published, at first anonymously, *Father and Son*, "a study of two temperaments."

1909 His first article on Gide appeared in the *Contemporary Review*.

1911 His first meeting with Gide occurred in London, followed by his first visit to Pontigny. He published his *Collected Poems*.

1912 *Father and Son* was published in French. Gosse made his second visit to Pontigny. *Portraits and Sketches* was published. Gosse entertained Gide in London and introduced him to Henry James and George Moore.

1913 He received the rosette of the Legion of Honor.

1914 He retired as Librarian to the House of Lords. (He was an ardent Francophile throughout World War I.)

1916 He entertained Maurice Barrès in London and spent a few days in France as guest of the French government. He published *Inter Arma* and "Reims Revisited."

1918 He published *Three French Moralists* and "The Gallantry of France."

1919 His literary outlet ceased to be the *Daily Chronicle* and became the *Sunday Times*.

1920 He published *Malherbe and the Classical Reaction in the Seventeenth Century*.

1921 He published *Books on the Table*. He received an honorary doctorate from the University of Strasbourg; he lectured in French to an audience of 2,000.

1924 As president of the Royal Society of Literature he had Gide elected an honorary fellow.

1925 He was knighted: he became a Commander of the Legion of Honor.

1928 His last trip to France and his last meeting with Gide came at the end of April. On May 16 he died.

A GIDE CHRONOLOGY, 1869–1928

1869   André Gide was born November 22 in Paris. His father Paul, a professor of law at the University of Paris, belonged to a Huguenot family of southern France; his mother, née Juliette Rondeaux, came from the well-to-do Protestant bourgeoisie of Normandy.

1877   Gide entered a Paris Protestant school, the Ecole Alsacienne.

1880   Paul Gide died of intestinal tuberculosis. André, a nervous child, grew up under the affectionate but very strict care of his mother.

1881   He became extremely attached to his first cousin, Madeleine, two years his elder. They spent their summer vacation in Normandy with Madeleine's sisters and brothers.

1885   He received his first Communion.

1887   He made friends with Pierre Louÿs and Marcel Drouin.

1889   He took his B. A. degree at Paris.

1891   He published *Les Cahiers d'André Walter*. He met Oscar Wilde in Paris and became a frequent guest at the weekly meetings at the house of Mallarmé.

1893   He traveled to northern Africa in the company of J. P. Laurens; he had his first homosexual experience.

1895   He returned to Africa, where he encountered Oscar Wilde and Lord Alfred Douglas. His mother died. On October 8 he married his cousin Madeleine at Etretat, Normandy.

1896   He spent his honeymoon in Africa.

1897   He published *Les Nourritures terrestres* and contributed to Edouard Ducoté's review, *L'Ermitage*.

1899   He published *Le Prométhée mal enchaîné, Philoctète,* and *El Hadj*.

1901   *Le Roi Candaule* appeared.

1902   *L'Immoraliste* was published.

1903   *Saül* and *Prétextes* appeared.

1904   Gide built his Paris house, Villa Montmorency. He was present at a banquet honoring Edmund Gosse and received his first letter from Gosse.

1906   *Amyntas* appeared.

1907   *Le Retour de l'enfant prodigue* was published.

1909   In February Gide and Jean Schlumberger, Jacques Copeau, André Ruyters, Henri Ghéon, and "Michel Arnaud" (Marcel Drouin) published the first number of the *Nouvelle Revue Française*. Gide himself published *La Porte étroite*.

1910   *Oscar Wilde* appeared.

1911   The first edition of *Corydon* was privately printed. *Isabelle* and *Nouveaux Prétextes* appeared. Gide's first adult trip to England came in July; he met Gosse in London and invited him to Pontigny, where they spent ten days in August. Gide's correspondence with Arnold Bennett began in March.

1912   Gide published *Le Retour de l'enfant prodigue*, preceded by *five* other *traités*. He and Gosse were together again at Pontigny in August.

1913   Gosse visited Gide in Paris.

1914   *Souvenirs de la Cour d'Assises* and *Les Caves du Vatican* were published. Gide traveled to Turkey. He stopped writing to work for the Foyer Franco-Belge.

1916   He left the Foyer and began to write his "posthumous works" —*Corydon* and his memoirs. He discovered the autobiographical novels of "Mark Rutherford" (William Hale White). In September he went to Paris to join Gosse.

1918   Gide took Marc Allégret to England in June and spent the summer in and near Cambridge.

1919   He published *La Symphonie pastorale*.

1923   Gide's daughter was born. He published *Dostoievsky*.

1924   *Incidences* and *Corydon* were published. Gide was elected honorary fellow by the Royal Society of Literature.

1925   Gide started for the Congo.

1926   He returned to France. *Les Faux-Monnayeurs, Si le Grain ne meurt,* and *Le Journal des faux-monnayeurs* were published.

1928   In late April Gide called on Gosse in Paris; in May Gosse died.

THE LAND OF FRANCE
by Edmund Gosse to André Gide [*1911*]

Sometimes at night before the fire I sit,
To ponder in that lonely hour of dream,
When o'er the earth the ghosts of memory flit,
And dear dead faces in the embers gleam;
The days in multitudes besides me stream,
While joy recaptures many a province fair,
Glowing, and luminous, and debonair.

Little it matters where my dream begin;
Since, like a feathery seed upon the wind,
Southward my fancy can but speed and spin,
Until beneath my poising brain I find
The soul of rustic loveliness, reclin'd
In some French woodland quivering to the west
Or clad with flower-gold on some French hill's crest.

Sands of Dunkirk are not too cold for me;
Nor dales of Roussillon too full of fire;
Down Tarn and Lot my memory leaps in glee;
Long miles of poplar'd Anjou cannot tire
Feet that to frost-capp'd Dauphiné aspire;
Shouting of waves which on black Penmarch fall—
Slow streams at Aigues-Mortes—I love them all!

France! take my hands in those kind hands of thine;
Like a child swallow to thy fields I fly!
Warmth, beauty, calm and happiness are mine
When o'er me bends that soft and radiant sky,
When in that vivid atmosphere I sigh—
Sigh—for pure gladness, while my pulses dance
A joyful measure to the praise of France.

LETTERS OF ANDRE GIDE TO PHILIP GOSSE, 1929–1930

February 4, 1929, from Paris

A newspaper item* tells me of your intention to collect Sir Edmund Gosse's letters and states your address, that letters may be sent directly to you.

I shall, however, await a letter from you confirming that intention, before sending you copies of the very fine and very important letters that I received from Sir Edmund Gosse, who was so kind as to give me the rarest friendship and for whom I still have the deepest gratitude, the highest veneration, and a warm affection.

---

* France lost last May, in the person of Sir Edmund Gosse, not only a friend but also a champion of her literature and art. At a time when English intellectuals, under the influence of Carlyle and others, were being captivated by German thought, Edmund Gosse never in fifty years relinquished his propagation of French thought on the other side of the Channel.

Dr. Philip Gosse, his son, and Sir Edmund's intimate friend Mr. Evan Charteris are preparing a biography of the famous writer, and to it they plan to add a selection of his letters. The author of the masterpiece *Father and Son* was a remarkable letter writer, and he kept up a close correspondence with most of his famous contemporaries in England as well as in other countries.

In France especially, which he was accustomed to visit several times a year, Sir Edmund Gosse had many contacts and faithful friends. Dr. Philip Gosse would be happy to hear from any persons who possess interesting letters written by his father. His address is 25 Argyll Road, London, W. 8. —*Le Temps* (undated, quoted by Gide).

February 8, 1929, from Paris

Our letters crossed. I am ransacking my papers—which are in great disorder, for I have just moved—for Sir Edmund Gosse's letters; I have carefully safeguarded all of them. You will receive them within a few days. I shrink from parting with them, but it is preferable that you have them copied: I am afraid that my secretary, who does not know English, might make many mistakes.

I trust that you will send them back to me as soon as possible. They vary in importance, but I am sending you all of them, leaving it to you to judge which ones will suit the importance of the publication.

February 22, 1929, from Paris

Here are the letters of Sir Edmund Gosse, which I have now found. I do not let them out of my hands without some qualms, and I should appreciate your letting me know shortly that you have received them.

March 11, 1930, from Paris

Permit me to express my concern about the letters of Sir Edmund Gosse that I sent you on February 23, 1929. In March, 1929, you kindly let me know that this priceless packet was in your hands. Your letter encouraged me in the hope of having the letters back "as soon as possible." This was just a year ago.

I shall not surprise you, I trust, by telling you how very highly I value those letters and how distressed I should be if I were not to get them back.

Furthermore, I intend to include in a small privately printed volume a letter that I wrote to Sir Edmund Gosse about *Si le Grain ne meurt*—a letter in answer to his insistent question why I had decided to publish that book while still living. I should like to quote the precise phrasing of his friendly question and of the several very pertinent and solicitous comments that he kindly wrote me about that publication. Few persons spoke of my book with so broad, enlightened, and generous understanding as your father. I wish the publication of those few lines might serve to make both his mind and his heart better known in France.

I should, then, be extremely grateful if you could give me, as soon as possible, the means of satisfying this friendly wish.

April 14, 1930, from Paris

May I remind you of the letter that I wrote you on March 11? I seem to remember that you answered my letter almost at once and in the friendliest manner. But inasmuch as I have since heard nothing, and inasmuch as you may have forgotten my request, permit me to subjoin to this note a copy of my earlier letter.*

The publisher of the book of which I told you is growing impatient. Be assured that otherwise I should not venture to disturb you once more. You would be doing me a great favor if, in lieu of the original letters—which, as I said, I value greatly and hope that you will soon be able to return to me—you were to give me now a copy of the letters, which no doubt you had typed with a view to printing them.

* When, in March, 1930, Philip Gosse was ready to send back the letters, he was at a loss for an address, for Gide's letters bore none. To make certain that his father's letters should not get lost, he asked the French embassy in London to take charge of returning them to Gide. It seems that the embassy did so.

SELECT BIBLIOGRAPHY

OF WORKS CONSULTED

Anonymous, "A Century of French Romance," *The Bookman,* February 1903.

Aubry, Georges Jean, *La Jeunesse de Valery Larbaud.* Monaco: Editions du Rocher, 1949.

Barrès, Maurice, *L'Ame Française et la guerre,* Vol. 10. Paris: Emile Paul, 1919.

Beaubourg, Maurice, "La liberté au théâtre," *La Revue Blanche,* 1er semestre, 1896.

Bellows, Williams, *Some Memoirs.* London: S. Cobden-Sanderson, 1929.

Bennett, Arnold, *Journal.* New York: The Viking Press, Inc., 1933.

Brée, Germaine, *André Gide, l'insaisissable Protée.* Paris: Les Belles lettres, 1953.

Charteris, Evan, *The Life and Letters of Sir Edmund Gosse.* London: Harper and Brothers, 1931.

Combelle, Lucien, *Je dois à André Gide.* Paris: F. Chambriaud, 1951.

Davray, Henry-D., "Lettres anglaises," *Mercure de France,* August 1904.

Dietz, J., "Paul Desjardins," *Cahiers de la Quinzaine,* 17ème – 19ème serie, June 20, 1930.

Du Bos, Charles, *Journal, 1924–1925.* Paris: Corréa, 1951.

— — —, *Lettres de Charles Du Bos à André Gide.* Paris: Corrêa, 1950.

Fadiman, Clifton, P., "Pure Novel," *The Nation,* October 26, 1927.

Farmer, Albert, *Le Mouvement Esthétique et Décadent en Angleterre.* Paris: Champion, 1931.

Fielding, Henry, *Tom Jones.* New York: Random House, 1950.

Fisher, Linette, "André Gide and the English Language," *Columbia Review,* Spring 1951.

Ghéon, Henri, "André Gide," *Mercure de France,* May 1897.

———, *Foi en la France. Poèmes du temps de guerre.* Paris: Nouvelle Revue Française, 1916.

Gide, André, *Les Cahiers d'André Walter.* Paris: L'Art indépendant, 1891.

———, *Paludes.* Paris: l'art indépendant, 1895.

———, "Wells: la guerre des mondes," *La Revue Blanche,* May 1900.

———, *Prétextes: Réflexions sur quelques points de littérature et de morale.* Paris: Mercure de France, 1903.

———, *Saül. Le Roi Candaule.* Paris: Mercure de France, 1904.

———, *Amyntas.* Paris: Mercure de France, 1905.

———, *La Porte étroite.* Paris: Mercure de France, 1909.

———, *Oscar Wilde,* In Memoriam (Souvenirs) Le De Profundis. Paris: Mercure de France, 1910.

———, *Nouveaux Prétextes: Réflexions sur quelques points de littérature et de morale.* Paris: Mercure de France, 1911.

———, *Isabelle.* Paris: Nouvelle Revue Française, Marcel Rivière et Cie, 1911.

———, *Le Retour de l'enfant prodigue, précédé de cinq autres traités.* Paris: Nouvelle Revue Française, Marcel Rivière et Cie, 1912.

———, "Les Caves du Vatican," *La Nouvelle Revue Française,* January, February, March, and April, 1914.

———, *Souvenirs de la Cour d'Assises.* Paris: Nouvelle Revue Française, 1914.

———, *La Symphonie Pastorale.* Paris: Nouvelle Revue Française, 1919.

———, *Dostoievsky.* Paris: Plon-Nourrit et Cie, 1923.

———, *Incidences.* Paris: Nouvelle Revue Française, 1924.

———, *Corydon.* Paris: Nouvelle Revue Française, 1924.

———, *Les Faux-Monnayeurs.* Paris: Nouvelle Revue Française, 1925.

———, *Le Journal des faux-monnayeurs.* Paris: Gallimard (1948).

———, *Voyage au Congo.* Paris: Nouvelle Revue Française, 1927.

———, *Si le grain ne meurt.* Paris: Nouvelle Revue Française, 1927.

———, *Le Retour du Tchad* suite du *Voyage au Congo.* Paris: Nouvelle Revue Française, 1928.

———, "Voyages dans la littérature anglaise," *Verve,* Vol. 1, No. 2, 1938.

———, *Interviews Imaginaires. La délivrance de Tunis.* New York: J. Schiffrin, 1943.

———, *Correspondance Paul Claudel–André Gide,* ed. R. Mallet. Paris: Gallimard, 1949.

———, *Correspondance Francis Jammes–André Gide,* ed. R. Mallet. Paris: Gallimard, 1948.

———, *Correspondance R. M. Rilke–André Gide,* ed. R. Lang. Paris: Corréa, 1952.

———, *Eloges.* Neuchâtel et Paris: Ides et Calendes, 1948.

———, *Journal 1889–1939.* Paris: Gallimard, 1948.

———, *Journal 1942–1949.* Paris: Gallimard, 1950.

———, *Et nunc manet in te,* suivi de *Journal Intime.* Neuchâtel et Paris: Ides et Calendes, 1951.

———, *Hommage à André Gide,* Paris: Nouvelle Revue Française, 1951.

———, *Ainsi soit-il.* Paris: Gallimard, 1952.

Gosse, Edmund, "Symbolism and M. Stephane Mallarmé," *The Academy,* January 1893.

———, *Questions at Issue.* London: William Heinemann, 1893.

———, *Critical Kit-Kats.* London, William Heinemann, 1895.

———, "Current French Literature," *Cosmopolis,* June 1896, December 1896, June 1897, December 1987, June 1898.

———, *Henry Fielding: An Essay.* London: Archibald Constable and Co., 1898.

———, "Some Recent Literature in France," *Contemporary Review,* December, 1898.

———, *The Life and Letters of John Donne, Dean of St. Paul's* (revised edition). Two volumes, London: William Heinemann, 1899.

———, *French Profiles.* London: William Heinemann, 1905.

———, *Sir Thomas Browne,* London: Macmillan and Company, Ltd., 1905.

———, *Father and Son: A study of Two Temperaments.* London: William Heinemann (1930).

———, "The Writings of M. A. Gide," *Contemporary Review,* September 1909.

———, *The Collected Poems of Edmund Gosse.* London: William Heinemann, 1911.

———, *The Life of Swinburne.* London: privately printed at the Chiswick Press, 1912.

———, *The Life of Algernon Charles Swinburne.* London: Macmillan and Company, Ltd., 1917.

———, *Portraits and Sketches.* London: William Heinemann, 1912.

———, *The Future of English Poetry.* London: The English Association, 1913.

———, "To our Dead," *London Times,* October 20, 1914.

———, *Inter-Arma: Being Essays written in Time of War*. London: William Heinemann, 1916.

———, "L'Unité française," *Mercure de France,* January 16, 1916.

———, "La France et l'Angleterre: l'avenir de leurs relations intellectuelles," *Revue des Deux Mondes,* October 1, 1916.

———, "Reims Revisited," *Fortnightly Review,* November 1916.

———, *Three French Moralists, and the Gallantry of France*. London: William Heinemann, 1918.

———, *Some Diversions of a Man of Letters*. London: William Heinemann, 1921.

———, *Books on the Table,* London: William Heinemann, 1921.

———, *Life of William Congreve,* revised edition. London: William Heinemann, 1924.

———, "Catalogue of Books and Manuscripts from the Library of M. André Gide," *Sunday Times,* May 3, 1925.

———, "The Coiners," *Sunday Times,* March 21, 1926.

———, "A Great French Critic," *Sunday Times,* November 13, 1927.

———, "The Book of Gosse 1875–1928." Manuscript, Cambridge University Library, Cambridge.

Gosse, Philip, *Memoirs of a Camp Follower*. London: Wyman and Son, 1934.

Gourmont, Rémy de, "Les Cahiers d'André Walter," *Mercure de France.* June 1891.

Herring, Ivor Jack, *History of Ireland*. Belfast: W. Mullan, 1947.

Hytier, Jean, *André Gide*. Paris: Charlot, 1945.

Kurtz, M., *Jacques Copeau: Biographie d'un théâtre*. Paris: Nagel, 1950.

Lafille, Pierre, *André Gide Romancier*. Paris: Hachette, 1954.

Lang, Renée, *André Gide et la Pensée Allemande*. Paris: Egloff, 1949.

Larbaud, Valery, *Lettres à André Gide*. Paris: Stols, 1948.

Leroy, Olivier, *Le Chevalier Thomas Browne*. Paris: Gambert, 1931.

Mallarmé, *Five Letters from Stéphane Mallarmé to Algernon Charles Swinburne*. London: privately printed by Hazell, Matson, and Viney, Ltd., 1922.

Mauclair, Camille, "Le Voyage d'Urien," *Mercure de France,* August 1893.

———, "Narcisse," *Mercure de France,* February 1894.

———, "Paludes," *Mercure de France,* July 1895.

Maugham, Somerset, *The Summing Up*. New York: Doubleday, Doran and Co., 1938.

Martin du Gard, Roger, *Notes sur André Gide, 1919–1951*. Paris: Gallimard, 1951.

Mauriac, Claude, *Conversations avec André Gide*. Paris: A. Michel, 1951.

Miomandre, Francis de, "Elémir Bourges et le culte des Héros," *Mercure de France,* February 1905.

———, "André Gide et l'inquiétude philosophique," *Mercure de France,* May 1902.

Morland, Jacques, "Enquête sur l'influence allemande," *Mercure de France,* November 1902.

Noël, Jean, "George Moore et Mallarmé," *Revue de Litterature Comparée,* Juillet–Septembre, 1958.

O'Brien, Justin, *The Journals of André Gide*. New York: Alfred A. Knopf, Inc., 1948.

———, *Portrait of André Gide*. New York: Alfred A. Knopf, Inc., 1953.

Peyre, Henri, *The Contemporary French Novel,* New York: Oxford University Press.

Pierre-Quint, Léon, *André Gide*. Paris: Stock, 1952.

Prudhon, P., "Le Jury Criminel," *Le Temps,* Octobre 13–Décembre 24, 1913.

Purdy Jr., Theodore, "A Spreading Plant," *Saturday Review of Literature,* November 12, 1927.

Rivière, Jacques, *Etudes*. Paris: Gallimard, 1936.

Roe, F. Ch., *Taine et l'Angleterre*. Paris: Champion, 1923.

Rops, Daniel, *Trois Tombes, Trois Visages*. Paris: La Colombe, éditions du Vieux-Colombier, 1946.

Schlumberger, Jean, "Portraits and Sketches," *La Nouvelle Revue Française,* February 1, 1913.

Signoret, Emmanuel, *Poésies Complètes*. Paris: Mercure de France, 1908.

Sitwell, Osbert, *Noble Essences*. London: Macmillan and Company, Ltd., 1950.

Stendhal, *Promenades dans Rome,* Paris: Le Divan, 1931.

———, "Lettre à Sutton Sharpe, 1822," *Mercure de France,* May 15, 1906.

———, *Lettres à ses amis*. Paris: Michel Lévy, 1855.

Stephens, W., *The Book of France*. Paris: Champion, 1915.

Stevenson, R. Louis, *Stevenson's Correspondence,* Vol. 4. New York: Charles Scribner's Sons, 1911.

Taine, Hippolyte, *Correspondance*. Paris: Hachette, 1927.

Tarde, A. de, "La question du Jury," *L'Opinion,* October 18, 1913.

Wharton, Edith, *A Backward Glance*. New York: Appleton Century, 1934.

Woolf, Virginia, *The Moment and other Essays,* New York: Harcourt, Brace & Co., 1948.

INDEX OF LETTERS

INDEX